G000097906

SuSE Linux

USER GUIDE

Authors:	Stefanie Haefner, Carsten Fischer, Viviane Glanz, Holger Hetterich, Johannes Meixner, Matthias Nagorny, Siegfried Olschner, Marcus Schäfer, Arvin Schnell, Adrian Schröter, Gabriele Strattner, Rebecca Walter
Translators:	Tino Tanner
Editors:	Antje Faber, Dennis Geider, Roland Haidl, Jana Jaeger, Edith Parzefall, Peter Reinhart, Marc Rührschneck, Thomas Schraitle, Martin Sommer, Rebecca Walter
Layout:	Manuela Piotrowski, Thomas Schraitle
Setting:	LaTeX

This book has been printed on 100 % chlorine-free bleached paper.

Contents

IV   Help   321

23 Help and Documentation   323

A SuSE Linux FAQ   333

B Glossary   339

Welcome

SuSE Linux is an easy-to-install Linux distribution. In the past few releases, the installation and configuration tool YaST2 has undergone serious development. Install with just a few clicks or choose to customize aspects of the installation to your specific needs. Both the quick install method and the customized method are explained in this manual. You can also find information to help new Linux users get started.

Configuration is also easy with YaST2. Aspects of configuration, such as hardware administration and Internet access, are the topic of the second part of the manual. It also discusses configuration of the desktop environments KDE and GNOME.

SuSE Linux includes a range of applications. Some of these are introduced in the third section. OpenOffice.org, which has replaced StarOffice as the standard office package in the distribution, is described extensively. Multimedia and graphics applications, such as those used for scanning and modifying images and playing sound files, are also introduced. Chapters discussing web browsers and e-mail programs can help you choose you ideal tools for the Internet.

SuSE also addresses your needs for more information and support in the final section. Find information about installation support and online help. Also get answers to frequently asked questions and, in the Glossary, definitions of important terms.

This book and the accompanying programs make obsolete the average user's need to borrow, rent, recruit, buy, or steal a geek for the purposes of installing and maintaining a Linux system. SuSE Linux is a system powerful enough for geeks, but friendly enough for the average user.

New Features in the User Guide

The documentation of the previous version (SuSE Linux 8.0) was modified as follows:

- The manuals *Applications* and *Basics* were combined to form this *User Guide*.
- The instructions for the installation and configuration with YaST2 were completely revised:
  - ▷ Apart from the quick installation, the user-defined installation is also covered in this manual.
  - ▷ The installation and configuration was structured exactly according to the actual procedure in YaST. Menus and modules are addressed.
  - ▷ Complex issues that only concern experts were moved to the *Administration Guide*.
- Due to the large number of new features, the following chapters have undergone substantial editing:
  - ▷ GNOME
  - ▷ OpenOffice.org (replacing StarOffice)
  - ▷ Sound
  - ▷ Kooka
- The following chapters were added to the applications section:
  - ▷ Opera
  - ▷ Digital Cameras in Linux
  - ▷ Evolution
  - ▷ K3b

Typographic Conventions

The following typographic conventions are used in this book:

Example	Meaning
YaST	programs
/etc/passwd	files or directories
⟨placeholder⟩	replace the character string placeholder (including the angle brackets) with the actual value
PATH	an environment variable called PATH
192.168.1.2	the value of a variable
ls	commands
user	users
earth:~ # **ls**	enter the command ls in the shell of the user root in his home directory on the host "Earth"
newbie@earth:~ > **ls**	enter the command ls in the shell of the user newbie in his home directory on the host "Earth"
C:\> **fdisk**	at the DOS prompt, enter the command fdisk
(Alt)	press this key; keys to press sequentially are separated by spaces
(Ctrl) + (Alt) + (Del)	keys to press simultaneously are connected with a '+'
"Permission denied"	system messages
'System update'	menu item or button text 'System update'
☞boot	reference to an entry in the glossary in the appendix

Acknowledgments

The list of all who contributed to the success of this distribution would fill a book. We would like to thank everyone who toiled to make this excellent SuSE Linux better than all previous versions — with an unfaltering commitment, countless cups of coffee, a great deal of overtime, and sleepless nights.

On a voluntary basis, the developers of Linux cooperate on a global scale to promote the development of Linux. We thank them for their efforts. Without them, this distribution would not exist.

Special thanks, of course, to Linus Torvalds.

Have a lot of fun!

Your SuSE Team

Part I

Installation

Getting Started with Linux

This chapter is intended mainly for people coming from other operating systems who are about to use Linux for the first time. We have organized the text as a list of questions and answers to talk about the most important doubts and issues arising when making initial forays into Linux. At the end of this manual, find a glossary explaining important concepts and a list of frequently asked questions about SuSE Linux. Both of them are a good complement to the present chapter.

The answers are based on a standard installation of SuSE Linux. If you have already customized your system, the answers still apply, but take into account the changed settings.

Important Requirements

- *How much hard disk space do I need? What will happen to my windows?*
  Naturally, a Linux installation requires an amount of hard disk space. About 1.5 GB of free space is required. Nevertheless, 400 MB may be sufficient for a minimum system. SuSE Linux can be installed as the only operating system on the computer. However, it can also share the hard disks with other operating systems. In this case, it needs at least one free partition.

  If you have installed Windows and there are several partitions (drive C: and other hard disk drives), theoretically you can install SuSE Linux on one of the additional partitions. If the partition in which to install Linux contains data, first save it to another partition.

  If your previous system consisted of a single partition that occupies the entire hard disk, SuSE Linux can easily and speedily resize it, provided it is a "FAT" file system (FAT or FAT32), which is the case with Windows 95, 98, and ME. If your Windows (NT, 2000, or XP) uses a partition with a NTFS file system, this partition cannot be resized by SuSE Linux.

  If Windows XP was preinstalled using the NTFS file system, but you have the installation CDs, you can reinstall Windows XP and select "FAT32" as file system for XP. This causes the hard disk to be formatted with the FAT file system, which can easily be resized during the Linux installation.

  Instructions for partitioning hard disks and resizing your Windows system are provided in *Resizing a Windows Partition* on page 30.

Working with Linux

- *Are there programs for Linux that I can use to read my old files created under Windows?*
  For the most part, you can continue to use your old files under Linux. Standard programs, such as StarOffice and The GIMP, can handle most of the file formats you have used so far, whether they are for documents, pictures or other graphics, or video or audio data. SuSE Linux comes with a suitable application for all of these and lets you work with your old files without difficulty.

- *Where can I get applications for Linux?*
  Your SuSE Linux comes with all the programs and applications needed
  for daily work. Just click the SuSE menu at the bottom left of your KDE
  desktop to find out about them. Many programs are available. Unless you
  installed all packages, even more applications can be installed from the
  distribution with YaST2.

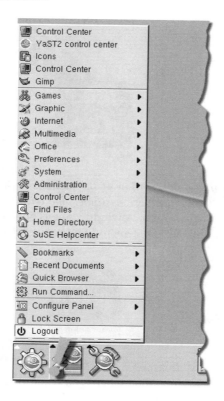

- *Why can't I simply switch off my computer?*
  You should not simply switch a computer off, but need to "shut it down" properly. Shutting the computer down properly avoids data losses. Simply switching a running system off is like a knock-out. A second user may using your computer by way of a network connection. If you simply switch the system off, you will also endanger the data the other user has not yet saved. The same also applies to your data. However, if you log out properly, you can be sure that your data is saved.

- *How do I format a floppy for Linux?*
  The easiest way to do this is with the KDE floppy formatter. To start this tool, click the SuSE menu at the bottom left of your desktop then select 'System' → 'Tools' → 'KFloppy'. Choose between the FAT format (used for DOS and Windows) and Linux's own ext2 file system format. You could also use mtools. More information is available in *Working with the Shell* on page 295.

- *Where can I find a description of the included software and how can I get help for the many programs that come with SuSE Linux?*
  Click the SuSE help button. A window opens on your desktop from which to access the SuSE Help System and find answers to all your questions.

- *What is a virtual desktop?*
  You may run into a situation where you want to have so many windows open that things get a little disorganized. Under Linux, this problem can

easily be avoided: look at the panel to find the numbered icons of the available virtual desktops, which represent different spaces where you can open and arrange windows. Then switch between virtual desktops at any moment to access the windows.

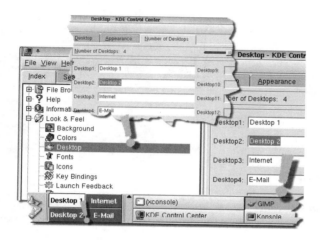

- *Where is the file manager?*
  Try Konqueror, which is not only a file manager, but also a web browser, viewer application, and more. Konqueror is the KDE program of choice for anything related to file management.

Files, Folders, and Directories

- *What happened to drive C:?*
  Drives are storage media, such as a floppy disk, a CD-ROM, or a hard disk. You have probably come to know these under the names A:, C:, D:, and so on. Unlike Windows, however, Linux incorporates all drives directly into the system's directory structure. The result is that drives are not accessed using names like C:, but using folders (i. e., names of storage areas) to tell the user where data is located.

- **What is root?**

  The root directory is identified by a slash ('/'). Linux file system normally holds a directory tree that starts at a / and is subdivided into many branches. These subdirectories have names like home, for instance (a subdirectory for personal files of users), or bin (which contains binary files — programs in most cases). The place where the entire directory tree originates is called the "root directory." From this point, access all the subdirectories. Theoretically it would be possible to call the root directory by a name, but it is historically known as /. Each directory or folder will also have a slash in front of its name. And in fact, each such folder could in turn be used as the root of another, separate file system.

- **Who is root?**

  Root is one of several users on your Linux system, a multiuser system. However, root is a very special user in that it is the most powerful one on your machine and consequently the one that requires the greatest degree of responsibility. Like a building manager for a building, root is responsible for the entire Linux system, making sure that it runs reliably, that the infrastructure works, that all programs are up to date, and that none of the "occupants" transgress the rights of others. Again like a building manager, root owns the master key for the entire Linux system, enabling this user to change things that are not possible for normal users. Also, root has access to the main directory / and all its subdirectories. For all these reasons, this user is called root.

Make it a rule only to log in as `root` on your system if that is really required for the job. Examples of this are the creation of a new user account or the installation of programs. In general, the system will explicitly prompt you to enter root's password (the master key) if a particular action requires it.

- *Where are things located in the file system?*
  Linux has a number of standard directories. The most important of them are explained below. For a more complete overview, see Figure 22.1 on page 297.

/home

> This is where the home directories of individual users are located. Your home directory contains all your data, personal configuration files, and anything else to which only you should have access. The majority of this data is readable for other users but can only be changed by the owner. This default setting can be changed at any time, of course. To learn more about this, read Section *File System Permissions* on page 305.

/root

> The home directory of the administrator `root`.

/usr/

> Most programs have some supporting files stored under this directory, such as documentation, help files, and other important data.

/bin and /sbin (executable files)

> These directories hold many programs closely related to the operating system itself, which are needed early in the boot procedure.

/opt (optional)

> Commercial software and very big packages not forming part of the system itself go into this directory. This includes things like KDE, Netscape, Mozilla, and some others.

/etc (configuration directory)
> Files related to the system configuration are stored in this folder. This includes things like the setup information for your Internet access, the boot configuration, and the configuration of individual programs, such as backup routines.

/boot (directory for system boot files)
> This is the place where any files and programs needed for booting are stored, such as the Linux kernel.

Others
> In addition to that, there are other folders containing information on the system and about the devices connected to it: /lib and /usr/lib (libraries), /var (variable data), /proc (processes), /media (removable storage media like the floppy and CD-ROM), /dev (all connected devices, such as printers, hard disks, and the keyboard).

More information on the topic can be found in *Files and Directories* on page 297.

About Passwords and Users

- *Why do I need a password?*
The password is the key to your home directory. Unlike other operating systems, Linux is a true multiuser system: files and settings of different users are managed while keeping them separate and those different users can access the system at the same time. If you imagine that your machine had two keyboards and two screens, you could use it alongside another user without getting in each other's way. Linux distributes system resources between active users in an intelligent way, so if that other keyboard and screen were located in another room (because they are connected to the system through a network), probably you would not even notice that there is another user at work.

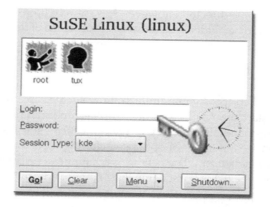

Each user has a directory of his own, the home directory. The home directory is used for all personal data as well as for personal configuration settings of applications. Examples of this are the web browser's bookmark list and the address book of an e-mail program. For security reasons, the whole area is protected with a password. Full access to this personal data is only granted if this password is known.

- *Why can I read some files but cannot delete them?*
  You do not have the necessary permissions. After reading the password that you have entered, the system will not only know about your home directory, but also about the permissions that you have as a user — the things you are allowed to do and those you are not.

For instance, you have the permissions to read most of the files in /etc, but changing them would require the permissions of the system administrator. Directories with files affecting the security and stability of the system are read-only for normal users or are completely inaccessible to them.

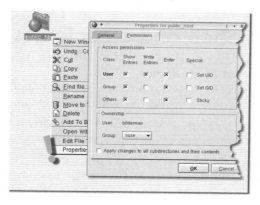

In your home directory, however, it is entirely up to you to decide which files should be hidden from other users or which of them can be shared with them. To set this in Konqueror, right-click the file then select 'Properties'.

- *How can I add or remove users?*
New users must be created by `root`. Always log in as `root` to perform tasks related to system administration, such as creating a new user. To do so, start the YaST2 Control Center as a normal user, enter the `root` password, and click the key to select 'Security and Users'. To the right, you can see a number of options, including 'User administration'. Select 'Create a new user'. The new user account can be created after you have filled out the fields (First name, Last name) and provided a password.

When entering a password, be sure to distinguish between uppercase and lowercase letters. A password should be at least five characters long and must not include special characters, such as accents. The characters #*,.;:._-+!$%&/ | ?{[()]} are allowed, however, as are spaces and any of the digits from 0 to 9. Normally you should make up a password consisting of about eight characters. To make certain the password has been entered correctly, it must be reentered in a second input field. Be sure to remember your password.

Let YaST2 create the user name for you then edit the field or create a user name yourself. A user name may only consist of lowercase letters (without umlauts), the three characters ._- and digits. The restrictions on user names are somewhat stronger than those on passwords.

To start working at the system, identify yourself by providing this user name and the password. This is commonly called the login procedure.

To delete a user, select the item 'Edit and create users'. In the dialog, select the corresponding user from the list and click 'Delete'.

Mounting, Shell, and Other Topics

- *What is meant by mounting?*
Mounting is an important procedure. Mounted floppies and CDs should not be removed from their drives without being unmounted.

On the other hand, putting the disks into the drives will not make them available to the system unless they are mounted.

The `mount` command integrates a storage medium (floppy disk, CD, zip drive, etc.) in the directory tree. Conversely, `umount` removes the medium from the directory tree. If you are using KDE, the whole procedure takes place in the background and is triggered by clicking the CD icon or the floppy icon, for instance.

Why is this needed?
This might seem a little Linux oddity at first, but it turns out quite practical if we have a closer look. To a Linux file system, it does not matter much what kind of medium is mounted in it: whether it is a floppy, a DVD, a hard disk, or a ZIP disk. By mounting them, they are registered with the system. On a system geared to multiple users, this is important, as there are potentially several users and several programs wanting access to the same medium at a given time.

Imagine that someone came to your office and exchanged the drawers in your desk because he needed to work at the place for an hour. When you come back after a while, you cannot find that draft contract that must be ready before tomorrow — the drawer is not where is used to be. Therefore, under Linux any drives or media (the "drawers" of the file system) need to be explicitly mounted and unmounted.

- *Working with the Shell*
  With Linux, there are always several ways to achieve a particular goal. This may be a bit confusing at first, but has many advantages. If a particular function should fail or become unavailable for some reason, the same commands can be given to the computer by other means.

  For instance, if a program cannot be started with a mouse click from a menu, you could enter the program name with the keyboard and still launch the application. As another example, to see the contents of a directory, use the text command ls.

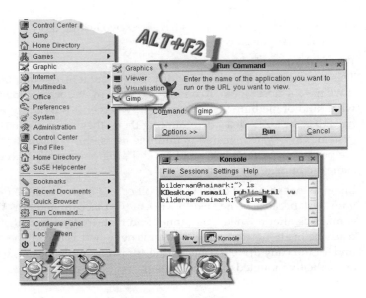

Such commands are entered in a text console, a small, no-frills text window (also referred to as the "shell") that enables you to control almost every aspect of your computer. Experienced users often prefer the console. It makes it possible to combine different commands into one long command line, which then might act like a new, small program. This may have practical advantages over using the mouse, depending on what you want to achieve. Learn more about working from the console in the Chapter *Introduction to Bash* on page 296.

Quick Installation

A few clicks are almost all you need to completely install SuSE Linux on your computer. If no Linux system was installed previously, your hard disk will be partitioned automatically, an existing Windows system (95/98/ME) will be resized, a variety of software will be installed, and your hard disk will be configured automatically.

If you do not like the suggestions offered by YaST2 or have special requirements, modify the installation suggestions manually. The Chapter *User-Defined Installation* on page 19 describes how this is done.

Step One: Selecting the Language

Start your computer and insert CD 1 or the DVD into the correct drive. Restart the computer. If your BIOS is configured to boot from the CD-ROM, your CD will be detected and the installation system will start. If the CD-ROM is not booted, reconfigure your BIOS to boot the CD-ROM drive before the hard drive.

Select the language for your system. The language configuration set here will be the default applied to your keyboard. The keyboard layout can be adjusted in the next step if required.

Step Two: Accept Suggestions

SuSE Linux scans all your hardware and scans for any previously installed operating systems. It lists the results here (see Figure 2.1 on the next page). Also see the suggested partitioning, including Windows reduction, and the installation option.

If this is your first Linux installation, you probably should accept the majority of these suggestions. Verify the recommended keyboard layout and time zone and correct them if needed.

The following suggestions are listed for your review. Alter YaST's suggested hardware and partitioning settings by clicking the respective parameter or by clicking 'Detailed'.

Caution

Do not change the boot loader, the partitioning, or the hardware settings unless you know what you are doing.

Caution

Installation Mode 'New Installation' is the default value here.

Keyboard Layout The layout is selected according to the language chosen in the first step.

Mouse The detected mouse type is listed here.

Partitioning Suggestion Lists the suggested partitioning for your system. If Windows 9x or ME is located on disk, the reduction rate will be specified here.

Software Selection   A default system with an office package is the default installation.

Boot Loader   Determines where SuSE Linux installs the boot manager. The Master Boot Record (MBR) is the default setting for this.

Time Settings   The local time zone is set here, based on the language settings. This setting often needs to be modified manually.

After changing a parameter, click 'Accept'. This returns you to the selection and continues the installation with the modified values.

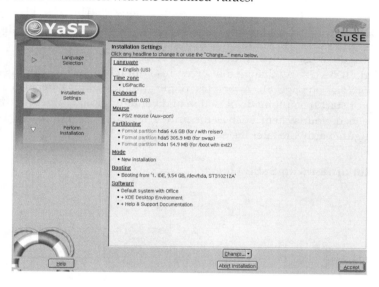

Figure 2.1: *Detected Hardware and Installation and Partitioning Suggestions*

Step Three: Installation

Start the installation by clicking 'Yes' in the green window. Depending on the performance of your computer, the complete installation of your system with about 350 program packages takes approximately fifteen minutes.

Configuration

Following the installation, make three important settings before you can start using SuSE Linux (refer to Chapter *System Configuration* on page 37 for detailed instructions). First, set a password for the system administrator, also referred to as the user ☞*root* or "superuser".

┌─ **Caution** ───

Be sure to remember the root password, as you can only modify the system or install programs using the `root` identity. Check the settings of your screen and graphics card, as incorrect settings could damage your monitor.

─── **Caution** ─┘

Then configure a user. Finally, the detected screen and the graphics card are displayed. If necessary, change the screen resolution or the color depth (see *Monitor Settings* on page 40). After a test of the graphics settings, decide whether to set up or start the automatic detection and configuration of other hardware components of your system, such as the printer, sound card, or modem. You can also configure hardware later instead.

Have a lot of fun with SuSE Linux!

User-Defined Installation

The previous chapter covered the quick standard installation procedure. This chapter provides detailed information about the individual parameters that you can modify from the suggestion window by starting the respective modules. This gives complete control over the installation. Thanks to the new design of YaST2, even the advanced installation of SuSE Linux and applications is easy.

Starting Your System from the CD-ROM

Insert the first SuSE Linux CD or the DVD into the drive. Then restart the computer to load SuSE Linux, install from the medium located in the drive, and set up your machine.

Possible Problems When Starting from the CD/DVD

If you can boot your machine from the CD, proceed with the installation using YaST2. Booting from the CD may not be possible for the following reasons:

- Your CD-ROM drive may not be able to read the "boot image" of the first CD. In this case, use CD 2 to boot the system. The second CD contains a conventional 1.44 MB boot image, which can be read even by older drives.

- The boot sequence of the machine may be incorrect. Information about changing the BIOS parameters are provided in the documentation of your motherboard and in the following paragraphs.

  The BIOS is a small utility used to start the basic functionalities of the computer. Motherboard manufacturers provide a BIOS adapted to the characteristics of the motherboard.

  The BIOS setup can only be entered at a specific time. At the system start-up, some hardware tests are performed, such as a memory test. You can see this from the system memory counter. At the same time, the key to press to enter the BIOS setup is displayed at the bottom of the screen. Usually this is done by pressing (Del), (F1), or (Esc). Press the respective key to enter the BIOS setup.

  When the BIOS setup has started, change the boot sequence as follows: In an AWARD BIOS, look for 'BIOS FEATURES SETUP'. Other manufacturers use similar entries, such as 'ADVANCED CMOS SETUP'. Select the respective entry and confirm with (↵).

  To change the boot sequence, look for the item defining the start sequence of the drives, usually C, A or A, C. In the first case, the machine first searches for the operating system on the hard disk (C) then in the floppy disk drive (A). Select 'Boot Sequence' and press (Page ↑) or (Page ↓) until the sequence A, CDROM, C is displayed.

  Exit the settings by pressing (Esc). To save the changes, select 'SAVE & EXIT SETUP' or press (F10). Confirm your settings with (Y). To undo the settings, press (N).

If you have a SCSI CD-ROM drive, start its BIOS (for example, for an Adaptec host adapter, press (Ctrl) + (A)). Select 'Disk Utilities'. The system checks and displays the connected hardware components. Make a note of the SCSI ID for your CD-ROM drive. Exit the menu with (Esc) then enter 'Configure Adapter Settings'. Under 'Additional Options', select 'Boot Device Options' and press (↵). Enter the ID of the CD-ROM drive and press (↵). Press (Esc) twice to return to the start screen of the SCSI BIOS. Exit this screen and confirm with 'Yes' to reboot the machine.

- Your CD-ROM drive may not be supported because it is an older model. To check whether your drive is supported, refer to the Hardware Database of SuSE Linux at `http://hardwaredb.suse.de/en/`.

The Opening Screen

As the boot screen appears, SuSE Linux is preparing for installation.

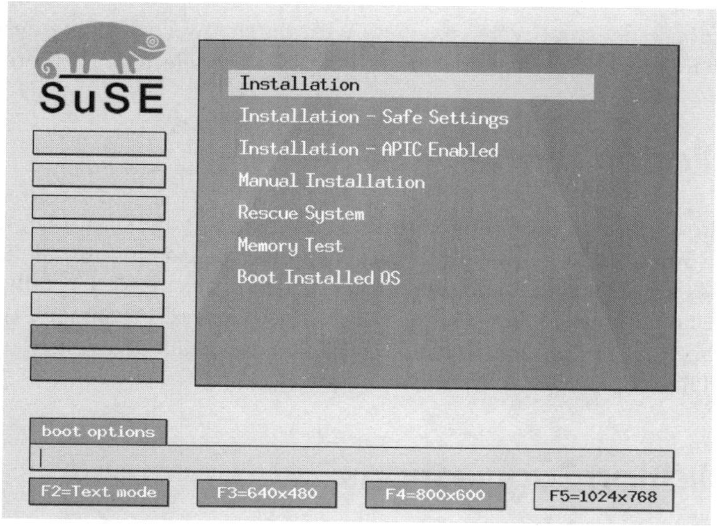

Figure 3.1: *The Boot Screen*

A few seconds later, SuSE Linux starts loading a minimal ☞*Linux system* that takes over the rest of the installation procedure. A number of messages and copyright notices then appear on the screen. At the end of the loading process, the YaST2 program starts and, a few seconds later, the graphical interface of YaST2, the SuSE Linux installation program, is displayed.

YaST2 Takes Over

Now the actual installation of SuSE Linux starts with the YaST2 installation program. All YaST2 screens have a common format. All entry fields, lists, and buttons on the YaST2 screens can be accessed with your mouse. If your cursor does not move, your mouse has not been automatically recognized by Linux. You will then need to use your keyboard.

Selecting a Language

SuSE Linux and YaST2 are adapted to use the language selected. English is the default setting for the international distribution of SuSE Linux. These settings can be changed individually.

If your mouse does not work, navigate with the arrow keys to the desired language then press (Tab) repeatedly until the 'Next' is selected. Then press (↵).

Installation Mode

If you already have a SuSE Linux version installed on your computer, decide whether to perform a 'New Installation', 'Update' the existing installation, or boot the existing system. If you do not have a SuSE Linux version installed, begin a new installation by clicking 'Next' to continue (Figure 3.3 on page 24). This chapter only covers the 'New Installation'. Information about a system update is provided in Chapter *System Update* on page 51.

Installation Suggestions

After the hardware has been detected and the mouse configured, YaST2 provides information about the detected hardware and the suggestions for the installation and the partitioning as described in Chapter *Quick Installation* on page 15 and Figure 2.1 on page 17). After you modify a suggestion, YaST2 returns to the suggestion window. The following sections explain the various configuration settings available.

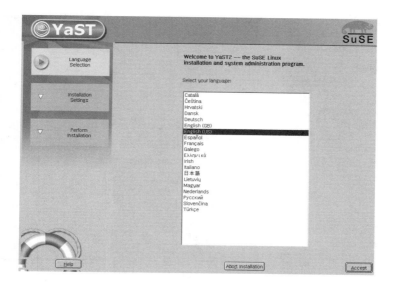

Figure 3.2: *Selecting the Language*

Mode

Here, change the installation mode selected before the suggestion window appeared if you already have a Linux system on your computer. You can also boot your installed system from here. This is useful if your system is no longer able to boot from the hard disk.

Keyboard Layout

Select a keyboard layout. By default, the layout corresponds to the language selected. After changing the layout, use the field to test special characters, Y, and Z to make sure the layout is correct. If they are not displayed correctly, the keyboard layout is not correct. Return to the suggestions with 'Next'.

Mouse

If YaST2 did not recognize your mouse type automatically, use Tab until 'Change' is highlighted. Press Space and the arrow keys until 'Mouse' is selected. Press

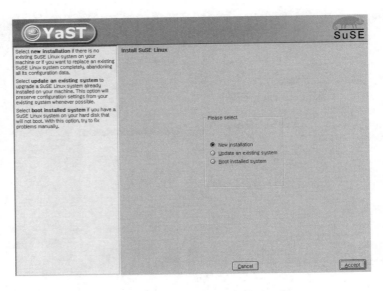

Figure 3.3: *Selecting the Installation Type*

⏎ to open a mouse type selection screen, illustrated in Figure 3.4 on the facing page.

To select your mouse type, use ⬆ and ⬇. Your mouse documentation should include a description of the mouse type. Select the mouse type from the list. Confirm your selection by pressing (Alt) + ⬆ or (Tab) and (⏎).

Now, test to see if your mouse is working. If the mouse cursor on the screen follows your mouse movements, your mouse is configured correctly. If the cursor does not move, select a different mouse type and try again.

Partitioning

If you are not familiar with Linux and its file systems, you may be concerned about how much disk space is required. It is also important to consider how to distribute this space. YaST2 usually provides a reasonable suggestion based on the available hard disk space. Modify this suggestion, if needed, to fit the needs of your system.

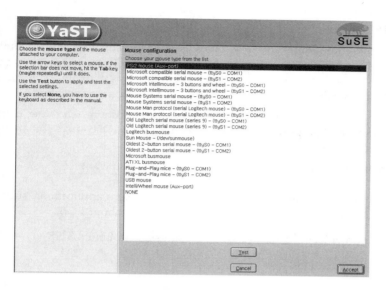

Figure 3.4: *Selecting the Mouse Type*

Partition Types

Every hard disk has a partition table with space for four entries. Each entry in the partition table can be a primary partition or an extended partition. Only *one* extended partition is possible.

Primary partitions are simple: they consist of a continuous range of cylinders assigned to one operating system. However, using primary partitions, you could set up no more than four partitions per hard disk. More do not fit in the partition table.

This is why extended partitions are used. The extended partition is also a continuous range of hard disk cylinders. However, the extended partition itself can be subdivided into *logical partitions* that do not require an entry in the partition table. In other words, the extended partition is a container for logical partitions.

If you need more than four partitions, make sure at least the fourth partition is an extended partition and assign it the entire free cylinder range. Subsequently, set up multiple logical partitions (the maximum is fifteen partitions for SCSI hard disks and 63 partitions for (E)IDE hard disks).

Linux does not care about the type of partitions (primary or logical) used for the installation.

Time to Decide

The absolute minumum for SuSE Linux is 180 MB. However, this limits the uses of the machine. For example, you can only use the console without the X Window System. To use X and start a few applications, the minimum value is 500 MB. Both values include the space required for the swap partition.

A reasonable amount is 1 GB including the swap partition — a rather modest requirement in this age of several gigabyte hard disks. Of course, you are free to use more hard disk space.

The amount of hard disk needed depends on what you want:

- For the X Window System together with modern applications, such as KDE, GNOME, OpenOffice.org, and Netscape: about 1 GB.

- For downloading lots of movies and music with Linux: 2 GB

- Both items: 3 GB.

- Writing CDs and the items listed above: 4 GB.

These guidelines can help develop a partitioning scheme for your system:

- For less than 4 GB: a swap partition (128–256 MB) and a root partition (/).

- For more than 4 GB (you can also proceed as described in the previous item): boot (/boot), swap, root (250 MB), home (/home) with about 200 MB for each user, and the rest for applications (/usr). Possibly consider a partition for /opt and one for /var.

The YaST2 Partitioner

The suggested partitioning appears with a confirmation option, allowing you to accept, change, or discard the suggestion. See *More Partitioning Tips* on page 32 regarding automatic entries in the file system table. Clicking 'Change' opens the 'Partitioner' (Figure 3.5 on the facing page).

YaST2 shows all ☞*partitions* present on the selected hard disk (Figure 3.5 on the next page). Any free storage space is shown and automatically selected. To assign more disk space to ☞*Linux*, assign more partitions following the order from the last to the first ☞*partition*. If you have three partitions, it is not possible to use the second one for Linux and the first and third for other operating systems.

If you choose 'Discard', a dialog appears containing the hard disk selection as shown in Figure 3.6 on page 28. All the hard disks on your system are listed here.

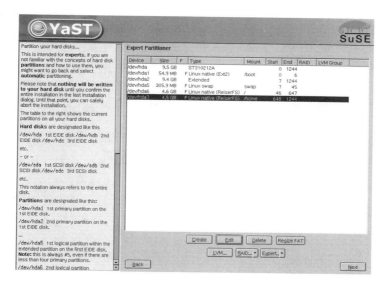

Figure 3.5: *The SuSE Linux Partitioner*

Decide where to install SuSE Linux. There is no risk associated with selecting the hard disk, as no changes are made at this time.

'Advanced Settings, Manual Partitioning' shows the previous partitioning of your system. It can be manually modified or reused for your new system.

By clicking 'Entire hard disk' in the following dialog window, the entire hard disk and all its partitions are activated for ☞*Linux*. If you already installed a Windows operating system with a FAT file system, you will be asked if you want to delete or shrink the Windows partition (refer to *Resizing a Windows Partition* on page 30).

During the course of the installation, YaST2 will verify whether there is sufficient space for a minimum installation and whether the three standard partitions used by Linux can be created. If this is not the case, you will prompted to alter your selection. If there is enough storage space, YaST2 will use your settings to apportion the entire hard disk or the selected ☞*partitions*.

⌐ **Caution** ───

If you choose 'Use entire hard disk', all information on your hard disk will be lost.

─────────────────────────────────────── **Caution** ⌐

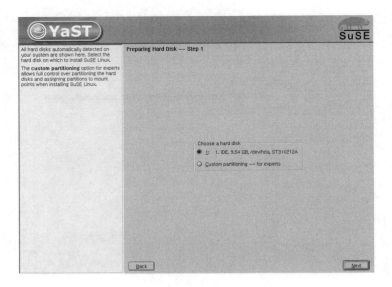

Figure 3.6: Selecting the Hard Disk

Manual Partitioning

With the 'Partitioner', shown in Figure 3.5 on the preceding page, the partitions of your hard disk can be modified manually. Partitions can be added, removed, or changed.

If you select 'Partitioning' in the suggestion screen and 'Base partition setup on this proposal' in the next dialog, the partitioner will list the hard disk and all available or suggested partitions. Disks are listed as devices without numbers (such as /dev/hda or /dev/sda). Partitions are listed as parts of the devices (for example, /dev/hda1 or /dev/sda1). The size, type, file system, and mount point are also displayed. The mount point describes where the partition is attached in the Linux file system tree.

Creating a Partition

To create a new partition:

1. Select the disk on which to create a partition (this will be done automatically if there is only one hard disk).

2. Select 'Create custom partition setup'. A dialog appears asking for the type of partition. You can create up to four primary partitions or up to

three primary partitions and one extended partition. Within the extended partition, you can create several "logical" partitions as explained in *Partition Types* on page 25).

3. Select the file system to use to format the hard disk and, if required, a mount point. YaST2 suggests a mount point for each partition created. Details of the parameters are provided in the next section.

4. Select 'OK' to apply your changes.

The new partition will be listed in the partition table. Selecting 'Next' writes the partition table to disk and formats partitions if necessary.

Partitioning Parameters

To add a partition to the file system tree, set the following parameters in the partitioner:

1. Select the partition

2. 'Edit' the partition and set the parameters:

   - File system ID (if you do not want to format the partition): This can be 'Linux swap', 'Linux', 'Linux LVM', or 'Linux RAID'. For details on LVM and RAID, refer to the *Administration Guide*.

   - File system (for formatting the partition): This can be 'Swap', 'Ext2', 'Ext3', 'ReiserFS', or 'JFS'. Swap is a special format that makes the partition usable as virtual memory. Every system should have at least one swap partition of at least 128 MB. By default, ReiserFS is used for the partitions. Like JFS and Ext3, it is a "Journaling File System". A journaling file system enables a quick recovery from a system crash or a bad unmount. Also ReiserFS is very fast in handling lots of small files. Ext2 is a not journaling file system. It is "rock solid" and good for smaller partitions, as it does not require too much disk space for the management.

   - Mount Point: Set the directory where the new partition should be connected in the file system tree. If you select the last entry in the list, enter your own directory name. 'Swap' is used for the special file system Swap.

3. Select 'Next' to format and enable the partition.

Resizing a Windows Partition

SuSE Linux can easily coexist with other operating systems on the machine.
If Microsoft Windows (9x/ME or XP on FAT 32) is already installed on your
computer and the hard disk selected for SuSE Linux only has one ☞*partition*
containing Windows (which is the case with most preinstalled computers), you
can reduce the part of the hard disk that is reserved for Windows without having
to remove this operating system to enable the installation of SuSE Linux.

This section assumes the hard disk selected contains Windows 9x or ME. The
following instructions also apply to Windows XP installed on a disk formatted
with the FAT file system. However, if Windows NT, 2000, or XP is installed on an
NTFS file system, the partition size cannot be reduced.

If there is insufficient empty space available for SuSE Linux, choose between two
options. Either completely delete Windows from the hard disk or reduce the
Windows partition to create enough space for the installation of SuSE Linux. See
Figure 3.7 on the facing page.

YaST2 gives a reasonable resizing suggestion for your Windows partition.
However, it can be modified manually. If you decide to delete Windows, all data
will be irrevocably lost during Linux installation.

Windows on NTFS

If you have a computer on which Windows XP was preinstalled, most likely it
uses an NTFS. Nevertheless, you have two possibilities for installing SuSE Linux
alongside XP. The easier option is to reinstall your Windows XP with the XP
installation CDs and choose FAT 32 as the file system. However, this might result
in a performance drop for your Windows, since it represents a migration from a
very modern NTFS to a much older FAT system.

The cleaner, though more complicated, solution is to use a partitioning tool of
your choice (such as fdisk or Partition Magic) to format part of the hard disk
with NTFS where you can subsequently install Windows XP with its modern file
system and leave part of the hard disk unformatted. Following the installation
of Windows XP, use this free space to install SuSE Linux. YaST2 automatically
detects the free space and can install Linux there without touching the XP
installation.

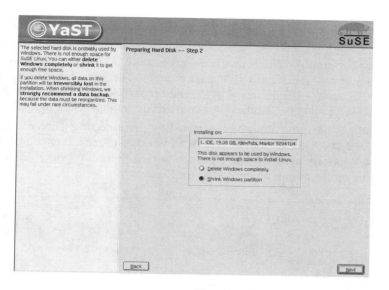

Figure 3.7: *Available Options for Windows Partitions*

The Windows Resizer

┌─ **Caution** ───

The Windows Resizer only works if your computer has a hard disk with exactly one Windows partition (usually the case for most preinstalled Windows computers). Otherwise, you will have to manually partition your hard disk.

─── **Caution** ─┘

Before reducing your Windows partition, ☞*boot* your Windows PC. Then run both Scandisk and Defrag programs. Scandisk and Defrag scan the files used by Windows then condense these files to the beginning of the hard disk. This speeds up the reduction process.

┌─ **Note** ───

Disable the Windows swap file and reboot windows before defragmenting your hard disk. Windows assigns its swap file a special, invisible ID that keeps Defrag from moving these file.

─── **Note** ─┘

After you go to 'Partitioning' in the suggestion screen and click 'Edit' in the screens that follow, use the mouse or arrow keys to highlight the Windows partition. Next, click 'Resize'.

In the first bar graph, YaST2 shows how much space is currently occupied by Windows and how much hard disk space remains. The second diagram, shown in Figure 3.8, gives a suggestion of how to best repartition your hard disk. Either accept this suggestion or define your own partition settings using the slider.

The 'Windows Resizer' can also be accessed by first selecting 'Discard' then 'Entire Hard Disk'. Next, you will be asked whether to reduce or completely delete the Windows partition (see Figure 3.7 on the preceding page). Choosing the resizing option allows you to access the Resizer.

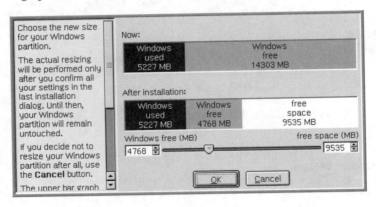

Figure 3.8: Resizing the Windows Partition

More Partitioning Tips

If the partitioning is performed by YaST2 and other partitions are detected on the system, these partitions will also be entered in the file /etc/fstab to enable easy access to this data. This file contains all partitions in the system with their properties (parameters), such as the file system, mount point, and user permissions. An excerpt is shown in File 1.

```
/dev/sda1          /data1  auto    noauto,user 0 0
/dev/sda8          /data2  auto    noauto,user 0 0
```

File 1:   /etc/fstab: Partition Data

The partitions, regardless of whether they are Linux or FAT partitions (Windows 95/98, ME), are specified with the options noauto and user. This allows any user to mount or unmount these partitions if needed. For security reasons, YaST2 does not automatically enter the `exec` option here. However, to run programs from there, you can enter this option yourself. This measure will be necessary if you encounter system messages such as "bad interpreter" or "Permission denied".

Detailed background information and tips for partitioning are provided in the *Administration Guide* in *Special Installation Procedures, Partitioning for Experts*.

Software

Here, determine which software to install on your machine. A default selection including KDE and OpenOffice.org is preset. If you click 'Software', a dialog offering the three basic systems for installation appears:

- Minimum system (only recommended for experts)

- Minimum graphical system

- Default system (with KDE and office packages)

If you click one of the three systems then click 'Detailed selection', the software installation module will start. The detailed software selection module was completely revised from earlier versions (see Figure 3.9 on the following page). It offers more functionality and flexibility than ever before.

Preselection

The module starts with the selection filter. At the top left next to 'Filter', 'Selection' is marked. These selections represent groups of program packages to select for installation or removal by clicking the respective check box. Below, see possible preselection groups of this filter, some of which are already selected as they belong to the default installation of SuSE Linux.

The right frame displays a list of the individual packages that belong to the selection. Packages selected for installation are checked to the left of the package name. Select and deselect individual packages according to your needs. To do this, click the symbol several times until the desired status is shown. A full description of the status marks and detailed instructions for this module are provided in the Section *Install/Remove Software* on page 48.

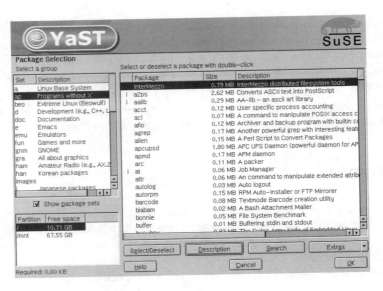

Figure 3.9: Installing and Removing Software

┌─ **Caution** ─────────────────────────────────────

The default selection offered for installation is usually suitable for both newcomers and advanced home users. It has been selected carefully based on our experience. Normally, you do not need to modify anything here. When deleting packages, observe the warnings and do not deselect any packages of the Linux base system (usually located in the package group 'System').

─── **Caution** ─┘

Other Filters

Click 'Filter' to see a selection of additional filters that can be used to structure the view of the packages. For example, there is a selection according to 'package groups', which is also defined as the default filter when you start the software selection in YaST after the system has been installed. Using this filter, the program packages are displayed according to subjects in a tree structure on the left side. The more you unfold the tree in a package group, the more detailed the selection will be and the smaller the number of related packages in the package list on the right side will be.

Booting

A boot loader is needed to start Linux. It can also offer a selection of operating systems. Programs that handle this task include the boot managers ☞ *LILO* , the "**LI**nux **LO**ader", and GRUB, "**GR**and **U**nified **B**ootloader".

Until version 8.1, LILO was the default boot manager of SuSE Linux. If you updated your old system, LILO was retained as boot manager. On the other hand, if you performed a new installation, your current boot loader is GRUB. The differences are insignificant to the average user.

By default, YaST2 suggests installing the boot loader in the Master Boot Record (MBR) of the hard disk. If you have several hard disks, it will recognize the boot hard disk from the ☞*BIOS* settings.

This is displayed in the proposal screen under 'Booting'. YaST2 will detect whether you have any other operating systems. There are several possibilities for installing the boot loader. The following paragraphs provide an introduction to the boot manager. For a detailed description (for experts), refer to the boot loader chapter in the *Administration Guide*. Enter the boot loader configuration by clicking 'Booting'. The dialog displayed in Figure 3.10 appears.

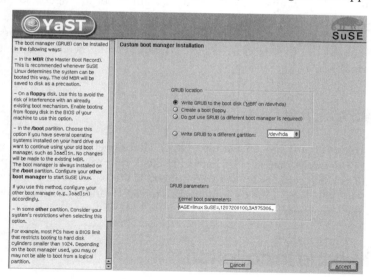

Figure 3.10: *Boot Loader Installation*

In this dialog, determine how and where the boot loader is to be installed. The following options are available:

- Write GRUB to the boot disk (☞*MBR* on /dev/hda)

- Create a boot floppy

- Write GRUB to a different ☞*partition*

- Do not use GRUB

The first option is usually suitable. This option installs the boot loader in the ☞*MBR* of your booting hard disk. Also use this option if you intend to use the Linux boot loader as a boot manager for multiple operating systems. However, make sure your operating system can be booted by LILO or GRUB (applies to MS-DOS, Windows 9x/ME, NT, 2000, XP, and OS/2).

If unsure or you do not want to modify the previous boot mechanism, use the option 'Create a boot floppy'. Linux boots if you insert the floppy disk in the drive before switching on your computer. If the floppy disk is not in the drive, the other operating system starts. The boot loader could later be installed to the hard disk with YaST2.

If you have already installed a different boot manager and want to include SuSE Linux in this boot manager, select 'Do not use GRUB'. Following the installation of SuSE Linux, reconfigure the existing boot manager and include SuSE Linux in the boot routine.

If your system requires additional kernel parameters for each start-up, enter these parameters in the respective field. Usually nothing needs to be entered for a normal home user system.

Time Settings

In this screen (Figure 3.11 on the next page), choose between Local Time and GMT in the field marked 'Set hardware clock to'. Your selection depends on the BIOS clock settings for your computer. If the hardware clock is set in the BIOS to GMT, SuSE Linux automatically reflects Standard and Daylight Savings time changes.

Starting the Installation

A click on 'Next' accepts the suggestions and any changes made. A green confirmation screen opens. After clicking 'Yes' here, the installation begins using your settings. The installation usually takes between fifteen and thirty minutes, depending on your machine's performance and your software selection.

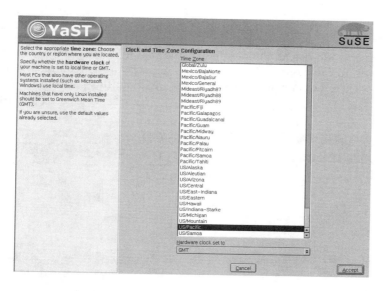

Figure 3.11: *Selecting the Time Zone*

System Configuration

After the installation of your system and selected software is complete, you need to make three more important settings before you can work with SuSE Linux: define a password for the system administrator `root`, create a normal user, and configure your monitor. The following sections show how this is done.

Root Password

`root` is the name of the ☞*superuser*, the ☞*system administrator*. `root` is permitted to do all the things normal users are not permitted to do. The superuser can make changes to the system, such as installing new applications or setting up new hardware. If users forget their passwords or have problems with software, `root` can help them. As a general rule, only log in as root to carry out administrative tasks, such as system maintenance or repairs. `root` is quite risky for everyday use, as root can delete files irreversibly.

For verification purposes, the password must be entered twice as in Figure 3.12 on the following page. Be particularly careful not to forget the `root` password. It cannot be retrieved later.

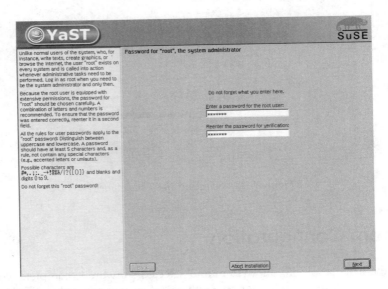

Figure 3.12: Setting the Root Password

User Name and Password

Linux is an operating system that allows several users to work on the same
system at the same time. For it to function smoothly, each user needs a ☞
user account, which allows them to log in to the system then to log out again
when finished. Setting up user accounts provides a strong basis for operating
security. Normal users cannot change or delete files needed for the system to
work properly. Similarly, a user's personal data may not be accessed, modified, or deleted by other users. Each user can set up his own working environment with preferred applications and settings. When users log in to the
Linux system, they find their personal environments unchanged.

Create such a user account yourself using the dialog as shown in Figure 3.13
on the next page. Enter the user's first name and last name. Also specify the

user name (login). If you cannot think of a suitable user name, click 'Suggestion' and the system will automatically generate one for you.

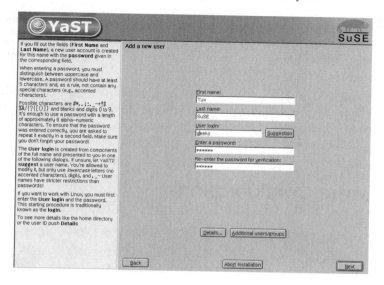

Figure 3.13: *Entering the User Name and Password*

Finally, enter a password for the user, which you must repeat to confirm. The user name tells the system who you are and the password verifies your identity.

Caution

Memorize your user name and password, as you will need this information every time you log in. To provide effective protection, a password should be between five and eight characters long. The maximum length for a password is 128 characters. However, if no special modules are loaded, only the first 8 characters are used to identify the password. Linux distinguishes between lowercase and uppercase letters in the password. Accented characters are not allowed. Special characters (such as *, ., # , ;) and the digits 0–9 may be used.

Caution

Monitor Settings

This shows graphics card and screen with a suitable configuration. In most cases, you can accept the suggestion. However, you can customize color depth, resolution, and the image repetition rate manually.

The settings will be tested once you have accepted the suggestion or entered your changes.

When you click 'Change', you have the option of configuring the graphical interface. For this purpose, the program SaX2 is started. Before modifying the suggested configuration of your graphical user interface, read the instructions in *Display and Input Devices (SaX2)* on page 62.

Hardware Configuration

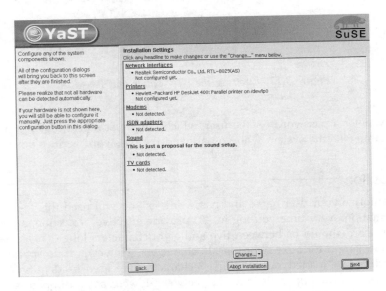

Figure 3.14: Configuring the System Components

Once your graphics card has been configured, you will see a screen like that shown in Figure 3.14. Now you have the option of configuring your system hardware, such as printer or sound card. The hardware configuration can also be done after the installation.

Start the hardware configuration by clicking each component. YaST2 will then automatically detect and configure the hardware. Click 'Finish installation' when completed.

Graphical Login

SuSE Linux is now installed and configured so you can log in to your system. Your monitor displays the graphical ☞*login*, as in Figure 3.15. Enter the user name specified earlier and the respective password to log in to your system.

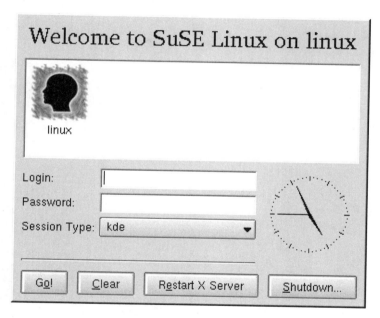

Figure 3.15: *Logging In*

Part II

Configuration

YaST2 — Configuration

YaST2, which you already used for the installation, is also the configuration tool for SuSE Linux. This chapter covers the configuration of your system with YaST2, which enables comfortable configuration of the main system components. This includes most of the hardware, the graphical user interface, Internet access, security settings, user administration, installation of software, and system updates and information. This chapter also provides instructions for using YaST2 in text mode.

Starting YaST2

The 'K' menu and the 'SuSE' menu (the icons at the bottom left on the KDE panel) offer several ways to access YaST2: via the 'Control Center', via 'SuSE' → 'Administration' → 'Configuration', and via 'Preferences'. Using the K menu, directly select the configuration module you need.

At start-up, YaST2 first opens a small dialog in which to enter the password for the user root (the system administrator). The configuration is performed as root because only root can modify Linux system files.

YaST2 can also the command line, but this is a bit more complicated. In the shell, change to the user root with the command sux –, enter the root password, then enter yast2. After you exit YaST2, use the command exit to change from the user root to the normal user.

To use YaST2 in text mode instead of with the graphical interface, refer to *Using YaST2 in Text Mode* on page 100. This version offers the same functionality with a different interface.

To change the language of YaST2 and your entire system, select 'System' → 'Select language' in the YaST2 Control Center. Choose a language, exit the YaST2 Control Center, log out from your computer, then log in again and start YaST2.

The YaST2 Control Center

When you start YaST2 in the graphical mode, the YaST2 Control Center (Figure 4.1 on the facing page) is opened first. In the left frame, you will see the categories 'Software', 'Hardware', 'Network/Basic', 'Network/Advanced', 'Security & Users', 'System', and 'Miscellaneous'. If you click one of icons, the respective contents are listed on the right-hand side. For example, click 'Sound' to open a window in which to configure the sound card. The configuration usually comprises several steps. Press 'Next' to proceed to the following dialog.

The left frame displays a help text for the respective topic, explaining the entries required. After the necessary specifications have been made, complete the procedure by pressing 'Finish' in the last configuration dialog. The configuration is saved.

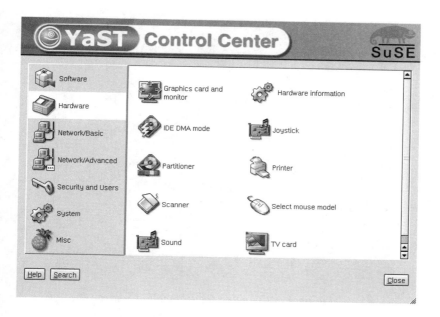

Figure 4.1: The YaST2 Control Center

Software

Change Installation Source

The installation source is the medium containing the software to install. Install from CD or DVD (the usual approach), from a network server, or from the hard disk. Refer to the detailed YaST2 help text.

When you exit the module with 'Save and exit', the settings are saved and applied to the configuration modules 'Install/Remove Software', 'System Update', and 'Boot and kernel configuration'. This module also offers the possibility to proceed with 'Install' to install or remove packages.

Online Update

The YaST Online Update (YOU) enables the installation of important upgrades and improvements. The respective patches are made available for download on the SuSE FTP server. The latest packages can be installed automatically. Use 'Manual update' to determine which patches will be installed in your SuSE Linux system.

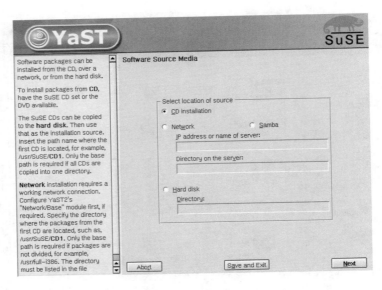

Figure 4.2: Changing the Installation Source

Press 'Next' to download a list of all available patches (if you selected 'Manual update'). Subsequently, the software installation module (see *Install/Remove Software* on the current page) starts, listing all downloaded patches. Here, select the packages for installation or simply accept YaST2's suggestion installation. The patches are installed like other packages.

Patch CD Update

Unlike the Online Update, the patches are not downloaded from the FTP server but installed from CD-ROM (provided to "SuSE Linux Enterprise Server" customers), which is much faster.

Install/Remove Software

This module enables you to install, update, or remove software on your computer. It was completely revised for SuSE Linux 8.1 (Figure 3.9 on page 34). To install from CD, insert the first CD in the drive.

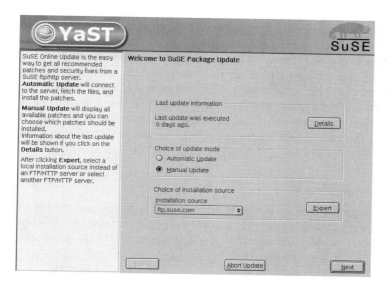

Figure 4.3: YaST2: Online Update

The Selection Filter

With 'Filter' at the top left of the main window, define the criterion for displaying the package selection. The default setting is 'Package groups'.

┌─ **Note** ───

If you are acquainted with previous versions of SuSE Linux, you will realize that you can no longer select packages from "package series". The reason is that the package database structure was completely revised. The packages are now organized in "groups".

─── **Note** ─┘

These package groups are displayed in a tree structure on the left-hand side. If you click one of the main groups (for example, 'Development' or 'Documentation'), all program packages belonging to this main group are listed at the top of the right frame. If you click one of the subgroups, the right frame only displays the packages of the respective subgroup.

Another interesting filter is the one that displays packages according to 'Selections'. You may have noticed this filter during the installation if you entered the software settings in the suggestion screen (see *Software* on page 33). Using the 'Selections' filter, install predefined selections for specific utilization areas with a single click. This is the only filter for which you can activate something in the left frame at this stage. If you click the check boxes of the selections in the left frame, all packages of the respective selection will be installed. If you deselect a package from the standard selection (such as KDE), all related packages will be uninstalled when you confirm. Along with each selection, the right frame displays the packages belonging to this selection together with their current state. Select and deselect individual packages as desired. The predefined selections include 'Development', 'Games', 'KDE', 'GNOME', 'Multimedia', 'Web Server', and 'Documentation'.

The Package Window

The package window to the right displays the following information for each package (from left to right): the status, the package name, a brief description, the size, the version, and the source column, which allows you to install the source code of the package.

The status of the package is indicated by various icons. The following are available:

- is already installed

- is not and will not be installed

- will be installed due to manual selection

- will be installed because it is required by another selected package (dependency)

- will be replaced by a newer version (update)

- will be deleted (uninstalled)

- has been renamed: this status cannot be selected manually (applies to packages that were replaced by a new package with a different name)

Refer to the 'Help' for this module. There, find detailed descriptions of the individual icons and information about which icon represents which status.

Switch the status by clicking the icon to the left of the package name. Only applicable ones are offered, which means a package that is not installed cannot have the status "uninstall". If you do not know what a certain status means, do not select it or do not modify it if it was set automatically.

Caution

You have the possibility to mark installed packages for deletion. Observe the alerts and do not delete any packages of the Linux base system (mostly located in the package group 'System').

Caution

The Info Window

The frame at the bottom rights displays several tabs under which to find information about the currently selected package, such as a detailed description, technical data, a list of files installed with this package, the packages this package requires, the packages that require this package, and possible conflicts with other packages already installed or selected for installation.

The Search

'Search' opens a search dialog in which you can search for specific package names or parts of package names. In the search result, determine what to do with the packages found.

System Update

This module enables you to update your system. The process consists of several steps. YaST2 checks which packages to update. If desired, decide individually for each package whether to perform an update. This approach cannot be used for the base system, which requires a boot from the installation medium, such as from CD.

┌─ **Note** ───

The system update is a very complex procedure. For each program package, YaST2 has to check which version is installed on the computer and what it needs to do to correctly replace the old version with the new version. YaST2 also tries to adopt any personal settings of the installed packages. However, some configurations may cause problems after the update if the old configuration is unable to handle the new program version as expected or if unexpected inconsistencies arise between various configurations.

The older the existing version is and the more the configuration of the packages to update diverges from the standard, the more problematic the update will be. Sometimes, the old configuration cannot be adopted correctly. In this case, an entirely new configuration must be made. Before starting the update, the existing configuration should be saved.

─── **Note** ─┘

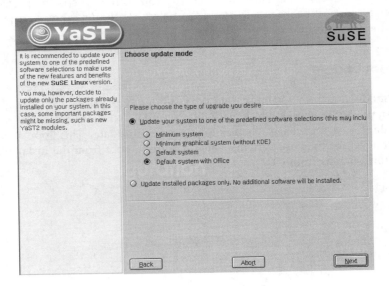

Figure 4.4: System Update

Hardware

New hardware must first be installed or connected as specified by the vendor. Switch on external devices, such as the printer or the modem, and start the respective YaST2 module. Most devices are automatically detected by YaST2 and the technical data is displayed. If the automatic detection fails, YaST2 offers a list of devices (model, vendor, etc.) from which to select the suitable device. Consult the documentation enclosed with your hardware for information.

Note

If your model is not included in the device list, try a similar model name. However, in some cases the model must match exactly, as similar designations do not always indicate compatibility. Unfortunately, devices with similar designations might not understand the same language.

— Note ⌐

Printer

Peculiarities of Printing in Linux

In Linux, printers are addressed by means of print queues. The data to print is temporarily stored in a print queue and subsequently sent to the printer by the printer spooler.

Usually, this data does not exist in a form that could be sent directly to the printer. For example, an image generally needs to be converted to a format the printer can print. The conversion to the printer language is handled by the print filter used by the printer spooler.

Some Standard Printer Languages

- ASCII text — Most printers can print ASCII text directly. However, there are printers that cannot print ASCII directly. Instead, they can be addressed by means of one of the following standard printer languages.

- PostScript — PostScript is the standard page description language in Unix and Linux for direct printing on PostScript printers.

- PCL3, PCL4, PCL5e, PCL6, ESC/P , ESC/P2, and ESC/P rasters — If no PostScript printer is connected, the printer filter uses the Ghostscript program for converting the data to one of these other standard printer languages. For this purpose, a driver that suits the respective printer model well is selected to take model-specific characteristics (such as color settings) into consideration.

Workflow of a Print Job in Linux

1. The user or an application generates a new print job.

2. The print data is temporarily stored in the print queue, from which it is sent to the print filter by the printer spooler.

3. Now the print filter does the following:

   (a) Determines the type of print data.

   (b) If the print data is not PostScript, it is first converted to the standard language PostScript. Normally, ASCII text is converted to PostScript using the a2ps utility.

   (c) If necessary, the PostScript data is converted to another printer language.

   - If a PostScript printer is connected, the PostScript data is sent directly to the printer.
   - If no PostScript printer is connected, the Ghostscript program uses a driver that is suitable for the respective printer model to generate the printer-specific data that will subsequently be sent to the printer.

4. After the entire print job has been sent to the printer, the printer spooler removes the print job from the print queue.

Various Print Systems

SuSE Linux supports two different print systems:

LPRng and lpdfilter This is a traditional print system that consists of the printer spooler LPRng and the print filter lpdfilter. In the traditional print system, the entire configuration of a queue is determined by the system administrator and the user can merely choose from the various queues. To choose from multiple configurations for one printer, several queues with different configurations must be set up for this printer.

CUPS In the CUPS print system, the user has the possibility to individually determine printer-specific settings for each printout, as the entire configuration of a queue is not determined by the system administrator. Rather, the options for printer-specific settings are stored in a "PPD file" (PostScript Printer Description) for each queue and can be offered to the user in a print dialog.

Since the configuration files of the two print systems conflict, only one of them can be installed at a time. For more information about CUPS, see http://www.cups.org/ and the *Administration Guide*.

Print Queues

Usually, several print queues are required for the following reasons:

- Various printers are addressed by means of various print queues.

- The print filter can be configured individually for each print queue. Accordingly, various queues are used for the same printer to use multiple configurations.

One standard configuration is sufficient for plain black-and-white printers (such as most laser printers), but color ink jet printers usually require at least two configurations (queues):

- An lp standard configuration for quick and inexpensive grayscale printing. There should always be a print queue called lp, because this is the traditional name of the default queue.

- A color color queue for color printing.

Supported Printers

Since printer drivers for Linux are usually not provided by the hardware manufacturer, the printer must be addressed using one the common printer languages.

Quality printers understand at least one of the common printer languages. Printers that do not know any common printer language, but only a proprietary protocol, are called "GDI printers" (this is the case with many inexpensive ink jet printers). These printers only work with the operating system version for which the manufacturer provides a driver. Because the control sequences of these printers do not adhere to any generally accepted standards, these devices often cause difficulties in Linux.

Nevertheless, many of these printers are supported by SuSE Linux. However, only a limited functional scope, such as low resolution black-and-white printing, is supported for some models. We cannot guarantee the reliability of the following information, as we do not test GDI printer drivers ourselves. The following printers can be configured directly with YaST:

- Brother HL 720/730/820/1020/1040, MFC 4650/6550MC/9050, and compatible models.

- HP DeskJet 710/712/720/722/820/1000 and compatible models.

- Lexmark 1000/1020/1100/2030/2050/2070/3200/5000/5700/7000/7200, Z11/42/43/51/52 and compatible models. Linux drivers from Lexmark are available at http://www.lexmark.com/printers/linuxprinters.html.

- Oki Okipage 4w/4w+/6w/8w/8wLite/8z/400w and compatible models.

- Samsung ML-200/210/1000/1010/1020/1200/1210/1220/4500/5080/6040 and compatible models.

As far as we know, the following GDI printers are not supported by SuSE Linux. This list is by no means complete.

- Brother DCP-1000, MP-21C, WL-660

- Canon BJC 5000/5100/8000/8500, LBP 460/600/660/800, MultiPASS L6000

- Epson AcuLaser C1000, EPL 5500W/5700L/5800L

- HP LaserJet 1000/3100/3150

- Lexmark Z12/22/23/31/32/33/82, Winwriter 100/150c/200

- Minolta PagePro 6L/1100L/18L, Color PagePro L, Magicolor 6100DeskLaser/2DeskLaserPlus/2DeskLaserDuplex

- Nec SuperScript 610plus/660/660plus

- Oki Okijet 2010

- Samsung ML 85G/5050G, QL 85G

- Sharp AJ 2100, AL 1000/800/840/F880/121

Configuration with YaST2

The YaST2 printer module in SuSE Linux 8.1 has changed considerably. The module was simplified, four buttons were reduced to one, and CUPS was defined as the standard print system. However, you can switch between the print systems CUPS and LPRng at any time. To change the print system, follow the instructions of YaST2 and keep your CDs ready.

┌─ **Note** ───

If you selected 'New Installation' during the installation of SuSE Linux 8.1, CUPS and all related program packages were installed automatically. If, however, you performed an update of your old SuSE Linux, you were asked if you wanted to change your system from LPRng to the new print system. If you decided to keep LPRng, you can now use the YaST2 printer module to change your system to CUPS, if desired. However, the LPRng configuration of previous SuSE Linux versions cannot be adopted by CUPS.

── **Note** ─┘

To set up the printer, start YaST2 and select 'Hardware' → 'Printers'. The main printer setup window appears. Here, see any printers already installed. To add a printer, click 'Add'. In the following dialog, select whether to detect the printer automatically or add it manually. If automatic detection fails, YaST2 opens the manual setup. If your printer is detected automatically, it appears in the upper part of the main window. The automatic configuration and the manual configuration are covered in the following sections.

Automatic Configuration

Under the following conditions, YaST2 enables the automatic configuration of the printer:

1. The parallel or USB port is set up correctly and the connected printer is detected automatically.

2. The detected printer is listed in the printer database. As this identification might be different from the model designation, the model may have to be selected manually.

3. The printer database contains at least one configuration for the respective model that is known to work without problems. Depending on the printer, up to five queues are configured automatically.

To make sure everything works properly, each configuration should be checked with the print test function of YaST2. Additionally, the YaST2 page provides important information about the configuration.

Manual Configuration

If one of the requirements for the automatic configuration is not met or if you want a specific individual configuration, configure the printer manually. Depending on the success of detection, YaST2 can automatically determine the required data or submit a useful preselection. The following parameters need to be configured:

Hardware Connection (Port)

- If YaST2 is able to detect the printer model automatically, this indicates that the printer connection works on the hardware level and no settings need to be configured here.
- If YaST2 is unable to detect the printer model automatically, the printer connection on the hardware level will not work without a manual configuration.

Name of the Queue

As the print queue name will be entered frequently for printing, use short names consisting of lowercase letters and possibly numbers.

Ghostscript Driver or Printer Language

As the Ghostscript driver generates the printer-specific data for non-PostScript printers, the configuration of the Ghostscript driver is the key to determining the type of printout. The selected Ghostscript driver and suitable driver-specific settings determine the appearance of the printout. Differences in the appearance of the printout generated by various configurations for the same printer are specified here.

If YaST2 has detected the printer model automatically or the model is listed in the printer database, a useful preselection of suitable Ghostscript drivers is provided. In this case, YaST2 usually offers several predefined configurations, such as:

- Black-and-white printing, 300 dpi
- Only LPRng: grayscale printing, 300 dpi
- Color printing, 300 dpi
- Only CUPS: color printing, 600 dpi

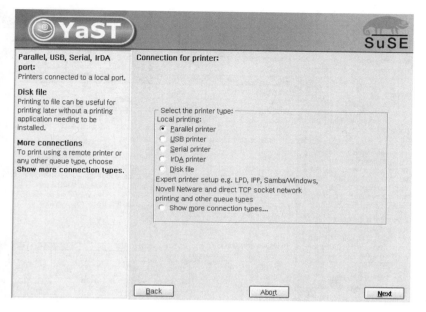

Figure 4.5: Selecting the Printer Interface

- Photo printing, 600 dpi

YaST2 indicates if a configuration is only supported by either CUPS or LPRng. A predefined configuration consists of a suitable Ghostscript driver and possibly some driver-specific settings for the respective type of printout.

Not all selectable combinations of individual driver settings may work with every printer mode, especially in connection with high resolutions.

Test the configuration by printing a YaST2 test page. If the test print produces nonsense (for example, lots of pages that are almost empty), you can normally abort the procedure immediately by extracting all paper from the printer then canceling the test print. However, in some cases printing will no longer be possible afterwards. Therefore, it is always better to cancel the test print first then wait for the end of the printout.

If the printer model is not listed in the printer database, YaST2 offers a selection of standard drivers for the standard printer languages.

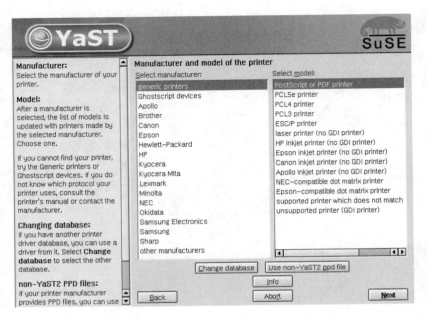

Figure 4.6: Selecting the Printer

Advanced Settings

Here, access the hardware-dependent (driver-specific) and the hardware-independent settings, allowing you to specify special settings for the queues as well as access limitations. Normally, you do not need and should not perform any changes here. For details regarding the options, refer to the printing chapter in the *Administration Guide*.

Configuration for Applications

Applications use the existing print queues in the same way as when printing on the command line. Normally, you do not need to configure the printer again. Simply use the existing print queues.

Printing from the Command Line

From the command line, print using the command
`lpr -Plp filename` (replace `filename` by the name of the file to print). In this example, the default print queue `lp` is used. The option `-P` allows you to explicitly specify the print queue. For example, `lpr -Pcolor filename` uses the print queue `color`.

Using the LPRng Print System

Applications use the `lpr` command for printing with this print system. In the application, select the name of an existing print queue, such as `lp` or `color`, or enter the appropriate print command, such as `lpr -Plp` or `lpr -Pcolor`, in the print dialog of the application.

Using the CUPS Print System

The `cups-client` package contains command-line tools for printing with CUPS, including the `lpr` command. Thus, the approach described above also works in CUPS.

Furthermore, programs such as xpp or KDE's integrated printer dialog kprinter can be used for selecting the print queue and setting CUPS standard options and printer-specific options of the PPD file with graphical selection menus.

Troubleshooting

If the communication between the computer and the printer is faulty, the printer will not be able to process the data sent and the result will be many sheets filled with unintelligible characters.

1. Take all paper out (ink jet printers) or open the paper trays (laser printers) to terminate the printing process.

2. As the print job will be removed from the print queue only after having been sent completely to the printer, usually it will still be in the print queue. Even a reboot will not remove print jobs from the print queue. Delete print jobs using a utility such as kprinter. Instructions for handling print jobs on the command line are provided in the *Administration Guide*.

3. Possibly some data is transmitted to the printer even though the print job was deleted from the print queue. Terminate all processes that still access the printer with the command `fuser`. Enter the following for a printer connected to the parallel port:

```
earth:~ #  fuser -k /dev/lp0
```

For a USB printer, enter the following:

```
earth:~ #  fuser -k /dev/usb/lp0
```

4. Reset the printer by switching the power off for some time. Then insert the paper and switch on the printer.

For More Information

Details on printing in Linux are provided in the Chapter *Printing* in the *Administration Guide*. This manual is included on the CDs and is installed by default. To view the book, start SuSE Help (the lifesaver on your KDE desktop) and click *Administration Guide*. You can also load the directory `/usr/share/doc/packages/suselinux-reference_en` in your browser and click the PDF file.

The documentation in the *Administration Guide* mainly describes general issues and their solution. You can find a solution for many special problems in the Support Database. The Support Database is located in the SuSE Help system; the latest version is available online at `http://sdb.suse.de/en/`. For printer problems, check the Support Database articles *Installing a Printer*, *Printer Configuration with SuSE Linux 8.0*, and *Installing a Printer Since SuSE Linux 6.4 and Up to 7.3*, which you can find by searching for the keyword "installation" or online at `http://sdb.suse.de/en/sdb/html/jsmeix_print-einrichten.html`
`http://sdb.suse.de/en/sdb/html/jsmeix_print-einrichten-80.html`
`http://sdb.suse.de/en/sdb/html/jsmeix_print-einrichten-64.html`

The main problems in each version are summarized in a central article, *Known Problems and Special Features in SuSE Linux 8.1* at `http://sdb.suse.de/en/sdb/html/bugs81.html`. If you are not able to find any solution in the documentation or the Support Database, make use of the SuSE Support Services at `http://www.suse.de/en/services/support/index.html`.

Display and Input Devices (SaX2)

The X server is the graphical input and display subsystem on Linux. All graphical programs talk through it to receive key presses and mouse actions and to display windows on screen.

Normally, the graphical interface is set up during the installation. To improve the values or connect a different monitor in the running system, use this YaST2 module. The current configuration is saved before any changes are made.

Configuration uses the same dialog as during the installation of SuSE Linux. Choose between 'Text mode only' and the graphical interface. The current values are displayed for the latter: the screen resolution, the color depth, the refresh rate, and the vendor and type of your monitor, if it was autodetected. If you are in the process of installing your system or have just installed a new graphics card that you want to initialize, a small dialog appears, asking whether to activate 3D acceleration for your graphics card.

Click 'Edit'. SaX2, the configuration tool for the input and display devices, is started in a separate window (Figure 4.7).

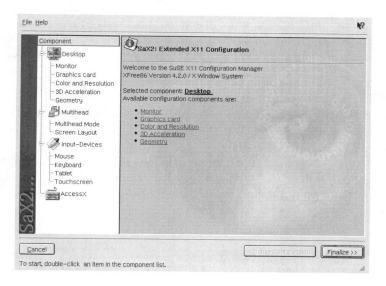

Figure 4.7: *The Main Window of the New SaX2*

SaX2— Main Window

In the left navigation bar, there are four main items: 'Display', 'Input devices', 'Multihead', and 'AccessX'. Configure your monitor, graphics card, color depth, resolution, and the position and size of the screen under 'Display'. The keyboard, mouse, touchscreen monitor, and graphics tablet can be configured under 'Input devices'. Use 'Multihead' to configure multiple screen operation (see *Multihead* on page 67). Here, set the multihead display mode and the layout of the screens on your desk. 'AccessX' is a useful tool for controlling the mouse pointer with the number pad. Adjust the speed of the mouse pointer controlled with the number pad.

Select your monitor and your graphics card. Usually, these are automatically detected by the system. In this case, you do not need to modify anything. If your monitor is not autodetected, automatically continue to the monitor selection dialog. Most likely, you can find your monitor in the comprehensive vendor and device list. You can also manually enter the values specified in the monitor documentation or select one of the preconfigured VESA modes.

After you click 'Finish' in the main window following the completion of the settings for your monitor and your graphics card, test your settings. Thus, ensure that your configuration is suitable for your devices. If the image is not steady, terminate the test immediately by pressing (Esc) and reduce the refresh rate or the resolution and color depth. Regardless of whether you run a test, all modifications are only activated when you restart the X server.

Display

If you go to 'Edit configuration' → 'Properties', a window with the tabs 'Monitor', 'Frequencies', and 'Expert' appears.

- 'Monitor' — In the left part of the window, select the vendor. In the right part, select your model. If you have floppy disks with Linux drivers for your monitor, install these by clicking 'Driver disk'.

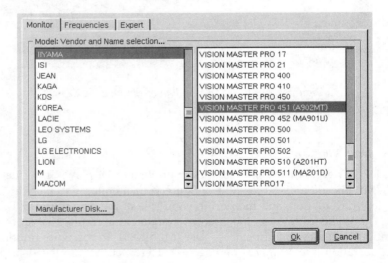

Figure 4.8: SaX2: Monitor Selection

- 'Frequencies' — Here, enter the horizontal and vertical frequencies for your screen. The vertical frequency is another designation for the image refresh rate. Normally, the acceptable value ranges are read from the model and entered here. Usually, they do not need to be changed.

- 'Expert' — Here, enter some options for your screen. In the upper selection field, define the method to use for the calculation of the screen resolution and screen geometry. Do not change anything unless the monitor is addressed incorrectly and the display is not stable. Furthermore, you can change the size of the displayed image and activate the power saving mode DPMS.

Graphics Card

The graphics card dialog has two tabs — 'General' and 'Expert'. In 'General' as in the monitor configuration, select the vendor of your graphics card on the left side and the model on the right.

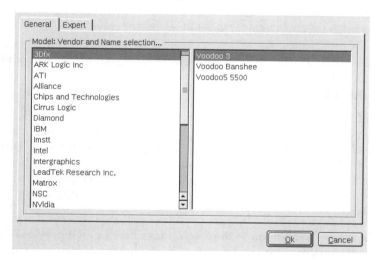

Figure 4.9: SaX2: Selecting the Graphics Cards

'Expert' offers more advanced configuration possibilites. On the right side, turn your screen to the left or to a vertical position (useful for some turnable TFT screens). The entries for the BusID are only relevant if you operate several screens. Normally, nothing needs to be changed here. You should not modify the card options unless you have experience in this field and know what the options mean. If necessary, check the documentation of your graphics card.

Colors and Resolutions

Here, see three tabs — 'Colors', 'Resolution', and 'Expert'.

- 'Colors' — Depending on the hardware used, select a color depth of 16,
  256, 32768, 65536, or 16.7 million colors (4, 8, 15, 16, or 24 bit). For a
  reasonable display quality, set at least 256 colors.

- 'Resolution' — When the hardware is detected, the resolution is
  queried. Therefore, the module usually only offers resolution and color
  depth combinations that your hardware can display correctly. This
  keeps the danger of damaging your hardware with wrong settings very
  low in SuSE Linux. If you change the resolution manually, consult the
  documentation of your hardware to make sure the value set can be displayed.

- 'Expert' — In addition to the resolutions offered in the previous tab,
  this tab enables you to add your own resolutions, which will subsequently be included for selection in the tab.

3D Acceleration

Optionally activate the 3D acceleration of your graphics card. A dialog is
displayed in which to activate the 3D properties of your graphics card.

Image Position and Size

Under these two tabs, precisely adjust the size and the position of the image
with the arrows (see Figure 4.11 on page 68). If you have a multihead environment (more than one screen), use the 'Next screen' button to move to
the other monitors to adjust their size and position. Press 'Save' to save your
settings.

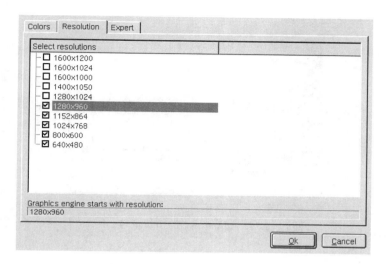

Figure 4.10: SaX2: *Configuring the Resolution*

Multihead

If you have installed more than one graphics card in your computer or a graphics card with multiple outputs, you can connect more than one screen to your system. If you operate two screens, this is referred to as "dualhead." More than two is referred to as "multihead." SaX2 automatically detects multiple graphics cards in the system and prepares the configuration accordingly. Set the multihead mode and the arrangement of the screens in the multihead dialog. Three modes are offered : 'Traditional' (default), 'One screen (Xinerama)', and 'Clone mode':

- 'Traditional multihead' — Each monitor represents an individual unit. The mouse pointer can switch between the screens.

- 'Cloned multihead' — In this mode, all monitors display the same contents. The mouse is only visible on the main screen.

- 'Xinerama multihead' — All screens combine to form a single large screen. Program windows can be positioned freely on all screens or scaled to a size that fills more than one monitor.

The layout of a multihead environment describes the arrangement of and the relationship between the individual screens. By default, SaX2 configures a

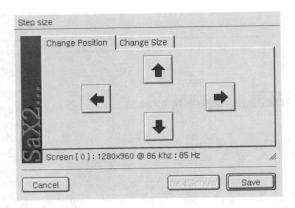

Figure 4.11: Adjusting the Image Geometry

standard layout that follows the sequence of the detected graphics cards, arranging all screens in a row from left to right. In the 'Layout' dialog of the multihead tool, determine the way the monitors are arranged on your screen by using the mouse to move the screen symbols in the grid. After you have completed the layout dialog, verify the new configuration by clicking 'Test'.

Linux currently does not offer 3D support for Xinerama multihead environments. In this case, SaX2 deactivates the 3D support.

Input Devices

Mouse If the mouse already works, you do not need to do anything. However, if the mouse does not work, control it with the number pad of the keyboard as described in *AccessX* on the next page.

If the automatic detection fails, use this dialog to configure your mouse manually. Refer to the documentation of your mouse for a description of the model. Select your model from the list of supported mouse types and confirm by pressing ⑤ on the number pad.

Keyboard The selection field at the top of this dialog enables you to specify the kind of keyboard to use. Then select the language for the keyboard layout (the country-specific position of the keys). Use the test field to check if special characters are displayed correctly.

The status of the check box used for activating and deactivating the entry of accented letters depends on the respective language and does not need to be changed. Click 'Finish' to apply the new settings to your system.

Touchscreen Currently XFree86 only supports Microtouch and Elo Touch-Systems touchscreens. SaX2 can only autodetect the monitor, not the toucher. The toucher is treated as an input device. Configure the toucher as follows:

1. Start SaX2 and select 'Input devices' → 'Touchscreens'.
2. Click 'Add' and add a touchscreen.
3. Save the configuration by clicking 'Finish'. You do not need to test the configuration.

Touchscreens feature a variety of options and usually have to be calibrated first. Unfortunately, there is no general tool for this purpose in Linux. The standard configuration contains suitable default values for the dimensions of the touchscreen. Normally, no additional configuration is required.

Graphics Tablet Currently XFree86 only supports a limited number of graphics tablets. SaX2 enables the configuration of graphics tablets connected to the USB port or the serial port. From the configuration perspective, a graphics tablet is like a mouse — as an input device. The following procedure is recommended:

1. Start SaX2 and select 'Input devices' → 'Graphics tablet'.
2. Click 'Add', select the vendor from the following dialog, and add a graphics tablet from the selection list.
3. Mark the check boxes to the right if you have connected a pen or eraser.
4. If your tablet is connected to the serial port, verify the port. /dev/ttyS0 refers to the first serial port. /dev/ttyS1 refers to the second. Additional ports use similar notation.
5. Save the configuration by clicking 'Finish'.

AccessX

If you operate your computer without a mouse and activate AccessX in SaX2, you can control the mouse pointer on your screen with the number pad of your keyboard. Use (%) as the left mouse button. (X) works as the middle mouse button. Use (÷) as the right mouse button. Press one of those keys to select a button. Then release it and use (5), (+), and (0) to click, double-click, or lock the button. Locking is a way of simulating keeping a button pressed. (Del) releases the button locked by (0). Move the cursor using the number pad keys (1), (2), (3), (4), (6), (7), (8), and (9). Use the slider to determine the speed of the mouse pointer when the respective keys are pressed.

For More Information

For more information about the X Window System, its history, and its properties, refer to the Chapter *Configuration of the X Window System with SaX2* in the *Administration Guide*.

Hardware Information

YaST2 performs a hardware detection for the configuration of hardware components. The detected technical data is displayed in this screen. This is especially useful, for example, if you want to submit a support request for which you need information about your hardware.

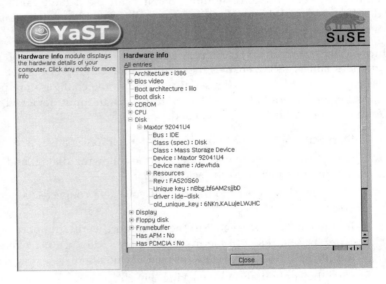

Figure 4.12: *Displaying Hardware Information*

IDE DMA Mode

This module enables you to activate and deactivate DMA mode for your IDE hard disks and your IDE CD and DVD drives in the installed system. This module does not have any function for SCSI devices. DMA modes can substantially increase the performance and data transfer speed in your system.

During the installation, the current SuSE Linux kernel automatically activates DMA for hard disks but not for CD drives, because default DMA activation for all drives often caused problems with CD drives. Use the DMA module to decide whether to activate DMA for your drives. If the drive supports the DMA mode smoothly, the data transfer rate of your CD drive can be increased by activating DMA.

┌─ **Note** ───

"DMA" (**D**irect **M**emory **A**ccess) means your data can be transferred directly to the RAM, bypassing the processor control.

── **Note** ┘

Joystick

Using this new module, easily configure your joystick by simply selecting the vendor and the model from the list. You can also access this module from the sound card configuration of which it is an integral part.

Partitioning

Although it is possible to modify the partitions in the installed system, this should only be done by experts who know exactly what they are doing. Otherwise, the risk of data loss is very high. If you still want to use this tool, refer to the description in *Partitioning* on page 24 (the partitioner during the installation is the same as in the installed system).

Scanner

If your scanner is connected and switched on, it should be detected automatically when this YaST2 module is started. In this case, the dialog for the installation of the scanner appears. If no scanner is detected, the manual configuration dialog appears. If you have already installed one or several scanners, a table listing existing scanners that can be modified or deleted appears. Press 'Add' to configure a new device.

Next, an installation is performed with default settings. If the installation is successful, a corresponding message appears. Now, test your scanner by inserting a document and clicking 'Test'.

Scanner Was Not Detected

Only supported scanners can be autodetected. Scanners connected to another network host will not be detected. The manual configuration distinguishes three types of scanners: USB scanners, SCSI scanners, and network scanners.

- USB scanner: Specify the vendor and model. YaST2 attempts to load USB modules. If your scanner is very new, the modules may not be loaded automatically. In this case, you will be taken to a dialog that enables you to load the USB module manually. Refer to the YaST2 help text for more information.

- SCSI scanner: Specify the device (such as `/dev/sg0`) SCSI scanners should not be connected or disconnected when the the system is running. Shut the system down first.

- Network scanner: You need the IP addresses or the host name.

You can use a scanner that is connected to a host in your network and configured as a network scanner. To configure a network scanner, refer to the Support Database article "Scanning in Linux" (`http://sdb.suse.de/en/`, keyword "scanner"). When selecting a network scanner, enter the host name or the IP address of the host to which the scanner is connected in the dialog.

If your scanner was not detected, probably the device is not supported. However, sometimes even supported scanners are not detected. If that is the case, proceed with the manual scanner selection. If you can identify your scanner in the list of vendors and models, select it. If not, select 'Cancel'. Information about scanners that work with Linux is provided at `http://cdb.suse.de/index.php?LANG=en`, `http://sdb.suse.de/en/`, and `http://www.mostang.com/sane`.

⌐ Caution ───

Only assign the scanner manually if you are absolutely sure. A wrong selection could damage your hardware.

── **Caution ⌐**

Troubleshooting

You scanner may not have been detected for one of the following reasons:

- The scanner is not supported. Check `http://sdb.suse.de/en/` for a list of devices compatible with Linux.

- Your SCSI controller was not installed correctly.

- There are termination problems with your SCSI port.

- Your SCSI cable is too long.

- Your scanner has a SCSI Light Controller that is not supported by Linux.

- Your scanner is defective.

┌─ **Caution** ─────────────────────────────────

SCSI scanners should not be connected or disconnected when the the system is running. Shut the system down first.

─────────────────────────────── **Caution** ─┘

For more information about scanning, refer to the chapter *Kooka — The Scanning Application* on page 265.

Sound

When the sound configuration tool is started, YaST2 tries to autodetect your sound card. Configure one or multiple sound cards. To use multiple sound cards, start by selecting one of the cards to configure. Press 'Configure' button to enter the 'Setup' dialog. 'Edit' opens 'Sound configuration', where you can edit sound cards already configured. 'Finish' saves the current settings and completes the sound configuration. If YaST2 is unable to autodetect your sound card, press 'Add sound card' in 'Sound configuration' to enter the 'Manual sound card selection', where you can select a sound card and the respective module.

Setup

With 'Quick automatic setup', you will not be required to go through any of the further configuration steps and no sound test is performed. The sound card is completely configured. 'Normal Setup' provides the option of controlling the output volume and playing a test sound. With 'Advanced setup', manually adapt the options of the sound module.

Set up your joystick by clicking the respective check box. Select the joystick type in the following dialog and click 'Next'. The same dialog appears when you click 'Joystick' in the YaST2 Control Center.

Sound Card Volume

Test your sound configuration in this test screen. Use the '+' and '-' buttons to adjust the volume. Start at about ten percent to avoid damage to your speakers or hearing. A test sound should be audible when you press 'Test'. If you cannot hear anything, adjust the volume. Press 'Continue' to complete the sound configuration. The volume will be saved.

Sound Configuration

Use 'Delete' to remove a sound card. Existing entries of already configured sound cards will be disabled in the file /etc/modules.conf. With 'Options', manually adjust the options for the various sound modules.

In 'Mixer', configure the individual settings for the input and output of each sound card. 'Next' saves the new values and 'Back' resets the default configuration. Under 'Add sound card...', configure additional sound cards. If YaST2 autodetects another sound card, continue to 'Configure a sound card'. If YaST2 does not detect a sound card, continue to 'Manual sound card selection'.

If you use a Creative Soundblaster Live or AWE, automatically copy SF2 sound fonts to your hard disk from the original Soundblaster driver CD-ROM with 'Install sound fonts'. They are saved in the /usr/share/sfbank/ creative/ directory.

The start-up of ALSA when booting the machine can be enabled or disabled with 'Start ALSA'. For playback of MIDI files, activate the check box 'Start sequencer'. This way, the sound modules required for sequencer support will be loaded along with the ALSA modules.

The volume and configuration of all sound cards installed will be saved when you click 'Finish'. The mixer settings are saved to the file /etc/ asound.conf and the ALSA configuration data appended to the end of the /etc/modules.conf file.

Configuring a Sound Card

If multiple sound cards were detected, select your preferred card under 'List of automatically recognized...'. Continue to 'Setup' with 'Next'. If the sound card was not autodetected, click 'Select from the list' and, with 'Next', proceed to 'Manual sound card selection'.

Manual Sound Card Selection

If your sound card was not autodetected, a list of sound card drivers and models are shown from which to choose. With 'All', see the entire list of supported cards.

Refer to your sound card documentation for the information required. A reference list of sound cards supported by ALSA with their corresponding sound modules is available in /usr/share/doc/packages/alsa/cards. txt and at http://www.alsa-project.org/~goemon/. After making your selection, click 'Next' to return to 'Setup'.

TV Cards

After starting and initializing this YaST2 module, the 'Setting Up the TV Card' dialog appears. If your TV card was autodetected, it is shown here. Highlight the line with the mouse then click 'Add'. If your TV card was not detected, configure the "other, not recognized" card, which activates the manual configuration. Use 'Edit' to change an existing configuration.

'Overview of the TV cards' appears after clicking 'Edit' or immediately after starting this YaST2 module if you have already installed and configured one or more TV cards. In this dialog, individually edit or remove the configuration of each card. 'Add' starts manual configuration.

In the 'Manual Configuration' screen, select your TV card type. If you need to choose a tuner type to obtain a functioning configuration, click 'Select Tuner' and highlight the tuner type. If you are unsure, leave the settings at 'Default (recognized)' for now and see whether it works. If none or not all the tuners can be configured, this could be because the autodetection of the tuner type was unsuccessful or because you selected the wrong type.

'Details' opens the expert configuration. Here, select the kernel module to use as the driver for your TV card and its parameters. All the TV card driver parameters can be adjusted. To do this, select the parameters to edit and enter the new value. Confirm the new values with 'Apply' or restore the default values with 'Reset'.

In the 'TV card, Audio' dialog, you can create the settings for watching TV on your computer with sound. Typically, a short cable comes with your TV card with which to connect to the audio input of the sound card. For this, the sound card must already be installed and the external input not on mute. Click 'Yes' in the screen and select a sound card in the next step. Here you also have the chance to configure your sound card. See also *Sound* on page 73.

Network/Basic

Basic Information on the Internet Access

This section explains a number of important terms in connection with Internet access, briefly introducing their aim and function. All the machines connected to the Internet make up a large network where various operating systems are running with different hardware. The Internet uses a standard communication protocol that can be understood regardless of hardware or software used. Communication is made with the Internet Protocol (IP), together with the Transmission Control Protocol (TCP), the User Datagram Protocol (UDP), and the Internet Control Message Protocol (ICMP). These protocols comprise the common "language" used by all machines on the Internet. The abbreviation for this is TCP/IP.

Every machine on the Internet has an ID number — the IP address. It can only be addressed by TCP/IP with this number. Normally, a machine also has a text name, used by application programs to refer to it. The Domain Name System (DNS) is responsible for converting the IP address to a text name. This particular service is offered by name servers. A machine or an application offering a service is called a server (for example, DNS server) and a machine or application making use of a service is called a client.

Below TCP/IP, there are various standardized protocols for forwarding the appropriate TCP/IP data transfers to the given transmission method. For network connections via a network card, this is the ethernet protocol. For modem and ISDN telephone connections, it is the Point-to-Point Protocol (PPP). For ADSL and T-DSL connections, the Point-to-Point over Ethernet Protocol (PPPoE) is used. The ethernet, PPP, or PPPoE connection, followed by the TCP/IP connection between your own machine and a machine on Internet provider, must be established before setting up an Internet connection.

On top of TCP/IP, there are various standardized protocols for proper data transfer to the application.

- The HyperText Transfer Protocol (HTTP) serves for the transfer of web sites in HyperText Markup Language (HTML) format.

- The Simple Mail Transfer Protocol (SMTP) is responsible for sending e-mails to another machine and Post Office Protocol (POP3) for downloading e-mails from a mail server.

- The File Transfer Protocol (FTP) is used to transfer files.

For several application programs, such as a web browser and an e-mail program, to use the same Internet connection at the same time, separate TCP/IP connections are used for each application. Large amounts of TCP/IP data are also divided into small packets, so HTTP packets from the web browser can be sent over its TCP/IP connection while alternating with SMTP or POP3 packet transfers from the e-mail program via other TCP/IP connections.

Since several applications are using the same Internet connection, the IP address, which only identifies the machine, is not enough. A port number is needed to sort out which TCP/IP data belongs to which application. These standard services are usually provided on their particular server at the following port numbers: DNS on port 53, HTTP on port 80, SMTP on port 25, POP3 on port 110, FTP on ports 20 and 21. The client can only implement the right service if it addresses the correct port number at the server.

Information about the Internet Dial-Up

If you activate 'Dial on demand' or 'Automatic dial-up' in the YaST2 modules, the Internet connection is established automatically whenever necessary, for example, when an external URL is entered in the browser or when e-mail is sent and retrieved. 'Dial on demand' or 'automatic' is only advisable if you have a flat rate for Internet access. With 'manual', the computer only establishes a connection to the Internet when you want it to do so. Background processes, such as retrieval of e-mail in regular intervals, frequently establish connections to the Internet, which can be expensive.

E-Mail

The configuration module allows you to adapt your mail settings if you send your mail with sendmail, postfix, or the SMTP server of your provider. Retrieve mail via SMTP or the fetchmail program, for which you can also enter the details of the POP3 server or IMAP server of your provider.

You can also use a mail program of your choice, such as KMail or Evolution, to set your POP and SMTP access data as usual (to receive mail with POP3 and send mail with SMTP). In this case, you do not need this module. The e-mail module is described in detail in the *Administration Guide*.

Network Card

With the help of YaST2, configure your network card for connection to the local network. You have the option of deciding between 'Automatic address setup (with DHCP)' and 'Static address configuration'.

'Automatic address setup (with DHCP)' DHCP (Dynamic Host Configuration Protocol) ensures that a host receives an IP address from a DHCP server. Configuring the network takes place automatically. This function can only be implemented if a DHCP server exists on your network.

'Static address configuration' This is the conventional method. Enter your IP address here. A network interface is already entered under 'Subnet mask', which is normally sufficient. Otherwise, this will have to be modified. Ask your system administrator for this information.

When you click 'Finish', continue to the next screen. Now, you will see a display of the port to which your network card is connected as well as the autodetected hardware if you have a PCI card. With ISA and ISA-PnP cards, make your selections manually. Also edit the settings or delete the configuration of a network card or add additional cards. If you are located in a wireless LAN, activate the check box for "Wireless support". After it has been activated, configure the options and the access to your wireless LAN. Press 'Next' to see a list of the configured cards. Complete the configuration by clicking 'Finish'.

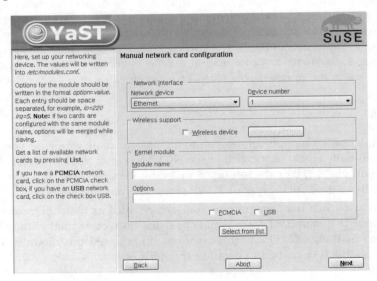

Figure 4.13: Configuration of the Network Card

Cable Modem

In some countries (US, Austria), Internet access via cable modems has become relatively widespread. The cable subscriber gets a modem-like device from the ISP, which is connected to the TV cable network on one side and to the computer on the other using a 10BaseT (twisted pair) cable and a network card. As far as the computer is concerned, this is basically a permanent network link with a static IP number.

Following your provider's specification, select either 'Automatic address setup (with DHCP)' or 'Static address configuration' for the configuration of your network card. Most providers today use DHCP. A static IP address is generally included in the provider's business package. In this case, the provider should have assigned a static IP address.

Regarding the setup and configuration of cable modems, refer to the Support Database article available online at `http://sdb.suse.de/en/sdb/html/cmodem8.html`.

Modem

In the YaST2 Control Center, find the modem configuration under 'Network/Basic'. If the autodetection fails, select the manual configuration. In the screen that opens, enter the port by 'Device' and any name for your modem by 'Modem name'.

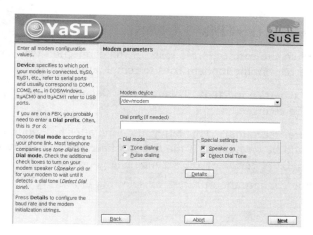

Figure 4.14: Modem Configuration

If a PBX is interposed, you may need to enter an extra number to dial out of the system (usually a zero, but you can find this out in the operation instructions for your telephone system). Also decide between tone and pulse dialing, whether the speaker should be switched on, and whether it should wait for the dial tone. The last option should not be used if your modem is connected to a PBX.

The baud rate and the initialization string settings for the modem can be specified under 'Details'. Only make changes if your modem has not automatically been recognized and special settings have to be made for data transfer. This is primarily the case for ISDN terminal adapters.

For an ISP (Internet Service Provider), select either a standard provider for your country or click 'New' and enter the ISP parameters manually: the names of the dial-up and the connection (for example, the name of the selected provider), the phone number (of the provider), and your user name.

Under 'Request for password', enter either your password or, if, for security reasons, you want to prevent the password from being saved to your hard disk, select 'Always ask me'. The next dialog allows you to make the previously-defined provider the default ISP and to set a default modem for each provider if you have several modems.

By selecting 'Dial on demand', tell the system to establish a connection automatically as soon as an application tries to reach the Internet. In general, this is only advisable if you have a flat-rate connection (also see *Information about the Internet Dial-Up* on page 77). By selecting 'Activate firewall', enable the Personal Firewall.

Under 'Details', activate additional features:

'Reconnect when the connection is lost' If the connection was terminated for some reason, the modem tries to redial automatically.

'Modify DNS when connected' This is set by default and usually does not need to be changed.

'Disconnect after (seconds)' This lets you define after how long the connection should be terminated if the line has been inactive (with no data transferred). A period of 180 seconds is a good value in most cases.

Finish the configuration process by selecting either 'Next' or 'Finish'.

DSL

Your network card must be properly configured to configure ADSL access. With YaST2, you can only set up connections based on the Point-to-Point-over-Ethernet protocol (PPPoE). Automatic IP addressing does not occur with the DHCP protocol. You cannot use 'Automatic address setup (with DHCP)'. Instead, use a static "dummy IP address". A good choice might be `192.168.22.1`, for example. In 'Subnet mask', enter `255.255.255.0`. For a stand-alone system, be certain that you do not make any entries in the 'Default gateway' field. The values for the 'IP address' of your machine and 'Subnet mask' are only placeholders. They do not have anything to do with setting up a connection with ADSL. They are only required for activating the network card.

Enter your user ID and your personal password in the screen. Finally, set the ethernet card to which your modem is connected (usually eth0). Sixty seconds 'Idle time' is recommended — the connection will automatically be terminated if data flow stops. With 'Finish', this procedure is completed.

To use 'Dial on demand' (see page 77) if you have a stand-alone system, you must enter a name server. Most providers today support dynamic DNS assignment, so a current IP address is forwarded to the name server each time the connection is set up. However, a suitable dummy name server IP must be entered in this dialog. `192.168.22.99` is a good choice. If you do not receive a dynamic name server assignment, enter the IP addresses of the name servers of your provider here.

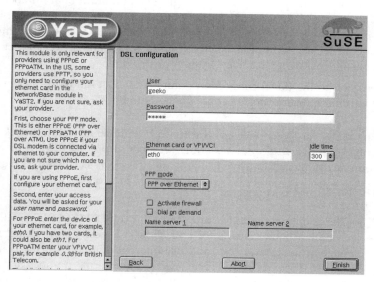

Figure 4.15: ADSL Configuration

Proceed for T-DSL (German Telekom) as you would for ADSL. To configure your T-DSL, you will need the following data: attachment identification, T-Online number, shared user ID, and your personal password. This information can be obtained from your T-DSL login sheet.

ISDN

If your ISDN card is successfully autodetected, a dialog appears in which to make your 'Selection of ISDN protocol'. 'Euro-ISDN (EDSS1)' is the standard for this (refer to scenarios 1 and 2a below) in Europe. '1TR6' is a protocol used by older and larger phone systems (refer to Scenario 2b below). 'NI1' is the standard in the USA. If this automatic detection fails, choose the correct ISDN card. Then specify the ISDN protocol and click 'Next'.

In the screen that follows, specify your country and provider. The ones listed here are "Call-by-Call" providers. To use a provider not included in this list, click 'New'. This opens the 'ISP parameters' screen in which to make all the necessary settings pertaining to your preferred provider. 'ISDN SyncPPP' is the standard 'ISDN type'. Specify the provider name for the 'Connection Name' then the provider's telephone number.

In the case of an interposed PBX, you might need an additional number in front of the phone number itself to dial out (usually a zero or nine, but it is best to refer to the instructions for your PBX). The entire telephone number may not contain any separators, such as commas or blank spaces. Enter the user name and password received from your provider.

Next, proceed to the ISDN connection parameters. The following scenarios require various specification for your 'Phone Number':

- The ISDN card is connected directly to the phone company's socket. Enter an MSN, Multiple Subscriber Number, if provided by your phone company. Otherwise, leave it blank and the ISDN card should work.

- The ISDN card is connected to a PBX:

  ▷ The telephone system's protocol is Euro-ISDN/EDSS1 (usually for "small" phone systems for households): These phone systems have an internal S0 bus and use internal numbers for the connected devices. In this case, specify the internal number as MSN. Further information can be obtained from your phone system documentation. One of the MSNs available for your phone system should work as long as this MSN is allowed external access. If all else fails, a single zero might work as well.

▷ The phone system's protocol for the internal ports is 1TR6 (mostly the case for "large" corporate telephone systems): the MSN is known here as "EAZ" and is usually the extension. Usually, you only need to enter the last digit of the EAZ for the Linux configuration. If all else fails, try the digits 1, 2, 3, 4, 5, 6, 7, 8, or 9.

Choose a dial mode of 'Manual', 'Automatic', or 'Off'. Look at *Information about the Internet Dial-Up* on page 77 regarding the 'Automatic' dial mode. It is best to choose 'Manual', so you can establish the connection to the Internet using kinternet and also disconnect without waiting for a time-out. Dial from the command line with `/usr/sbin/isdnctrl dial ippp0` and hang up with `/usr/sbin/isdnctrl hangup ippp0`.

You can also configure after how many seconds the connection should be terminated if data transfer is no longer taking place. Sixty seconds is recommended for this. When enabled, 'ChargeHUP' makes sure that the connection is not terminated until the next payable unit. However, this does not work with every provider.

It is highly recommended to select 'Initialize ISDN system when booting' so the necessary drivers are loaded automatically. This alone will not set up an Internet connection.

If there is only the one local host, you do not need to change anything in 'IP settings'. YaST2 will suggest the most appropriate local and remote IP address to accept.

The preselected items 'Dynamic IP Address' and 'Dynamic DNS' ensure that the IP address and name server assigned by the provider are forwarded during the connection, which is usually necessary. Under 'Callback settings', 'Callback off' should be selected, as the other choices are — at least for private use — irrelevant. 'Next' and 'Finish' complete the configuration.

Starting or Stopping System Services

This tool allows you to determine which network services (such as telnet, finger, talk, and ftp) to start when SuSE Linux boots. These services enable external hosts to connect to your computer. Also configure various parameters for each service. By default, the master service that manages the individual services (inetd) is not started. It must first be activated. Can choose between a standard configuration and user-defined settings.

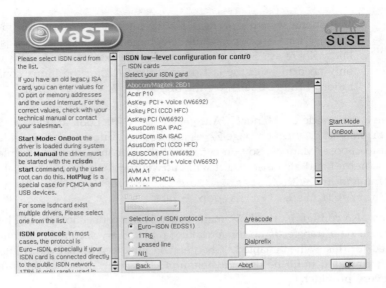

Figure 4.16: ISDN Configuration

┌─ Caution ─────────────────────────────────

This is an expert tool. Only make modifications if you are familiar with network services and know exactly what you are doing.

──────────────────────────────── Caution ─┘

Network/Advanced

This group mostly contains tools for professionals and for the system administrator. If you have SuSE Linux Personal Edition, some of the tools covered in this section will not exist in this group, as they are only installed in the Professional Edition.

The tools 'LDAP client', 'NIS server', 'NIS client', and 'NIS+ client' will not be addressed here, as these are genuine expert tools that are usually only used in company networks. More information about these modules is provided in the *Administration Guide*.

Host Name and DNS

The host name and the domain name can be changed here. If the provider has been configured correctly for DSL, modem, or ISDN access, the list of name servers contain entries made automatically as they were retrieved from the provider data. If you are located in a local network, you might receive your host name via DHCP, in which case you should not modify the name.

NFS Client and NFS Server

You need these two tools only if you are located in a network. In this case, you have the possibility to operate a file server that can be accessed by members of your network. On this file server, make programs, files, or storage space available for users. Use the 'NFS server' module to set up your computer as an NFS server and to determine which directories to export for use by the network users. The NFS server should be set up by an expert. To configure an NFS server, refer to the brief instructions in the *Administration Guide* under *Linux in the Network: NFS*.

Subsequently, any user (with the needed permissions) can mount these directories in his own file tree. The easiest way to do this is by means of the 'NFS client' module, in which the user merely needs to enter the host name of the computer acting as NFS server and the mount point on his computer. To do this, select 'Add' in the first dialog and enter the said data (see Figure 4.17).

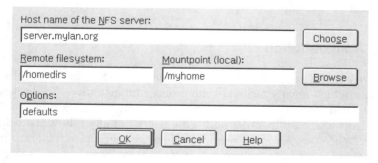

Figure 4.17: Configuration of NFS Clients

Routing

This tool is only needed if you are located in a local network or are connected to the Internet by way of a network card, as is the case with DSL.

As indicated in *DSL* on page 80, for DSL the gateway data is only needed to configure the network card correctly. However, the entries are dummies that do not have any function. The value is important only if you are located in a local network and use your own computer as gateway (the gateway to the Internet).

Security and Users

A basic aspect of Linux is that it is a multiuser system. Consequently, several users can work independently on the same Linux system. Each user has a user account identified by a login name and a personal password for logging in to the system. All users have their own home directories where personal files and configurations are stored.

User Administration

First, verify that 'User Administration' is marked. YaST2 provides a list of all users, which greatly facilitates the user administration. To delete a user, select it from the list (the line will be highlighted dark blue) and click 'Delete'. To 'Add' a user, simply fill in the required fields. Subsequently, the new user can log in to the computer with the login name and password. Edit details under 'Edit' → 'Details'.

Group Administration

First, verify that 'Group administration' is marked. YaST2 provides a list of all groups, which greatly facilitates the group administration. To delete a group, select it from the list (the line will be highlighted dark blue) and click 'Delete'. It is also easy to 'Add' and 'Edit' users. Simply follow the help texts in YaST2. When you enter the members of the new group in the entry field at the bottom, make sure the user names are entered without any space after the comma. YaST2 suggests a group ID that you can accept.

Security Settings

In the start screen 'Local security configuration', which can be accessed under 'Security&Users', there are four selection items: Level 1 is for stand-alone computers (preconfigured). Level 2 is for workstations with a network

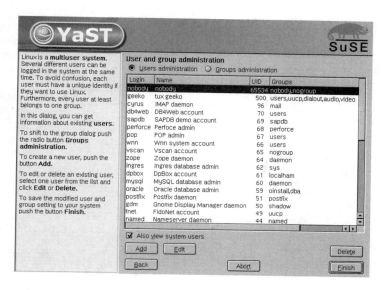

Figure 4.18: *User Administration*

(preconfigured). Level 3 is for a server with a network (preconfigured). Use 'Custom Settings' for your own configuration.

If you click one of the three items, have the option of incorporating one of the levels of preconfigured system security options. To do this, simply click 'Finish'. Under 'Details', access the individual settings that can be modified. If you choose 'Custom settings', proceed to the different dialogs with 'Next'. Here, find the default installation values.

'Password settings' Define how long the password should be for future users (minimum and maximum length). Five to eight characters is an acceptable value. Specify for how long a password should be valid, when it will expire, and how many days in advance an expiration warning should be issued (the warning is issued when logging in to the text console).

'Boot settings' This screen involves two things. First, it sets how the key combination (Ctrl) + (Alt) + (Del) should be interpreted. Usually, this combination, entered in the text console, causes the system to restart. Leave it at that unless your machine or server is publicly accessible and you are afraid someone could carry out this action without authorization. If you select 'Stop', this key combination will cause the system to shut

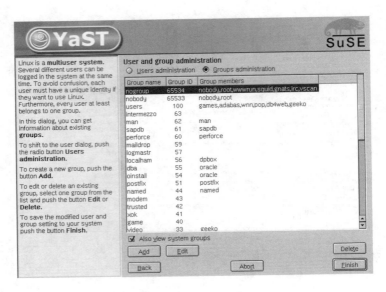

Figure 4.19: Group Administration

down. With 'Ignore', this key combination is ignored. Second, it sets who is permitted to shut down the system from KDM (KDE Display Manager — the graphical login). The options are 'Only root' (the system administrator), 'All users', 'Nobody', or 'Local users'. If 'Nobody' is selected, the system can only be shut down via the text console.

'Login settings' Typically, following a failed login attempt, there is a waiting period lasting a few seconds before another login is possible. The purpose of this is to make it more difficult for "password sniffers". In addition, you have the option of activating 'Record failed login attempts' and 'Record successful login attempts'. If you suspect someone is trying to find out your password, check the entries in the system log files in /var/log.

'Add user settings' Every user has a numerical and an alphabetical user ID. The correlation between these is established via the file /etc/passwd and should be as unique as possible.

Using the data in this screen, define the range of numbers assigned to the numerical part of the user ID when a new user is added. A minimum of 500 is reasonable for users.

'Miscellaneous settings' For 'Setting of file permissions', there are three selection options: 'Easy', 'Secure', and 'Paranoid'. The first one should be sufficient for most users. The YaST2 help text provides information about the three security levels.

The 'Paranoid' setting is extremely restrictive and should serve as the basic level of operation for system administrator settings. If you select 'Paranoid', take into account possible disturbances and malfunctions when using certain programs, because you will no longer have the permissions to access various files.

Also in this dialog, define which users can start the updatedb program. This program, which automatically runs either on a daily basis or after booting, generates a database (locatedb) where the location of each file on your computer is stored (locatedb can be searched by running the locate command). If you select 'Nobody', any user can find only the paths in the database that can be seen by any other (unprivileged) user. If root is selected, all local files are indexed, because the user root, as superuser, may access all directories.

Another option is to activate 'Omit current directory from the path of user root', a reasonable selection. Finally, there is the option 'Disable telnet login for user root'. It is also a good idea to choose this item. If not, it is possible to to log in to your machine as root via telnet, over which the root password is transmitted as plain text.

Press 'Finish' to complete your security configuration.

Firewall

This module can be used to activate and configure the SuSE Firewall. If you are connected to the Internet, you should make use of this protective measure. The SuSE Firewall protects you efficiently.

When the module is started, four dialogs appear consecutively. In the first dialog, select the interface you want to protect (see Figure 4.21 on page 91). 'External interface' is the interface for the Internet. 'Internal interface' is only required if you are located in an internal network and intend to use the firewall to protect your computer against internal attacks. In this case, your computer would be in a "demilitarized zone" (DMZ). Normally, a configuration with DMZ is only used for company networks.

After selecting your interface, selectively activate the services of your computer for which to allow access from the Internet (see Figure 4.22 on page 92). If you do not operate a server with one of these services but only

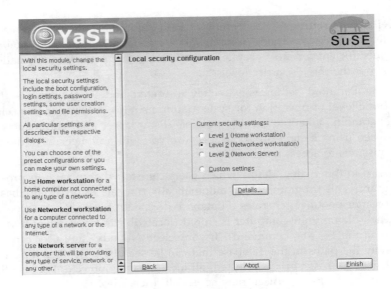

Figure 4.20: YaST2: Security Settings

want to surf the Internet and send and receive e-mail, do not activate any of these services (the more "doors" to the outside are closed, the fewer possibilities an attacker will have to intrude).

If you are not familiar with the terms masquerading and traceroute, simply accept the third dialog without any modifications. You can also accept the final dialog, as the default log options are usually sufficient.

When you click 'Next', a small window asks for confirmation. Then the new configuration is saved to your hard disk. The next time your Internet connection is started, your computer is protected effectively against attacks.

For more information about the SuSE Firewall, refer to the *Administration Guide* under *Linux in the Network*: *Firewall*.

System

Creating a System Backup

The YaST2 backup module enables you to create a backup of your system. The backup created by the module does not comprise the entire system, but

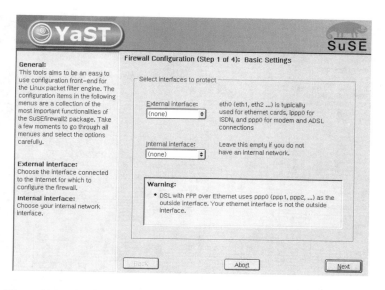

Figure 4.21: *YaST2: SuSE Firewall: Selecting the Interfaces to Protect*

only saves information about changed packages and copies of critical storage areas and configuration files.

Define the kind of data to save in the backup. By default, the backup includes information about any packages changed since the last installation run. In addition, it may include data that does not belong to packages themselves, such as many of the configuration files in /etc or in the directories under /home. Apart from that, the backup can include important storage areas on your hard disk that may be crucial when trying to restore a system, such as the partition table or the master boot record (MBR).

Creating a Boot, Rescue, or Module Disk

Using the YaST2 module, create two different types of boot disks, a rescue disk, and four kinds of module disks. Both boot disks enable initial installation if you have problems booting from CD. The disks are actually not intended for booting an already installed system. With a little trick, however, you can use them to boot an installed system.

'Boot disks' The standard boot disks contain a complete minimum system with all files needed for starting SuSE Linux, including the kernel. You can also create a boot disk for i386 and older Cyrix processors.

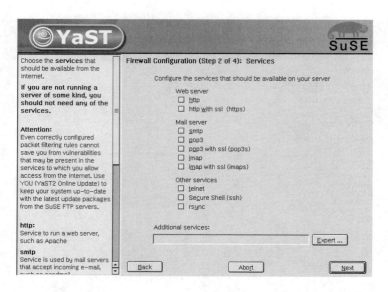

Figure 4.22: YaST2: SuSE Firewall: Externally Accessible Services

---

┌─ Note ───

These boot disks should not be confused with boot disks that
boot an installed system. A boot disk for the installed system is
created during the installation or with the boot loader module in
YaST2 and starts the Linux system that is installed on the hard
disk if it is inserted when the computer is booted. It does not
contain any system, but only the boot loader.

─── **Note ─┘**

If all else fails, you can also start an already installed system with the
boot disk created above. For this, boot from the floppy disk then, when
it asks you to insert the first CD, exit the dialog to prevent the start of
a reinstallation. After making the language and keyboard entries, reach
a menu where can choose 'Start installation or system'. In the following
window, select 'Boot installed system'.

'Rescue disk' The rescue disk allows you to regain control of your system.
A minimum Linux system containing all the helpful tools needed to
resolve most problems is loaded.

'Module disks' If you need additional hardware modules or drivers for the

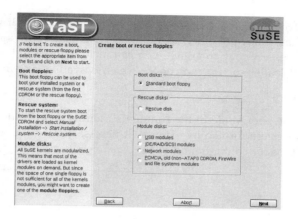

Figure 4.23: Creating a Boot or Module Disk

installation (for instance, if you install via the network), create one of the following disks:

- Modules 1: USB drivers
- Modules 2: IDE, RAID, and SCSI modules
- Modules 3: Network modules
- Modules 4: CD-ROM, PCMCIA, Firewire, file systems

Select the appropriate item in the dialog, insert a disk (preferably empty or formatted), and click 'Next'. The respective content is then written to the floppy disk.

Boot Loader Configuration

The boot mode is normally specified during the installation (see *Booting* on page 35). If your SuSE Linux can be booted, you do not need to change anything, unless you formerly booted from a floppy disk and now want to boot from the hard disk.

The boot loader configuration was substantially expanded. Apart from the the main dialog, which is described here, normal users can usually ignore most of the other dialogs that are accessed with 'Next' (if 'Edit' was selected), as these mostly concern expert settings. However, the dialog that enables the inclusion of new partitions in the boot loader start-up screen (which appears when the system is booted) may be of interest to home users. If you have installed Linux and there are other operating systems (such as Windows, OS/2, or another Linux) on your computer, you can include these in the selection list of the boot loader so you can choose which operating system to boot.

LVM

The "Logical Volume Manager" (LVM) is a tool for individually partitioning hard disks by means of logical drives. As this is a genuine expert tool, no additional information is provided within the scope of this user guide. For information, refer to the *Administration Guide*.

Profile Manager (SCPM)

The SCPM (System Configuration Profile Management) module offers the possibility to create, manage, and switch between entire individual system configurations. This is especially useful for mobile computers that are used in different locations (in different networks) and by different users. Nevertheless, this feature is useful even for stationary machines, as it enables the use of various hardware components or test configurations. Although the module with the accompanying help is easy to use, the configuration of profiles is a task that should be performed by experts or system administrators.

For information about the basics and utilization of SCPM, please refer to the respective sections in the *Administration Guide*.

Restore

This module (Figure 4.24 on the facing page) enables you to restore your system from a backup archive. Follow the instructions in YaST2. Press 'Next' to proceed to the individual dialogs. First, specify where the archives are located (removable media, local hard disks, or network file systems). As you continue, a description and the contents of the individual archives is displayed, so you can decide what to restore from the archives.

Additionally, there are two dialogs for uninstalling packages that were added since the last backup and for the renewed installation of packages that were deleted since the last backup. These two steps enable you to restore the exact system state at the time of the last backup.

┌─ Caution ──────────────────────────────────

As this module normally installs, replaces, or uninstalls many packages and files, you should use it only if you have experience with backups, as otherwise you may lose data.

─────────────────────────────── **Caution ─┘**

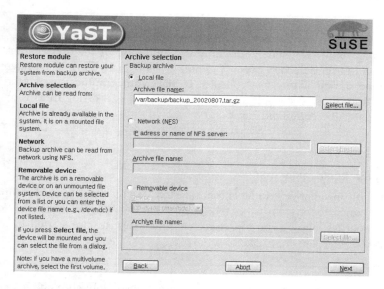

Figure 4.24: YaST2: *Start Window of the Restore Module*

Runlevel Editor

The Runlevels in SuSE Linux

SuSE Linux can be operated in several runlevels. By default, the system starts in runlevel 5, which offers multiuser mode, network access, and the graphical user interface (X Window System). The other runlevels offer multiuser mode with network but without X (runlevel 3), multiuser mode without network (runlevel 2), single-user mode (runlevel 1 and S), system halt (runlevel 0), and system reboot (runlevel 6).

The various runlevels are especially useful if problems in connection with a particular service (X or network) are encountered in a higher runlevel. In this case, the system can be started in a lower runlevel to repair the service. Moreover, many servers operate without a graphical user interface and must be booted in a runlevel without X, such as runlevel 3.

Usually home users only need the standard runlevel (5). However, if the graphical user interface freezes at any time, you can restart the X Window system by switching to a text console with (Ctrl) + (Alt) + (F1), logging in as root, and switching to runlevel 3 with the command init 3. This shuts down your X Window System. Restart it by entering init 5.

Tip

If you simply want to try out what happens in a different runlevel, such as runlevel 3, start your computer and wait for the boot loader screen to appear. Then press (↑), enter (3), and press (↵). The system will be started with a text console. To start your graphical user interface from the text console, log in and enter startx or log in as root and enter the command init 5.

Tip

Setting the Runlevel in YaST2

In a default installation, runlevel 5 is selected. If you want to start a different runlevel when the system is booted, change the default runlevel here. 'Runlevel properties' allows you to determine which services are started in which runlevel.

Caution

Do not modify anything unless you are not absolutely sure about what you are doing. If you deactivate certain services for a runlevel by mistake, your system may not work properly afterwards.

Caution

For more information on the runlevels in SuSE Linux, refer to the *Administration Guide* under *The Boot Concept*: *The Runlevels*.

Sysconfig Editor

The directory /etc/sysconfig contains the files with the most important settings for SuSE Linux (formerly centrally administered in the file /etc/rc.config). The sysconfig editor displays all settings in a transparent form.

The values can be modified and saved to the individual configuration files. Generally manual editing is not necessary, since the files are automatically adapted when a package is installed or a service is configured.

Caution ───

This is a professional tool. Do not edit the files in /etc/sysconfig if you do not know exactly what you are doing, because this could be very detrimental to the functionality of your system.

─── **Caution** ┘

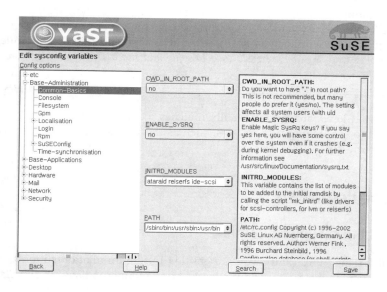

Figure 4.25: YaST2: Configuration of the sysconfig Editor

More information is provided in the *Administration Guide* under *The Boot Concept*.

Time Zone Selection

The time zone was already set during the installation, but you can make changes here. Click your country or region in the list and select 'Local time' or 'GMT' (Greenwich Mean Time). 'GMT' is often used in Linux systems. Machines with additional operating systems, such as Microsoft Windows, mostly use the local time.

Language Selection

Here, set the language for your Linux system. The language can be changed at any time. The language selected in YaST2 applies to the entire system, including YaST2 and the desktop environment KDE 3.

Keyboard Layout Selection

> **Note**
>
> You should only use this module if you work on a system without the X Window System and a graphical user interface. If you use a graphical system (such as KDE), set up the keyboard with the module 'Display and Input Devices'. (see *Display and Input Devices (SaX2)* on page 62).
>
> **Note**

The desired keyboard layout usually matches the selected language. Use the test field to see if special characters, such as the pipe symbol ' | ', are displayed correctly.

Miscellaneous

Submitting a Support Request

By purchasing SuSE Linux, you are entitled to free installation support. Information such as the scope, address, and phone number is listed in *Installation Support* on page 324.

YaST2 offers the possibility to directly send a support request by e-mail to the SuSE team. Registration is required first. Start by entering the respective data — your registration code is located at the back of the CD cover. Regarding your query, select the problem category in the following window and provide a description of the problem (Figure 4.26 on the next page). Also read the YaST2 help text, which explains how to best describe the problem so the Support team can help you.

> **Tip**
>
> If you need advanced support (such as for special problems), consider using of the SuSE Professional Services. Check http://www.suse.de/en/support/ for details.
>
> **Tip**

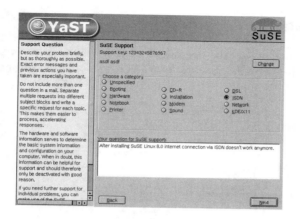

Figure 4.26: *Submitting a Support Request*

Start Protocol

The start protocol contains the screen messages displayed when the computer is started. The start protocol is logged to /var/log/boot.msg. Use this YaST2 module to view the protocol, for example, to check if all services and functions were started as expected.

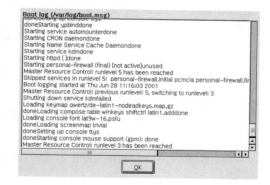

Figure 4.27: *Display Start Protocol*

System Protocol

The system protocol logs the operations of your computer to `/var/log/messsages`. Kernel messages are recorded here, sorted according to date and time.

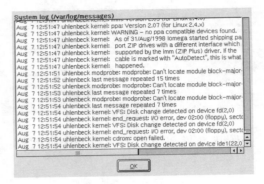

Figure 4.28: *Display System Protocol*

Loading a Vendor's Driver CD

With this module, automatically install device drivers from a Linux driver CD that contains drivers for SuSE Linux. When installing SuSE Linux from scratch, use this YaST2 module to load the required drivers from the vendor CD after the installation.

Using YaST2 in Text Mode

This version of YaST2 is excellent for administering a system without X or when X is not functioning properly. To start YaST2 in text mode, enter `yast` as `root` at the ☞*prompt*.

The text-based version of YaST2 replaces YaST1 after its development was discontinued. A text-mode YaST2 had already been provided, but was rarely used. YaST2 in text mode is operated with the keyboard just like YaST1. YaST2-ncurses has a different look and feel and YaST1 shortcuts no longer function.

Controls

Usage may be unfamiliar, but is very simple. The whole program can, in principle, be operated with (Tab), (Alt) + (Tab), (Space), Arrow ((↑) and (↓)), and (Enter) as well as with shortcuts. When YaST2 is started in text mode, the main window appears first (see Figure 4.29).

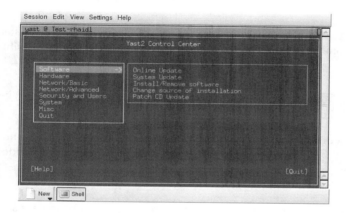

Figure 4.29: *The YaST2-ncurses Main Window with Active Module Frame*

There are three areas here: The left column features the categories to which the various modules belong. The modules of the category selected with an **x** are in a white frame to the right. The two buttons for aborting or starting the module marked in the frame are at the bottom.

After starting, the cursor is placed on the topmost field 'All', so the field is color-highlighted (normally green). However, 'Software' is selected, which can be recognized by the bracketed "**x**". Pressing (Tab) switches from one item to the next in the left column. The green-colored category is activated with (Space). The modules of this category then appear in the right-hand frame. The coloring of the marked items depends on the current terminal settings.

Press (Tab) repeatedly until the thin white frame to the right becomes prominent. Normally, it is possible to move backwards (Alt) + (Tab) or with (↑ Shift) + (Tab) (see Section *Module Operation* on the next page). Highlighting the white frame switches focus to the right-hand window in which a module can be selected for starting. The arrow keys move back and forth among the modules. Start the desired module by pressing (Enter) when it is marked green. Alternatively, press (Tab) to select 'Start'. Then start the selected module by pressing (Enter).

Different buttons or selection fields also contain a differently-colored letter (yellow with the standard settings). The combination (Alt) + (letter) selects the button directly, bypassing the TAB navigation.

Restriction of Key Combinations

It is possible that the (Alt) combinations in YaST2 do not work if system-wide (Alt) key combinations are set by a running X server. It is also possible that keys like (Alt) or (⇧ Shift) are captured for the terminal used.

Replacing (Alt) with (Esc): (Alt) shortcuts can be executed with (Esc) instead of (Alt). For example, (Esc) + (H) replaces (Alt) + (H).

Replacement of backward and forward navigation by (Ctrl) + (F) and (Ctrl) + (B) If the (Alt) and (⇧ Shift) combinations are occupied by the window manager or the terminal, the combinations (Ctrl) + (F) (forward) and (Ctrl) + (B) (backward) can be used instead.

Restriction of function keys: In SuSE Linux 8.1, the function keys are also shortcuts (see *Module Operation* on the facing page). Certain function keys could equally be occupied by the choice of terminal and are possibly not available for YaST The (Alt) key combinations and function keys should, however, be fully available on a pure text console.

Module Operation

In the following, it is assumed that the (Alt) key combinations are functional. Make appropriate substitutions or switch to a pure text console, if needed.

Navigation between buttons and selection lists: (Tab) and (Alt) + (Tab) navigates back and forth between buttons and frames containing selection lists and among the frames.

Navigation in selection lists: (↑) and (↓) always navigate among the single items within an activated frame containing a selection list. These can, for instance, be the single modules of a module group in the control center.

Checking of radio buttons and check boxes The selection of buttons with empty square brackets (check box [ ]) or of the module groups with parentheses (radio buttons ( )) on the left-hand side of the control center is done in the same way as the selection of packages during installation with (Space) or (Enter). The buttons at the bottom of the various modules or of the control center are activated with (Enter) when color-highlighted or with (Alt) + (yellow key).

The function keys: The function keys ((F1) to (F12)) provide quick access to the various available buttons. Which function keys are actually mapped to buttons depends on which YaST module is active, because the different modules offer different buttons. These include details, info, add, and delete. Like in YaST, 'OK', 'Continue', and 'Cancel' have been assigned to (F10). The various functions mapped to the function keys are explained in the help, accessible with (F1).

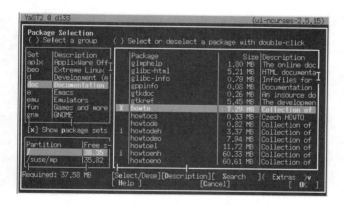

Figure 4.30: The Software Installation Module

Starting Individual Modules

Each YaST module can also be started directly. The modules can simply be started with `yast ⟨module name⟩`. The network module, for instance, is started with the command `yast lan`. Access a list of the names of the modules available on a system by running `yast -l` or `yast --list`. The various module descriptions can be found on page 53.

KDE — The Desktop

The K Desktop Environment (KDE for short) is the standard desktop for SuSE Linux. All information for optimizing your work with your desktop system can be found here. This chapter shows the graphical elements, summarizes some of the applications, and introduces KDE Internet connections. This chapter assumes that you have successfully installed SuSE Linux and set up the X server correctly.

The History of KDE

The story of KDE sounds like a modern fairy tale. To the great agony of a frustrated computer science student from Tübingen, Germany, previous Unix and Linux desktops were lacking in uniformity. For this reason, he developed the popular graphical user interface for the X Window System: KDE. In those days, Matthias Ettrich would have never guessed his appeal would spawn a newsgroup. He looked for some volunteers for his project "**K Desktop Environment**" (KDE) and it met with a lively reaction.

Soon, the first executable version was compiled and KDE became more popular. Improvements followed, bringing the KDE project to a critical mass and allowing it to take off on its own. Today hundreds programmers all over world are involved in developing even more improvements to KDE.

The First Start

When you start KDE for the first time, a configuration assistant will appear on the screen. First, select the country and language, then the system behavior (KDE, Unix, Windows, Apple OS), various effects, and desktop design in five easy steps. Finally, start the control center and further customize KDE to meet your needs. Start the configuration assistant manually by pressing (Alt) + (F2) and entering `kpersonalizer`.

Help

If, at some point, you are not able to get any farther in KDE, press (F1) or select 'Contents...' under the application's 'Help' menu. The KDE Help Center appears. A panel on the left-hand side has two tabs, 'Contents' and 'Search'.

Contents

'Contents' lists the various documents that belong to the KDE system and to the Linux system — man pages and info pages. With a click on 'Application manuals', for example, see the same menu structure as in the K menu. Explore the submenus and see the help documentation displayed in the field to the right.

Browse the traditional Unix man pages with 'Unix man pages'. The structure is historically based. The man pages are divided into nine or ten sections.

Click the corresponding section to display the items. Click the desired information. Find information about a particular command from a man page by entering the number sign ('#') and the name of the command in the URL field.

Operating KDE

In KDE, there are various ways to change the configuration and open files and applications. The KDE desktop, the menu bar, title, window, and control panels are available for this purpose. These various options are introduced in the following subsections.

The KDE Desktop

The desktop is the central switchboard in KDE. After starting KDE, find various icons on the desktop that enable quick access to CD-ROM disks or hard disks and allow easy file saving and set up of links to directories and files. Actually, the desktop is only one folder on your hard disk. It is located in your home directory under Desktop. All files stored here will be displayed by KDE on the desktop. To change this path, refer to *Look and Feel* on page 123.

The Menu Bar

If desired, position a menu bar in KDE on the upper margin of the desktop. Access the menu bar by right-clicking the desktop with the right mouse button. In the pop-up menu that appears, find 'Enable desktop menu' or 'Disable desktop menu'. Activate or deactivate the desktop menu by clicking this item. The following list provides an overview of the available items and the options with which to simplify your work in KDE.

'File' Execute various commands, start applications, lock your screen, or log out.

'New' Set up directories, links to FTP files, WWW files, and various applications so you can find them more quickly later.

'Bookmarks' Manage your bookmarks. This way, have easy access to frequently visited addresses and files. KDE automatically manages bookmarks from other browsers as well (currently Netscape and Mozilla).

'Desktop' Realign and organize your windows and icons and configure the background and desktop. Also deactivate the menu bar.

'Window' Displays all the desktops along with open applications.

'Help' Get information about KDE or report bugs and make requests.

The Title Bar

The title bar is the area at the top of a window containing its name and some icons, depending on the window decoration selected. In the default decoration, KDE2 exhibits the following title bar layout: the window panel menu, the "pushpin" symbol, the respective window name, and the minimizing, enlarging, and closing symbols. Sometimes, a question mark may appear before the minimizing symbol, the "What is that?" symbol. Figure 5.1 illustrates the title bar's composition.

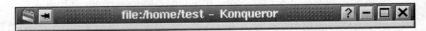

Figure 5.1: KDE2 Title Bar

Obtain more functions by right-clicking the title bar. A pop-up menu opens in which to configure the current window or create settings for the layout of all the windows. The pop-up menu contains the following items:

'Move' The window follows the movement of the mouse until dropped by left-clicking.

'Size' Change the horizontal and vertical dimensions of the window by moving them with the mouse. Confirm with a left click.

'Minimize' Minimize the current window. The application remains open, but its window disappears from the desktop and only appears as an icon in the task bar. To reopen the window, click the icon in the taskbar.

'Maximize' Maximize the current window. The application now occupies the entire screen. By clicking it again, restore the window to its original size.

'Shade' The current window is reduced to just a title bar.

'Always On Top' The current window will remain visible on your desktop until you deactivate this function or close the window.

'Store Settings' Saves your specifications.

'Settings...' Specify the properties and decoration in the window that opens.

'To desktop' By selecting from the submenu, move the window to another desktop.

'Close' Close the current window.

The Control Panel

After starting KDE, the taskbar appears on the lower margin (default setting). Inside this margin, find the SuSE menu and various quick-start icons for frequently used applications, such as a shell and Konqueror. Several "applets", introduced in *The Applets: Miniprograms* on the following page, are also available.

The KDE and SuSE Menu Structure

The SuSE KDE packages include two menus: the normal K menu and the extended SuSE menu. The K menu is the "traditional" menu. It only contains KDE applications. The SuSE menu's classification scheme is a little different. After initial start-up, this menu is built into the default configuration. Find all KDE applications and more in the SuSE menu. This allows you, for example, to start all GNOME and X applications.

The following categories are at your disposal: development, games, graphics, Internet, multimedia, office programs, settings, system, and service applications. Next to them, also find items like SuSE Help and Control Center.

Switch from one menu to another in the Control Center under 'Look&Feel' → 'Menu settings'. Here, also integrate additional menus for the start panel, such as the task menu or the administrator menu. These offer a presorted listing of frequently used applications.

Basically, all KDE applications are accessible from the K menu as well as from the SuSE menu. Decide for yourself which menu structure you prefer.

Figure 5.2: A Selection of Applets

The Applets: Miniprograms

The control panel also provides space for applets, which can be embedded there. For instance, display the time of day.

Figure 5.2 shows, from left to right, switchboard, quickstarter, system monitor, eyes, newsticker, the system portion of the control bar, and the time. Next to every applet is a small arrow that opens a menu. The applet can be moved or deleted there. The menu can be also used to open a settings dialog if one exists for that program. To add similar useful applications, right-click an open space and select 'Add' → 'Applet'.

The Taskbar — The taskbar helps to quickly and easily jump between open applications. Sort the applications according to desktops or group respective windows together. Select the menu items 'Look&Feel' → 'Taskbar' in the Control Center and explore the different setting options.

Figure 5.3: Taskbar: Displays All Active Desktop Windows.

The Switchboard — KDE provides multiple desktops. Configure up to sixteen "virtual desktops" to which you can also assign names.

Figure 5.4 on the facing page actually shows the same switchboard (from left to right), displayed with a numerical view, preview, and name view, respectively.

With a right-click inside the switchboard, open pop-up menu. Select 'Preview', 'Number', or 'Name'.

By clicking 'Enable Desktop Preview', an arrow appears next to it. Click this to open a small window showing a preview of the desktops. Activate a window by clicking directly in it.

Newsticker — If you have a working Internet connection, receive up-to-date news. The news reports appear in running text in a small applet

Figure 5.4: *Three Switchboard Displays*

program. Section *Network* on page 129 goes into more detail regarding this useful tool.

Selected KDE Applications

There are a multitude of KDE applications. Because of limited space, we are not able to introduce all the applications in detail. The selection in the list that follows by no means indicates a comparison of quality.

Hard Disk Management

Both kdf and kwikdisk help mount or unmount data media available on your system quickly and easily.

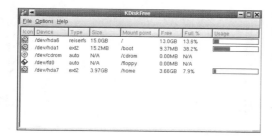

Figure 5.5: *Overview of Data Media with kdf*

- kwikdisk is an applet, so it can be integrated into the control panel. When you right-click the icon, a menu opens with which to mount or unmount the respective data medium. For a graphical overview, select 'Start KDiskFree'.

- kdf and KDiskFree show an overview of your data media obtained from the /etc/fstab file, similar to the df command. The window includes the data medium icon, the type, the size, the mount point, the available disk space, percentage of occupied disk space, and a graphical representation.

If you right-click an entry item, a pop-up menu opens. Integrate the data medium into your system with 'Mount device' or remove it with 'Unmount device'. The menu item 'Open data medium' starts a new Konqueror window listing the contents of the data medium.

DVI, PostScript, and PDF Viewers

Among the most important formats in Linux are DVI and PostScript. They can be viewed with ease using the DVI viewer, kdvi, or the PostScript and PDF viewer, kghostview. Both applications are set up intuitively. Figure 5.6 shows the KDvi window.

One of the features of these viewers is that they can be integrated into a Konqueror window. This makes it very easy to display files without needing to start the necessary application manually.

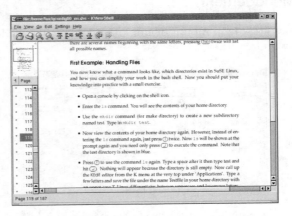

Figure 5.6: KDvi Document Viewer

In kghostview (see Figure 5.7 on the facing page), load any PostScript or PDF document and view it. Use 'File' → 'Open' and select the corresponding document. In the 'View' menu, choose various displays that automatically show the contents to size. To rotate the image ninety degrees, use 'View' → 'Orientation'.

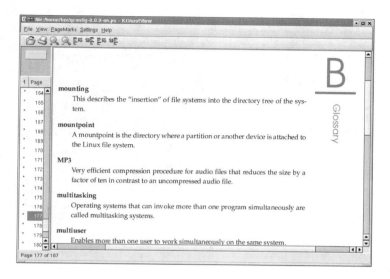

Figure 5.7: KGhostview Document Viewer

Setting Appointments with KOrganizer

With korganizer, manage appointments and get easy reminders of birthdays and important events. Define tasks and record your progress. The application can be found in the `kdepim3` package. It can be installed using YaST2. Start it by pressing (Alt) + (F2) and entering `korganizer`.

To set a new appointment, click 'Actions' → 'New Appointment'. A window appears in which to enter general information on the appointment, who will attend, and frequency of recurrence. If an entry recurs weekly, for example, set this under the 'Recurrence' tab. For this, 'Recurring Event' must be checked under the 'General' tab.

Under the 'General' tab, enter a 'Summary' and set the beginning and ending date along with the start time. You can also be reminded of this appointment. Activate the field 'Reminder' and set the time you want korganizer to remind you of your appointment. In the text field underneath, enter more detailed text.

To organize your appointments, define *categories*. Click 'Categories' to open a window in which to select the corresponding event. If the type of event to schedule is not listed, add the new name in 'New Categories' and press (↵). Close the window by clicking 'OK'.

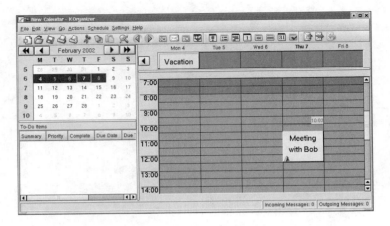

Figure 5.8: KOrganizer: KDE Daily Planner

The following illustrates how to effectively add a new appointment. To do this, it is best to use 'Actions' → 'New Event'.

Example First, schedule a simple appointment. To do this, enter the type of appointment in the 'Summary' field. Define the date with 'Start Date' and 'End Date'. Set a time that makes sense in 'Start Time' and 'End Time'. If you do not want to set a time, simply activate 'No time associated'.

To be reminded of this appointment, activate 'Reminder'. Now, the entry field next to it is available for setting the reminder in minutes, hours, or days. In the text field underneath, enter the details of the appointment. With 'Categories', calender entries can be sorted.

To specify other attendees, click 'Attendees'. Enter their names and e-mail addresses. Define which role the participant has (such as participant only or organizer) and which status he has (such as needs preparation, accepted, or confirmed). Select the participant with 'Address Book...' and the name and e-mail address are automatically added.

When you click 'Apply', your appointment is added to the calendar. This button leaves the window open, so you can still make small changes. To close the window, click 'OK'.

With KOrganizer, not only manage appointments, but also organize tasks. In 'Actions', find 'New To-Do'. Just try out some of the many options KOrganizer offers.

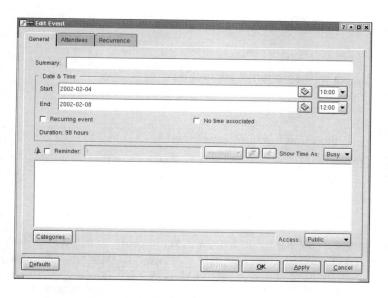

Figure 5.9: *Setting a New Appointment*

KInternet — Connecting to the Internet

To surf the Internet or send and receive e-mail, you need a modem, ethernet, or ISDN card connected to your computer and configured in SuSE Linux. This takes place with the help of the installation and configuration tool YaST2. When you have configured the device accordingly, use the application KInternet to manage your dial-up Internet connection.

KDE loads KInternet at start-up. The application independently evaluates whether an Internet connection can be established. If so, the application icon automatically appears in the lower right corner of the KDE panel in the form of a plug.

 No existing Internet connection.

 Connection is being set up.

 Connection has been established.

 Internet connection does not exist, but will be established once the data is retrieved from the Internet.

 Data is being transferred either to or from the Internet.

If you right-click the KInternet icon, a menu appears, which will assist in your KInternet configuration and help manage your data connection to your provider. Configuring access to one of your selected providers is easily accomplished with YaST2. Most common providers are preconfigured.

KInternet also offers a series of additional useful features, such as the proxy server WWW-Offle, a cache for all your web sites (regardless of which web browser you are using). This enables viewing of previously downloaded sites without having to redial the Internet. Web sites requested while offline will automatically be downloaded once you go back online. To use these features, install the package `wwwoffle`. Also enter the proxy `localhost`, `Port 8080`, in your web browser. In Netscape Navigator, this option can be found under 'Edit' → 'Preferences' → 'Advanced' → 'Proxies'. In Konqueror, select 'Settings' → 'Configure Konqueror'. Make your settings under 'Proxies'.

Frequently Asked Questions and Answers

1. **How can I access a CD or DVD?**

   An icon is located on your KDE desktop with an image of a CD. Insert your CD or DVD in your drive and left-click the icon. The CD will be mounted and its contents displayed in your Konqueror window.

2. **There isn't a CD icon on my desktop. How do I create one?**

   Right-click the desktop. Select 'Create new...' → 'CD-ROM Device'. A window opens. Under 'General', rename the icon on the desktop. Enter the device name of your CD or DVD drive under 'Device'.

3. **Can I put the control panel somewhere else?**

   Yes, of course. Left-click a free space in the panel and drag it to any other edge. After you have released the mouse button, the control panel will be placed there.

4. **I want another control panel. Is that possible?**

   Yes. Right-click an open space in the already existing control panel. Select 'Add' → 'Extension' → 'External Taskbar'. A taskbar opens. Now add files and directories there with the help of Konqueror. Alternatively, right-click the panel and select the corresponding items under 'Add'.

5. **How do I add programs and other items to the control panel?**

   For this, there are two options:

   (a) Right-click a free space in the control panel. A pop-up menu opens. Select 'Add' → 'Button' and you will see the entries as they appear in the K menu. Add your preferred item to the control panel by clicking 'Add this menu'. Also select the desired program directly by clicking it. In both cases, the corresponding icon will appear in the control panel.

   (b) Programs and folders can be added by selecting them straight from Konqueror with the left mouse button and, keeping the mouse button pressed, dropping the object into the control panel and releasing the mouse again.

6. **I want to find out more about my system. Where can I find this information?**

   There are two options here: Press (Alt) + (F2) and enter the application name ksysguard in the command dialog window. Another window opens. Use the "sensor browser" on the left-hand side to click individual monitoring modules and drag them into the main window. Another option is the Control Center. All the resources and devices associated with your computer are located under 'Information'.

7. **How can I display PostScript or PDF files?**

   In KDE, the program KGhostview serves this purpose. Section *DVI, PostScript, and PDF Viewers* on page 112 provides more details on this program.

8. **How can I view graphics files?**

   Use KView. Start it by entering (Alt) + (F2) and kview. The application supports several graphics formats.

9. **Can I play back my WAV, MP3, and other sound files in KDE?**

   Yes, press (Alt) + (F2) and enter noatun. A window opens. Load your audio file under 'File' → 'Open'.

10. **How can I play back an audio CD?**

    Insert the audio CD into the drive, start the application noatum ((Alt) + (F2) then enter noatun). Adjust the volume using kmix.

11. **How can I dial into the Internet?**

    Via the KInternet application. An detailed description of it is in *KInternet — Connecting to the Internet* on page 115.

12. **How can I read my e-mails?**
    With the KMail application.

For More Information

If you need more information about KDE, check the following web pages:

http://www.kde.org	*The* KDE page
http://www.konqueror.org	All about the Konqueror application
http://i18n.kde.org	Internationalizing KDE
http://kde.themes.org	All you ever wanted to know about design and other topics related to KDE
http://artist.kde.org	All about icons, clip art, and other graphics KDE
http://lists.kde.org	Mailing lists
http://bugs.kde.org	Known KDE bugs

KDE — Configuration

This chapter is intended to illustrate how to change the look and feel of KDE using the Control Center. It also shows how to configure the file manager, web browser, and other tools to meet your demands. The KDE Control Center enables configuration of KDE to meet individual needs. This chapter only focuses on the main aspects of KDE configuration.

The KDE Control Center

The KDE Control Center can be accessed directly via the control panel icon or in the K Menu and the SuSE menu under 'Control Center'. A window, as shown in Figure 6.1, opens.

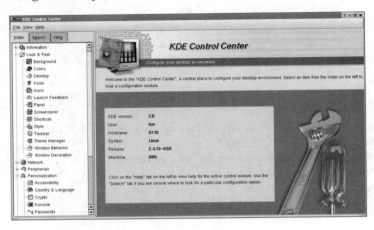

Figure 6.1: *The KDE Control Center*

The Control Center is divided into a menu bar and left and right panels. The left panel shows a list of configuration modules. After clicking a menu, the related modules in the right panel display some information. Clicking the module again starts the settings dialog in the panel to the right. Below it, find up to four buttons:

'Help' — View a short help text

'Use default settings' — Restore the default settings

'Apply' — Confirm changes

'Reset' — Revert changes

The menu bar contains the following menus:

'File' — Close the Control Center with 'Quit'

'View' — Select the layout of the Control Center. In 'Mode', decide whether to work with a structured 'Tree View' or with a simple 'Icon View'. Specify the 'Icon Size' of the latter.

'Help' — View the Control Center help pages via 'Contents'. Obtain informational text by using 'What is this?' and selecting an icon with the mouse. Write a 'Bug Report Regarding ...' to the program author or find information about KDE or the Control Center.

If you are unsure what a particular setting does, consult the tool tips by pressing ⇧ Shift + F1 then clicking the element in question. Its help text appears.

Peripheral Devices

Includes 'Printer Management', 'Mouse', 'Smartcards', and 'Keyboard'.

Mouse The 'General' tab defines left-handed or right-handed mouse or track ball usage, whether files or folders should be opened with a single-click or a double-click, if icons should change when they are touched by the mouse, and if the mouse pointer itself should change when resting over an icon.

The 'Advanced' tab includes configuration options for correlation between mouse movements and the movement of the cursor on the screen ('Cursor speed'), how quickly the second mouse click must follow the first one to be interpreted as a double-click ('double-click interval'), how the lines should change when using the scroll wheel of the mouse ('Mouse wheel regenerates scroll'), and similar options.

Keyboard To switch keyboard layouts, select a different layout here. In the 'Advanced' tab, configure the number pad (the item 'Lock number pad when starting KDE') and the key repetition rate.

File Display

This menu contains the modules 'File Manager' and 'File Associations'.

File Manager This module contains the setting options 'Behavior', 'Appearance', and 'Trash'.

Under 'Behavior', decide whether directories should open in a separate window. 'Display network processes in a single window' allows all processes to be combined into a single, easy-to-read window. 'Appearance' sets the visual layout of the Konqueror window (font, font size, etc.) Trash settings can be made in the third tab.

File Associations Assign specific programs file types — also known as "MIME" (Multipurpose Internet Mail Extension) types. Typically, these only pertain to file attachments in e-mails. File associations include rules for file recognition, a description, icon, and list of applications that can be used to open the given file type. File associations are classified as 'application', 'audio', 'image', 'inode', 'message', 'print', 'text', or 'video' and displayed in a menu labeled 'Known Types'. The following is a summary of the different features.

To automatically *search according to MIME type*, enter the file name in 'Find filename pattern' (see Figure 6.2). A manual search is initiated by double-clicking a type, opening it, and browsing its associated MIME types.

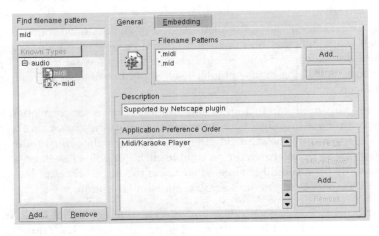

Figure 6.2: Editing a MIME Type

Create a new MIME type by clicking 'Add' in the lower left-hand corner of the widow. This will open a small dialog box in which to select an appropriate category from the list. Give it a 'Name' in the corresponding field.

Edit a MIME type by selecting the one to modify (see Figure 6.2). Make your selection from the list of available file types. The corresponding settings then appear in the right window panel.

Under 'General', specify the icon, the file pattern, and a short description. Applications capable of processing this type can be added with 'Add'.

The option 'Integrate' determines whether the file should be integrated into Konqueror or it should appear in its own window. Integration requires an application that works as a plug-in.

Power Control

Using the modules in this menu item, enable your computer's energy-saving features. Configure a certain command to run or a sound to be issued in cases of a power shortage. Today's computers can be switched to standby mode after a certain period of inactivity. This functionality requires APM support, included in most modern PCs.

Look and Feel

This module provides a variety of settings for your KDE system. They include the modules 'Desktop', 'Screensaver', 'Theme Manager', 'Colors', 'Window Decoration', 'Window Behavior', 'Taskbar', 'Background', 'Panel', 'Launch Feedback', 'Fonts', 'Style', 'Icons', and 'Key Bindings'.

┌─ **Note** ───

Keep your computer's memory capabilities in mind when changing KDE's look and feel. Styles with a lot of color variations and background images require more memory and processor capacity.

── **Note** ─┘

Most dialogs are self-explanatory. However, the following discusses a few important modules.

Desktop   'Desktop' defines the vertical positioning of the desktop, how hidden files are displayed, and enables the menu panel. Also enable previews for certain files (such as HTML). The most important settings listed here are for the KDE path, such as the one in which the desktop is stored.

Under 'Appearance', select the font size, default font, plain text color display, and the corresponding background color. Enable or disable underscoring of file names.

Under 'Number of Desktops', set the number and names of your desktops.

┌─ **Tip** ───

 Press Ctrl and any function key Fx, where x stands for the desktop number, or navigate through the desktops using Ctrl + Tab.
 ─── **Tip** ─┘

Screensaver To enable a screensaver, click the box in front of 'Enable screensaver'. Select the desired one from the list. To adjust setting options for
the individual screensavers, click 'Setup'.

Theme Manager This module provides the option of creating, saving, or
deleting themes (desktop designs). Under 'Installation', select a theme
from the list. Make fine adjustments in 'Contents'. This controls which
elements, such as colors, sound, and icons, are included. To obtain
more information, go to 'About'.

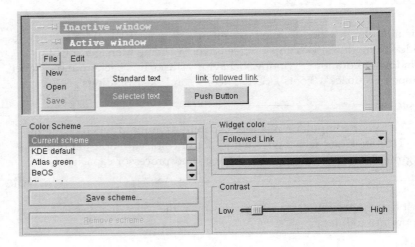

Figure 6.3: Color Adjustments to Your Desktop

Colors Here, change the color scheme of your KDE desktop and make individual color adjustments (see Figure 6.3), all of which are applied to
most KDE applications. Some preset color schemes are already listed.
Your changes are displayed in the sample window at the top as you
click them.

Window Decoration Decorate your window margins and title bars using
this module. The following tabs ('Buttons', 'Configure [Quartz]', etc.)

are activated, depending on the features of the decoration module selected. Then make your fine adjustments.

Window Behavior In this module, configure the window behavior when clicking, moving, or resizing windows. If you have selected a window manager other than KWin, which is 'KDE2 (Default)' in the 'Window Decoration' menu, the settings may not be applied.

Taskbar In this module, decide whether only the open applications on the current desktop or all open applications should appear in the taskbar. Also display the button for the taskbar in the taskbar itself, group related windows, or sort open applications according to desktops. It is recommended at least to check 'Show application icons' for the benefit of a better overview.

Background In this module, assign desktops a common background, different backgrounds, or color gradients. To assign backgrounds or color gradients, select a desktop from the list. To the right of it is a preview window. At the bottom of the window, find the tabs 'Background', 'Wallpaper', 'Advanced', and 'Optimization'.

Under 'Background', configure a mode, such as a pattern or a horizontal or vertical color gradient. The colors for this are located just below the mode drop-box.

'Wallpaper' specifies one or more wallpaper images for your desktop. Also define a mode here (centered, tiled, etc.). If you do not want to use these options, select 'No Wallpaper'.

'Advanced' provides options for blending your wallpaper background. Several options are available, including horizontal, vertical, and pyramidal.

'Optimization' provides options for memory optimization (for experts).

Panel In this module, set the position, size, and appearance of your panel (or "kicker"). Find dividers in this module.

Under 'Position', configure the panel's positioning on your screen (left, right, above, below), style (tiny, small, medium, large), and size.

To hide your panel, specify this in 'Hiding'.

'Look & Feel' defines various backgrounds for particular menus. First, make sure the box next to 'Enable background tiles' is checked (if it is not, click it) before the menus below are activated.

In 'Menus', define how the K menu layout should look — which additional items should appear there. Furthermore, integrate a quick browser menu, set up a menu cache, or use other options.

Specify the security level for the panel applets via the 'Applets' tab. Start these in two ways: internally or externally. The internal method is preferable to the external one, but can lead to instability and security gaps if the applets are poorly programmed. Select the appropriate security level here.

The last tab is labeled 'Extensions' and is responsible for setting up additional external taskbars, such as the positioning, automatic blending, or hide buttons.

Launch Feedback To see the status of a launching application, make several settings in this menu.

'Enable Busy Cursor' to receive feedback output to your mouse. Furthermore, decide if this feedback should occur coupled with a blinking effect and how long the launch feedback should be active.

Optionally, have the feedback notify you that a program is starting. This is also displayed in the panel if 'Enable taskbar notification' is checked. Make settings here as to how long the launch feedback should be active.

Fonts If the default font settings are not satisfactory, adjust them according to your own needs. Click 'Select' next to the font to change. Set the font style and size in the dialog and confirm your selection with 'OK'.

Style A style is the presentation of buttons, lists, menus, and other such desktop elements. Some preset options are already listed. To apply GNOME and GTK styles, click 'Import GTK Design...'. A window opens, guiding you through the installation.

Icons This module allows specification of the icon display. Also define special effects to apply to the icons.

Under 'Theme', decide whether to have the icons displayed with fewer colors or with rich colors and more shades. Install another design via 'Install New Theme'.

Under 'Advanced', decide whether to add effects to icons. Also set several icon sizes in the various panels and desktops.

Key Bindings If the previous keyboard shortcuts do not suit you, redefine the various key shortcuts for actions and applications in this module.

Define key combinations for your desktop under 'Global Shortcuts'. Attribute a key shortcut to an action in the list. For example, (Alt) + (F2) opens the 'Run command' window.

'Shortcut Sequences' defines the shortcuts to use for switching between desktops or moving a window to a desktop. The 'Application Shortcuts' tab defines certain key combinations to use for various actions frequently occurring in many applications, such as copying and pasting.

Information

To view your system information, browse through the various modules here. The information originates, for the most part, from the /proc directory. The items are self-explanatory and normally display hardware-specific information. This way, easily ascertain whether certain Linux devices are addressed correctly.

Sound

Use this module to configure use of your sound card.

Audio CD This module is responsible for setting up the input and output module for audio CDs. It is started by entering audiocd:/ in the URL field in the Konqueror. Settings can be made for the automatic detection of audio CDs, error correction, the file formats "Ogg-Vorbis" and "MP3", and settings for connecting to a music database on the Internet.

Midi Select the MIDI device to use for playing MIDI files.

Mixer In this module, basic kmix (KDE Mixer) sound card settings can be made. Save a default volume level or load already saved volume levels in the first section. Autoload preferred settings at KDE start-up via 'Load volumes on login'.

In the 'Hardware Settings' section, define, with 'Maximum number of probed mixers', how many sound cards kmix should detect at start-up. With 'Maximum number of probed devices per mixer', set how many devices should be detected on each sound card.

System Bell Set a system bell to use instead of system reports. Its volume, pitch, and duration can be set in this module.

Sound Server This module sets up the KDE αRts sound server, which you can use to listen to system sounds, MP3 files, and other sound events.

System Notifications Settings can be made in this module to report occurring events or to document such events.

Select one of the applications or application categories. Open the item by clicking the + symbol in front of it until presented with four options. 'Log to file' saves the messages to a file without issuing any

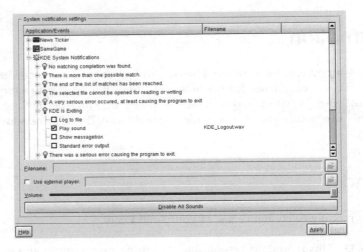

Figure 6.4: KDE System Notifications

acoustic or optical signals. 'Play sound' plays the configured sound file. 'Show message box' displays a message window. 'Standard error output' causes error output to be regulated by the application itself.

Next to 'Filename', define the sound file to play. Enter the file name itself here or select it from the list that appears after the directory icon is clicked.

After selecting a sound file, test it using the play button (the arrow icon) to the right of the directory icon. The playback volume can be regulated with the slider next to 'Volume'. To use an external playback application, click the box in front of 'Use external player' and select the desired application with the directory icon.

Network

Make network-related settings here.

Email Enter user information in this module, such as name, organization, e-mail address, and reply address. Specify your preferred e-mail application.

Preferences Configure the behavior of KDE applications in conjunction with the Internet and networks: time-out values and FTP options.

LAN Browsing Set up the LAN information server LISa in this module. You can only make changes as `root`.

News Ticker Use this module to configure the KNewsTicker applet. Four tab windows provide setting options for this purpose.

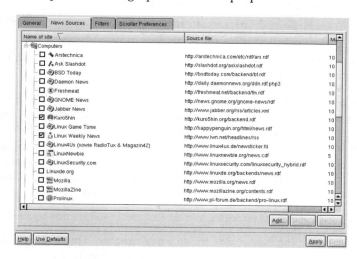

Figure 6.5: Configuring the KDE News Ticker

Under 'General', adjust the sensitivity of the mouse wheel, if using that type of mouse, and the news query interval. Also set whether running text should be slowed down.

Find available Internet addresses capable of issuing a news query under 'News sources'. To change these news source settings, such as source file, icon, category, or maximum articles, click 'Modify'. Use 'Add' to add a news source.

If you are only interested in certain types of news, define 'Filter' rules under the next tab. The last tab, 'Scroller Preferences', controls the scroll speed, ticker direction, and the appearance of the font, foreground, background, and highlighted color. Use the 'Miscellaneous' tab to set the underscoring of the current headline display, the icon display, infinite scrolling, or highlighted headlines.

SOCKS   This module enables the setup of KDE support for a SOCKS server or proxy.

Talk Configuration   Communicate with others over the network. You need a talk daemon to do this. Extensive setting options are available under the three tabs.

Use the tab 'Announcement' to set the application to announce the talk request and the talk application to launch. Set if an acoustic signal should be issued when talk requests arrive.

Set up an answering machine to receive text messages if you are not there to receive incoming talk requests.

Under 'Forwarding', settings can be made to relay incoming talk requests to other machines.

Windows Shares   Use this module to make settings for accessing drives and directories available over networks. Before accessing the data, authenticate your user identity. To enable this feature, fill out the fields for this in this module. The combination of a server with its authentication is referred to as assignment. When accessing a share already assigned, KDE automatically takes care of the authentication for you. If you have already entered a password, you will not be asked for it again.

> ┌─ **Caution** ─────────────────────────────────────
>
> Avoid saving passwords for security reasons. This is especially important in highly sensitive network environments.
>
> ─────────────────────────────────── **Caution** ─┘

Personalization

There are several modules under this menu item for customizing KDE.

Country & Language   Make the language, numbering, and date settings for your region. Selecting the respective 'Country' is usually sufficient. Make any extra settings under 'Numbers', 'Money', and 'Time & Date'.

If the language desired is not listed, try installing the necessary KDE language package. The name of the package starts with `kde3-i18n-` and ends with an abbreviation for the language, such as `de` for German or `es` for Spanish (for example, `kde3-i18n-de` for the German package).

> **Tip** ──
>
> See how your settings will be applied in the module preview at the bottom of the window.
>
> ── **Tip** ┘

Passwords   Decide whether blank spaces or asterisks should appear when entering your password. Restrict the storage time for any password is recommended.

Spell Checking   Define settings such as the spelling dictionary, character encoding, and the spell checking application. Both ASpell (KDE) and ISpell (non-KDE) are supported.

Crypto   This module provides SSL (Secure Socket Library) setup options, certification, authentication, and the configuration of other security-related aspects. For more information, click 'Help'.

Accessibility   For error messages to be issued by acoustic or visible signals other than the standard system bell, make these settings in the 'Bell' window of this module.

Set the key delays in the 'Keyboard' window. This sets the minimum time a key must be pressed before considered input.

To operate the mouse using the number pad, check the box next to 'Move mouse with keyboard (using the Num pad)' under the 'Mouse' tab. In addition, set the delay, acceleration, repetition rate, and more for this.

System

The menu contains modules for settings regarding your system behavior.

> **Caution**
>
> Since the settings for the modules 'Login Manager' and 'Date & Time' affect your whole system, you can only make changes here as `root`.
>
> **Caution**

Login Manager With this module, set up the graphical login procedure in KDE by modifying the appearance of the opening screen. Also adjust other features, such as who can access the login manager or who has the permissions to shut it down.

Under 'Appearance', configure the appearance of the login screen with a greeting and a logo. Set the visual display and the language, with the language independent of the user-defined language settings. Define a global or a customized setting for the position of the login manager.

Use 'Font' to choose the fonts the login manager should use for the greeting text and user name. For a special background or simple wall-paper color for your login screen, make these settings in the 'Background' window.

Under 'Sessions', decide which session types, such as 'KDE' or 'fail-safe', should be displayed in the login manager. Also set by whom and from where the machine may be shut down. Furthermore, decide which commands should be executed when shutting down or restarting your system.

Use the 'Users' window to set which existing users on the network appear in the login manager. Automatic user login and other miscellaneous features can be defined under 'Convenience'.

> **Caution**
>
> Saving passwords presents a security risk. Therefore, avoid this type of "convenience".
>
> **Caution**

Date & Time Define the system date, time, and time zone.

Linux Kernel Configurator KDE provides a graphical interface for compiling your own Linux kernel. To do this, you need the kernel source code (package `kernel-source`). This module is only for experts, as experience is required.

Console Configure the terminal application in KDE using this module by making global settings and modifying the color schemes in the following menus.

Under 'General', define which application to use as your default terminal. Also specify the position of the panels and margins and even the basic font layout.

Create your own personal color palette under 'Schema'. In the last tab, specify which sessions should be saved.

Font Installer When initially starting this module, you will be greeted by an assistant that will guide you through installing the fonts. Normally, you will not have to change too much here, since there are already default settings for this feature.

Session Manager With this module, define whether a confirmation should follow the login or if the previous session settings should simply be restored.

Web Browser

This menu includes modules for configuring Konqueror as a web browser.

Cookies These files are responsible for storing and querying information about your machine and your activities, which can be obtained by web servers through your browser. Sometimes, cookies can be helpful, such as when they contain Internet site settings so your browser does not need to recalibrate all the settings each time you visit the same web site. Web sites often save and query data from cookies without your knowledge. The queried information is used for statistics or for placing banner ads targeted to your consumer profile. This module allows you to set rules to restrict the use of cookies or to allow cookies coming from particular servers.

Enhanced Browsing With this module, activate two more Konqueror functions: The option 'Enable Internet Keywords' helps you find trade names in the Internet, such as companies, celebrities, or organizations. Instead of entering `http://www.kde.org/`, for instance, in the URL field in Konqueror, simply type "K Desktop Environment". The name entered there will then be interpreted as a URL and loaded.

In the 'Enable Web Shortcuts' section, find shortcuts for accessing certain search engines, adjustable to fit your needs. To perform a search, enter the shortcut for the search engine in the URL field in Konqueror, then a colon followed by the desired search term. To use "google" to search for "icq", for example, enter `gg:icq` in the URL field.

Konqueror Browser Use this module to configure the browser functions in Konqueror. The setting options are divided into several tabs. Under 'HTML', adjust settings such as automatic text completion in text fields and how often this should occur. Select the fonts, their size, and their encoding for web site display under 'Appearance'.

⌐ Caution

Active contents, such as Java and JavaScript applications, pose a security risk, even if the damage potential is not great. Specify only domain-specific settings if possible.

Caution ⌐

Decide whether embedded 'Java' applications should be able to run in web sites at all. Make these settings domain-specific or configure them to be activated only during the run time of the relevant applications. Determine whether embedded 'JavaScript' applications should be able to run on web sites. Make global settings for 'Plugins' under the last tab.

Netscape Plugins Plug-ins allow the contents of external applications, such as Flash, to be displayed inside the respective browser. Configure an automatic search for the plug-ins to be performed every time KDE starts, if desired. Under 'Plugins', find a detailed listing of your installed Netscape plug-ins. Konqueror can also use them.

Proxies & Cache Make your proxy server settings in this module.

Stylesheets "CSS" files contain information for standardizing the display of HTML pages. Each style element is attributed a format, such as headers. Specify the stylesheet to use under 'General'. Click 'Use user-defined stylesheet' to use the generated stylesheet under the 'Customize' tab.

User Agent When Konqueror establishes a connection to a web site, some basic user identification data is transferred in the form of a "user agent" login. Intelligent web sites evaluate this information to adjust their sites' HTML code to match the requirements of the browser used to visit it. This is a useful feature, as not all web browsers work in the same way. Some web servers refuse the connection to "inadequate" browsers. Spoof them by using a different "user agent" login.

GNOME — The Desktop

With the recent release of GNOME2, GNOME provides an amazingly fast option for the Linux desktop. This speed is offered without sacrificing features
or convenience. GNOME (GNU Network Object Model Environment) is an
effective desktop as well as a flexible and sophisticated developer's environment. It was developed to make the user interface more uniform, streamlin-
ing the various aspects of the look and feel. As well as components for managing the windows, additional components ensure that applications can share
data with each other, featuring a uniform operating concept and help system.
Modularization allows reusable program elements to be integrated into other
applications so the wheel does not have to be reinvented for each individual
scenario.

This chapter focuses on how to work with GNOME and how to customize
the environment and applications. It also provides an overview of some of
the core applications.

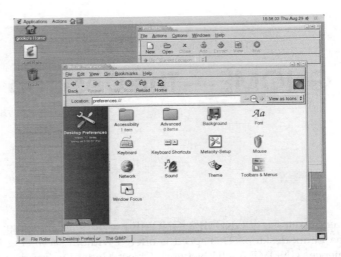

Figure 7.1: GNOME2 *Desktop with Open Applications*

Changing to GNOME2

Although the core GNOME2 desktop has been released, the changeover for applications is somewhat more time consuming. SuSE Linux 8.1 includes GNOME2 applications as much as possible. When the application has not yet been updated to the newer environment, the most recent GNOME 1.4 version is included.

These applications can be easily used in GNOME2, but do not offer the configuration integration provided by GNOME2 applications. Unfortunately, applets created for GNOME 1.4 are not compatible with the GNOME2 panels. As many applications and applets as possible are included in the distribution. To find additional GNOME2 packages, refer frequently to `http://www.suse.com` for updates.

For more information about changes between GNOME and GNOME2, refer to the release notes at `http://www.gnome.org/start/2.0/releasenotes.html`. These notes provide specific information about changes in the GNOME desktop from the developers themselves.

Starting GNOME2

A GNOME2 session is available from the graphical display managers included in SuSE Linux. It can also be started with `startx gnome2`. A reasonable default configuration is included for both regular users and the root user. It is also possible for the system administrator to modify this configuration or provide additional options.

GNOME2 and Window Managers

As well as GNOME2, a window manager must be used. The window manager controls how windows are drawn on the desktop. GNOME2 offers two window managers — Metacity and Sawfish2. Sawfish2 is a port of the Sawfish window manager commonly used with earlier GNOME versions. Metacity is a new window manager designed with GNOME2 in mind. It is lighter and faster than Sawfish and offers simplified configuration. Metacity is now the default GNOME2 window manager in SuSE Linux.

Help

GNOME2 includes extensive help and documentation. Yelp, the GNOME2 help browser, also provides easy access to other documentation on your system, like man pages. Access the help by selecting 'Help' from the menu. Many configuration dialogs and applications also offer help from menus or buttons.

Configuring GNOME

If the default configuration does not suit your needs, it can be modified extensively.

GConf

GNOME2 offers a new configuration method. The intention is to simplify and unify configuration in programs. For example, instead of changing the font in each application, you can change the font once and it will be applied to all applications compatible with GConf. GConf can also be used by system administrators to make configuration layouts. The GConf Editor can be useful for administrators and experienced users. The basic functionality of GConf is offered by the 'Desktop Preferences' and the individual application's configuration dialogs.

Desktop Preferences

If this is your first start, try the 'Start Here' icon on the desktop then select 'Desktop Preferences'. If this icon is not available, open Nautilus, the default GNOME file manager and viewer, by right-clicking the desktop and selecting 'New Window'. Under 'Location:', enter `preferences://`. Double-click the icon to access the dialog. The configuration options available here can also be opened from the menu.

Accessibility

GNOME2 is intended to be highly accessible for people with disabilities. Special accessibility options, such as keyboard controls, are in this folder.

Advanced

The 'Advanced' folder contains more complication configuration dialogs. Use them for selecting what applications are used for different file types, controlling access to a CD database, and other things. The subfolder 'Sawfish' contains the configuration for the Sawfish2 window manager. Unless you have specifically selected to use Sawfish, ignore this configuration and use the 'Metacity Setup' dialog described below.

The 'Preferred Applications' dialog is very useful. Use it to select your default web browser and text editor.

Background

Your GNOME background can be a picture or just a gradient. To select a picture, drag and drop one from an open Nautilus window or click the 'Picture' image to open a file browser. Select how the options are displayed under 'Picture Options'. Use 'No Picture' if you do not want a picture. Under 'Background Style' and 'Color', set the color background used with 'No Picture' or behind the picture.

Font

Select your 'Standard Application Font' and 'Desktop Font'. Click the listed font to open a selection dialog. The 'Standard Application Font' applies to all applications compatible with GNOME2 configuration.

Keyboard

In this dialog, make special settings for your keyboard. You can also configure the blinking of the cursor here.

Keyboard Shortcuts

It is possible to control a wide range of window manager functions with the keyboard. The default setup includes many reasonable keyboard shortcuts. To check the shortcuts or modify them to your own preferences, use this dialog. Two schemes are available: 'Default' and 'Emacs'. The Emacs scheme can be very convenient for emacs users. Either scheme can be modified to your needs. To enter a new shortcut, select the one to change. Press the keys to use for this function in the future.

Metacity Setup

This configuration tool only applies if you are using the Metacity window manager. This window manager is the default in SuSE Linux. Select a theme from the list. It will be used immediately, so you can see how it will look if used. To use a font other than that set in the 'Font Preferences' dialog, uncheck the 'Use Default Font' check box and select the desired font. With 'Focus Selector', set how windows are given focus. 'Click' gives focus only when a window is clicked. Both 'Mouse' and 'Sloppy' give focus when the mouse cursor is moved onto a window. When 'Mouse' is used, a window loses focus when the cursor leaves that window. Select how many workspaces to use with the 'Workspace Selector'.

Mouse

Use the 'Buttons' tab to configure your mouse for left-handed or right-handed use. Also set the 'Double-click Delay'. Under 'Cursor', configure the display of the mouse cursor and optionally set for an animated highlight around the cursor when (Ctrl) is pressed. 'Motion' contains settings for mouse acceleration and sensitivity and a threshold distance for dragging an item.

Network

If you use a proxy for accessing the web, configure its setup here. This will then be applied to all GConf-compliant applications.

Sound

Under 'General', select to enable or disable the sound server on start-up. If the sound server is enabled, optionally enable 'Sounds for events'. Use the list under 'Sound events' to configure individual sounds for events in compatible applications.

Theme

This selection controls the Gtk+ theme used in compatible applications. The Gtk+ theme selects the controls used in applications, including buttons, check boxes, and radio buttons. The titlebar and window borders are controlled by the window manager theme, set with the appropriate window manager configuration tool.

Toolbars & Menus

Use this to control the appearance and functioning of toolbars and menus. Select how text and icons are used in the toolbars, whether or not toolbars can be moved, and if menu items can have icons.

Panels

GNOME panels are easy to configure, add, and remove. A panel can be used to provide menus, applets, drawers, and launchers. Applets are small applications providing useful functionalities. Launchers are icons used to start a program. Drawers are like a subpanel that can contain other panel objects. To access panel controls, right-click an existing panel in an empty space to open the panel menu. If you right-click an existing launcher or applet, only the menu for that item is opened.

Configuring Panels

If available, use 'Properties' from the panel menu to make panel-specific settings. The settings available vary based on the panel type. The 'Hiding' settings are available with most panel types. 'Auto-hide' removes the panel from view when it is not being used. The panel is retrieved when the mouse moves to the panel location. Hide buttons enable the user to collapse and expand the panel as desired. The 'Background' tab has settings for the background color or image of the panel

Creating a Panel

GNOME offers five types of panels — menu, edge, corner, sliding, and floating. The menu panel is the panel at the top of the screen with the menu and clock in it. Edge panels are full-length panels placed along one of the four edges of the screen. Corner panels are short panels that can be positioned in the ends or middle of an edge. Sliding panels are short panels that can be middle-clicked and dragged into the desired position along an edge. Floating panels can be middle-clicked and dragged anywhere on the screen.

To create a new panel, right-click an existing panel and select 'Create Panel'. Select the desired panel type. Right-click the new panel to configure it or add items. Middle-click and drag to move it.

Adding Items

To add something to a panel, right-click an empty space and select 'Add to Panel'. Available applets are listed by category in the submenus. Launchers can be added manually or from the menu. Select the item to add. If you select 'Launcher', a dialog opens. Enter a specific and generic name for the item. Also enter a comment if desired. For 'Command', enter the command used to start the program, such as xchat to start xchat. If the application should be run in a terminal, select the 'Run in Terminal' check box. Click 'No Icon' to select an icon for the application. Things under 'Advanced' are not required.

Rearranging Panel Items

Things like applets, launchers, and drawers can be rearranged. Just drag items into place or right-click the item and select 'Move'. Items can be dragged from one panel to another. Remove items by right-clicking and selecting 'Remove from Panel'.

Removing Panels

To remove a panel, right-click and select 'Delete this panel...'. When a panel is deleted, all items in the panel and all configuration settings are lost. If you want items in the panel to be available in a different panel, move them to another panel before deleting the panel.

Nautilus

Nautilus is the GNOME2 file manager and viewer. It also supplies the icons on the desktop. For GNOME2, Nautilus has undergone extensive changes that have drastically improved its speed. If you have tried Nautilus before and disliked it, you may want to give it another chance. The information provided here is just a brief overview of the basic functionality of Nautilus. Refer to the internal help for more information.

Controlling Your Desktop

The default configuration provides several useful icons on the desktop. Double-click the desktop icon to start the application or open the folder in Nautilus. To make changes to the icon, such as rename it, right-click the icon and select the appropriate option from the menu. Use 'Properties' to select a different icon or make other changes. 'Rename' can be used to simply rename an icon. To delete the icon that launches a program, just throw it into the trash. Use caution doing the same with icons representing folders or data. If the icon is a folder or file, the actual data is deleted. If the icon is a link to a directory or file, only the link will be deleted.

If you right-click an empty space on the desktop, a menu of options opens. To create a new folder on the desktop for storing items, select 'New Folder'. To create a launcher for an application, select 'New Launcher'. Enter the name and command for the application and select an icon. Check 'Run in Terminal' if the application needs to be run in a terminal window.

To create a link on the desktop to an existing folder or file, open to it in Nautilus (double-click your home icon then navigate to the correct location). Right-click the item to which to link and select 'Make Link'. Drag the link from the Nautilus window and drop it onto the desktop.

Navigating in Nautilus

Nautilus navigation is similar to most existing web browsers. To open a new window, right-click an empty space on the desktop and select 'New Window'. The default opening location for Nautilus is your home directory. This can be changed.

The default window layout is shown in Figure 7.2 on the next page. The toolbar has icons for going forward and back, up a directory level, stopping, reloading, and returning to the home page. The path to the currently displayed directory or file is listed in 'Location'. A new path can be entered directly into this bar.

The left pane shows the current item being viewed and some information about that item. The bottom of the pane has 'History' and 'Notes' tabs.

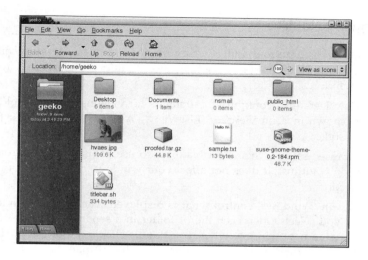

Figure 7.2: Nautilus Showing Home Directory

'Notes' can be used to make notes about an item. They are stored with the item. 'History' shows items you have accessed. To return to the default view, click the tab at the top.

Nautilus attempts to select appropriate icons for items based on what it can determine about the file type. A small preview is displayed for image and text files. Double-clicking a file opens the file in a viewer. The left tab will then display a list of possible applications with which to open the file. The file in the viewer cannot be edited within Nautilus.

You can also store bookmarks in Nautilus. Use 'Bookmarks' to add, edit, or access your bookmarks.

Managing Files

Files can be managed in Nautilus with drag and drop. To move files from one directory to another, use 'New Window' from the right-click menu or the 'File' menu in Nautilus to open two windows. In one window, open to the items to move. In the other, open to the destination. To move a file, just drag it to the new location and drop it. Copying is slightly more complicated. Right-click the item to copy and select 'Duplicate'. Then drag the copy to the new location. The menu displayed when an item is right-clicked has items for renaming files and editing other properties.

Configuring Nautilus

Nautilus takes its base font and other information from the desktop configuration. To make Nautilus-specific settings, use 'Edit' → 'Preferences' from a Nautilus window.

Under 'View Defaults', configure the defaults for viewing. Select if folders should be shown in 'Icon View' or 'List View'. Also set the sort order for both view styles.

In 'Appearance', select a theme for Nautilus to use. This theme controls the colors inside Nautilus. It does not affect your window manager or Gtk+ theme selections.

The settings in 'Windows' control what is displayed when a new window is opened. If you select 'Open each file or folder in a separate window', Nautilus will open a new window when you double-click a file or folder. Each item will have its own window. The sidebar is the left pane.

'Desktop & Trash' has options for the Nautilus desktop, the desktop directory, and the trash. Using the trash helps protect items from being accidentally deleted.

'Icon & List Views' has settings that control click behavior and sort order. Under 'Executable Text Files', set whether scripts should be run or displayed when clicked or if you should be asked each time. 'Show/Hide Options' controls listing of special file types.

'Icon Captions' controls the information available under icons. 'Sidebar Panels' controls what is available in the sidebar.

'Speed Tradeoffs' is useful for balancing between speed and display. Adjust the various settings to meet your needs.

Useful GNOME Applets and Applications

GNOME2 includes a variety of applets and applications. This is just an introduction to some of the most useful or interesting ones. These are all compliant with the GNOME2 configuration scheme.

Panel Applets

Dictionary

Dictionary is a useful applet for looking up the spellings and meanings of words. It accesses an online dictionary, so an Internet connection is required. Add it to a panel with 'Add to Panel' → 'Accessories' → 'Dictionary Lookup'.

Inbox Monitor

Inbox Monitor is a nice applet for checking if new mail has arrived. It can play a sound on arrival and can be configured to check a range of mailbox types and locations. Add it with 'Add to Panel' → 'Internet' → 'Inbox Monitor'.

Disk Mounter

This convenient applet is useful for mounting and unmounting drives. It can be configured to any mount point and offers a range of icons. Add it with 'Add to Panel' → 'Utility' 'Disk Mounter'.

Fish

For those who like silly amusements in the panel, try the GNOME fish. Historically named Wanda, the fish is fully configurable — offering several animations and customized naming. By default, Wanda the fish offers a fortune when clicked. Add a fish (or snarling monkey) with 'Add to Panel' → 'Amusements' → 'Fish'.

GNOME Terminal

Use GNOME Terminal to access the command line. Start it with 'Applications' → 'System Tools' → 'Terminal'. The default font is based on your font preferences. A new feature of this version of GNOME Terminal is profiles. Using these profiles, make a variety of setting options for different purposes and easily switch profiles. For example, if you connect to different machines, you may want to use different terminal settings for each machine.

To create, edit, or manage profiles, select 'Edit' → 'Profiles'. Set the default profile used for new terminals in this dialog. To create a new terminal, click 'New'. Enter a name for the profile and select the existing profile on which to base the settings. Click 'Create'. Select the new profile from the list and click 'Edit'. Also use this to edit an existing profile. Under the various tabs, make settings for the new profile.

To switch profiles in an open terminal window, select 'Terminal' → 'Profile' then select the desired profile. This change takes effect immediately. Additional terminals can be opened as new windows or tabs from the 'File' menu. Keyboard shortcuts for the application can be configured under 'Edit' → 'Keybindings'.

File Roller

File Roller is a convenient user interface for creating a variety of archived files. It can create and extract archives as well as add or extract items from an archive. In addition to using the menu items and buttons for adding items, you can add items by dragging them from a Nautilus window and dropping them into File Roller. Start File Roller with 'Applications' → 'Accessories' → 'File Roller'.

Games

GNOME2 includes a wide selection of games in the menu under 'Games'. Aisleriot is a card solitaire game including several different solitaire layouts. Iagno is a similar to Othello. Tangrams is a game in which you use geometrically-shaped pieces to form a predetemined shape, such as a chicken.

For More Information

To find out more about the GNOME desktop, check the following links.

http://www.gnome.org	The GNOME project home page
http://www.gtk.org/	GIMP Toolkit (GTK) home page
http://www.sunshineinabag.co.uk/	A Resource for GNOME2 Theme
http://www.gnome.org/faqs/	Frequently Answered Questions Answers

Ergonomics in the Workplace

This chapter is a short discussion of the ergonomic issues involved in the layout of computer workplaces. This text should not be seen as a substitute for studying the respective standards. No citations from these are included here and footnotes with references to other literature are completely omitted to preserve readability. It attempts to summarize the latest research findings in a short and concise manner, however, much will remain unmentioned. The items referred to in each section are mostly gathered from German literature and are almost always based on regulations and policies in the Federal Republic of Germany. This information is still useful in designing an ergonomic work area.

The Working Environment

If ergonomics specialists examined the home workstations of computer users systematically, they would probably burst into tears at the sight of the most curious constructions. Unfortunately, no standard has yet prevented individual users from buying so-called "special computer tables". The low-priced metal-tube frames with "practical rollers" (little stability), "ergonomically retractable keyboard tray" (no wrist pad), "integrated PC case holder and printer stand with paper mounting" (little stacking space and sometimes little legroom), "swiveling mouse pad" (unstable and insufficient working space), and "good view of the screen" (too close, too high) allow you to use a computer for a short time only. They should not be used at professional terminal workstations as they hardly meet any criteria of the corresponding standards. You will not find much of this kind of computer furniture in professional computer equipment catalogs, because manufacturers indirectly keep an eye on the employees' health by observing the minimum standards of computer workstations. The term "minimum standards" means they could be improved.

The Right Desk

A table at the wrong height strains arm and back muscles. The resulting cramped posture especially strains the spine. Too little leg room can force an unnatural body posture and cause disorders to the blood supply.

Choosing the right table is very easy. It should be as wide and deep as possible. An individual adjustment of the table height would be optimal. Working tables at which you can change between sitting and standing by turning the table into a writing stand, often just at the push of a button, are a luxury, but changing between a sitting and standing position brings relief.

- The flexible arrangement of working materials requires a table top of at least 160 x 80 cm.

- Workstations made of several interlinked boards are recommended.

- Tables that cannot be vertically adjusted must be 72 cm high. Tables that are vertically adjustable must be between 68 and 76 cm high.

- Even more width is needed for certain working tasks, such as CAD workstations. When changing between screen work and other kinds of work, at least 200 cm is required.

- There should be at least 60 cm leg room. Previous experience has shown, however, that this leg room is often too little.

- When using large screens, tables should be 100 or even 120 cm deep.

- The table surface should not be in bright colors and should have minimal reflection. A lot of office furniture is available in a subdued grey only.

Sitting Correctly on the Right Working Chair

Sitting in a working chair makes you sit in the same posture for a long time unlike in an easy chair, where you can move around easily. Constant sitting in the wrong position, such as bending forward or twisting to the side, can harm the respiratory and digestive organs. This leads to premature fatigue, circulatory disturbances, and backache resulting from overstraining the spine and the vertebrate disks. In extreme cases, years of sitting in the wrong position can lead to muscular and skeletal illnesses.

Correct sitting means a frequent change of posture. Different parts of the body are then constantly being used. Basically, it is a question of the correct adjustment. The height of your working chair is best when your forearms lying on the table are at right angles to your upper arms. You should be able to place your feet completely on the floor and your thighs and lower legs should also be at right angles. Gymnastic balls and balancing chairs offer an alternative to conventional seating arrangements Unfortunately, a good chair, constructed according to ergonomic criteria, is relatively expensive, but the investment in your health is worth it.

Important features of a good chair include:

- a backrest reaching to the shoulder blades and with an adjustable kinetic resistance

- support for the lumbar spinal column

- a seat that is also adjustable and can be tilted forwards or backwards

- automatic regulation of backrest and seat to retain an ideal angle

- springs that softly cushion the weight when sitting down

- stability provided with the help of at least five foot legs with rollers that are restrained when you stand

- adjustable height of the seat (according to standards, 42 to 53 cm) and backrest

- individual adjustment of arm rests, if there are any (luxury)

- a footrest if your feet do not reach the floor

Good Lighting for Productive Work

Generally speaking, workplace lighting does not come close to the intensity of light outdoors. This difference is unnoticed because the human faculty of perception is very flexible. The influence of lighting conditions on our own efficiency is often underestimated. If the light is too bright, you cannot see what is on the screen. If it is too dark, sharpness of vision decreases. The wrong lighting overstrains the visual system and, eventually, causes symptoms of fatigue and stress.

It is assumed that a combination of general lighting and individual workstation lighting is best. For the workstation at home, the combination of a high-powered ceiling lamp (500 watts, preferably with a dimmer) and one or two workplace lamps is recommended. The fluorescent lamps usually found in offices for general lighting should be supplemented by individual workstation lamps. The lighting should, however, not be too intense and be individually adjustable. Stark contrasts should be avoided. Be careful with strong desk lamps. Good illumination is, unfortunately, very expensive and the minimum requirements of lighting can also be fulfilled with cheaper illumination layouts.

However, individual sources of light are often problematic. If they are too strong, the contrast with the general lighting will be too apparent. Harmonizing, flowing transitions are considered more pleasant.

Keep the following points in mind when planning workstation lighting:

- First of all, it is important that you are exposed to daylight. A view outside is important.

- General lighting is considered pleasant if it is not below 250 lx (usually 500 lx is required, 1000 lx for an open plan office).

- 500–750 lx should be emitted by the individual workstation lighting.

- The lighting should not flicker. In the case of worn-out fluorescent lamps, a flickering can sometimes be noticed from the corner of the eye.

- Avoid dark shadows.

- Ceiling lights should emit light diagonally from above. Lighting strips should be set perpendicular to the screen table. The line of sight at the screen table should thus run parallel to the lighting strips.

- Whether the lighting is considered to be pleasant or not depends on the color temperature and light color of the lamp type. Warm white or neutral white is recommended.

- The light requirement depends not only on the working task, but also on age: older people need more light. The fact that older people often have only a small lamp in their homes has nothing to do with their light requirement, but rather with the fact that they want to save electricity.

- A screen workstation near daylight requires optimum shielding against direct and reflex glare, especially when the line of sight is directly out the window or at a 45° angle to it. The built-in antiglare facilities should be variable. Under no circumstances should artificial illumination cause reflex glare on the screen.

Optimum Climate

The room climate determines our well-being to a great extent. Problems arise more often if it is too cold, too warm, too drafty, or too dry. Low relative humidity can lead to burning eyes, dry mucous membranes, skin irritations, and increased susceptibility to colds. Things get complicated when people who work in the same room are accustomed to different basic temperatures.

For your well-being, it is important to observe the recommended basic values for temperature and humidity and to avoid strong air movement. The working material itself should not contribute to the increase of temperature.

- For activities in a sitting position or simple work, a room temperature of 20 to 22 °C is recommended. In summer, the temperature should be 26 °C at the most. This value should only be exceeded for a short time when the outdoor temperature is higher.

- A lot of equipment, as well as people, emit heat and influence room air conditions. This should be reduced as much as possible.

- Humidity should be between 40 (sometimes 50) and 65 percent and should be checked. This value is especially influenced by central heating.

- Draft (possibly from open windows and doors or air conditioning) should not exceed 0.1 to 0.15 m/s. Draft on individual parts of the body should be avoided.

- An air conditioner should be individually adjustable. It should be serviced regularly.

- The windows should be able to be opened and have sunshades to avoid glare effects. Sunlight can increase the room temperature considerably. Sunshades attached to the outside of the building provide the best protection.

- Plants can improve room conditions and are therefore recommended in all cases. They increase the relative humidity and filter pollutants from the air.

Too Much Noise Causes Stress

Noise is a physically powerful stress factor. Although it is often played down, too much noise makes you ill. Apart from health impairments, such as defective hearing, vegetative disorders, and psychic changes, noise affects our efficiency by impairing our ability to concentrate. Furthermore, discontent can reduce working motivation. The fact that proper noise abatement can possibly cost a lot of money is also problematic.

A calm working environment improves efficiency. Work at terminal workstations is often characterized as "mental activity". Therefore the maximum load value for scientific work or programming is 55 dB (A). The dB (A) represent a weighted evaluation of the acoustic pressure. The A-filter curve most resembles human perception. An increase of the sound level by 10 dB (A) is normally perceived as a duplication of volume.

- Since mainly mental work is done at terminal workstations, quiet working materials should be used from the start.

- The maximum limiting value for office work is 55 dB (A). With especially high mental demands or necessary communication of language, as low as 35–45 dB (A) is required. This is the case, for instance, for specialized work, scientific work, or programming.

- Furthermore, the evaluation level of a maximum of 55 dB (A) is important. If 70 dB (A) is measured for a quarter of an hour, the noise in the remaining time should be less than or equal to 55 dB (A).

- Workstations can be equipped with dividing walls, sound-absorbing floors, appropriately wallpapered walls, curtains, and other sound-dampening devices.

- Loud working equipment, such as matrix printers, should be installed in sound-absorbing cases. The permissible noise levels for office equipment are determined in the DIN standards.

- An air conditioner should not increase the normal noise level.

- Strain caused by excessive noise can also be reduced by an organizational restructuring of work.

Office Equipment

Buying a Screen

If you already have poor sharpness of vision, low-quality screens can make things even worse. Apart from eye problems, tenseness, fatigue, and many other disorders can be caused.

The latest technological developments are triniton, or black-matrix, screens and TFT flat screens. Unfortunately, flat screens are still relatively expensive. There are extensive standards which regulate the readability of the depicted information. When buying a screen, it is recommended to study the extensive standards to avoid a wrong purchase. One thing is certain: a good screen is usually expensive. The normal tube screens do not last forever. They only retain their focus and contrast for a few years.

- All depicted characters should be sharply defined and clearly legible up to the edges of the screen. A positive representation (dark characters on a light background, such as in a book) is recommended.

- As the depicted characters must be large enough, a 17-inch monitor is recommended, at least for graphical user interfaces (like KDE). For the processing of CAD, layout, and graphics, it should be 21 inches.

- It is especially important that the screen does not flicker. In concrete terms, the minimum sync frequency with 15-inch monitors should be at least 73 Hz. However, 85 Hz is recommended. For larger screens, such as 21-inch, 100 Hz.

- Luminosity and contrast should be variable. The focus of the characters should not differ with adjustments of brightness or contrast.

- The image should be free from distortion and show no color errors.

- To avoid reflex glare, a good antireflective coating of the screen surface is recommended.

- The screen should be rotatable and inclinable. A vertical adjustment is recommended.

- Color representation leads to a better intake of the information shown. However, the display of colors can also overstrain the eyes because different colors are broken up differently by the lenses. For red colors, people are farsighted, but for blue colors we are nearsighted. Older screens often have convergence errors — the three beams of the screen tube are no longer justified exactly, so colored edges form around letters, for example.

- Electromagnetic radiation emitting from the screen should be kept to a minimum.

Screen Location

A screen put in the wrong place leads to a cramped posture at work, which can cause illnesses. A work table that has insufficient depth often prevents the screen from being placed reasonably. The natural position of the head and arms is designed for work that lies in front of us. Ergonomics specialists have developed their own guidelines for the so-called "vision and gripping area." These reject placing the screen to the side. An exception is only when the screen is rarely used. A reason for this placement is the fact that even the required minimum 80 cm worktable depth is insufficient with a large screen and the use of working documents. Often the screen is placed — as shown in many PC manual pictures — on top of the computer case. This also leads to an unnatural posture. Observe yourself while you are reading. Are you looking straight ahead or slightly down?

- Shoulder, keyboard, and screen should be in one line so you always look directly at the screen. This rule that does not necessarily have to be observed all the time.

- Ultimately, the workstation should be individually adapted to the person and the working task. Flexibility is the key. Easily movable, rotatable, and, ideally, screens that retract into the table are encouraged.

- A comfortable visual distance varies individually. At least 50 cm is required. Some people need considerably more.

- It is a good idea for users to look away from the screen from time to time. In this way, their eyes can adapt to a different distance.

- If a document is being copied, it should be at the same distance as the screen to avoid frequent changes of focus.

- The difference in luminance between the direct working area, the screen, and the immediately surrounding areas, such as the screen case, should not be more than three to one. For this reason, computer cases in offices are not black. The difference between the working area and the surroundings should not be more than ten to one. Shiny areas create large differences of luminance. This is why office furniture is not available in bright colors and has a matt surface.

- To minimize the reflex glare on the screen, the screen and the keyboard should be arranged so the line of vision is parallel to window panes. The further the screen is away from the window, the better.

- The screen should not be directly under a lighting strip, but to the side of it. The line of vision should be parallel to the lighting strip.

The Keyboard and the Wrists

It has been well-known for some time that the keyboard arrangement derived from the typewriter is not necessarily ergonomic. During typing, the fingers, hands, arms, and shoulder-area are strained. This leads to tenseness. All the strain caused by a keyboard of inferior quality adds up over time. Unfortunately, the micromovements produced while typing are very difficult to measure. The RSI syndrome is a risk.

The keyboard is, without doubt, the input device of the computer used most. Therefore, it must be especially well constructed. Ergonomic specialists are always criticizing the fact that ⇑ Shift keys and Enter keys are too small. Another basic problem is the cable, which is often too short, preventing a comfortable individual placement. The question arises why so many people are willing to spend a thousand dollars on a PC, but only twenty dollars on an appropriate keyboard. You should also buy an extension cord along with your keyboard.

- The keyboard should be separate from the screen. It should also be inclinable, but set in a stable position (sufficiently large, rubber-coated feet).

- The middle key row should not be more than 30 mm above the surface of the table.

- There should be room to rest your hands in front of the keyboard. If there is no built-in wrist pad, get one.

- The marking must contrast with the color of the plastic and be easy to read. The keyboard should have no intense color and a satin-matt finish. For the keyboard legend, a dark script on a light background is recommended. Black keys are not ergonomic.

- The form of the keys should enable light and accurate typing. The lift of key should be 2–4 mm and the working point should be distinctly felt. Here 50–80 g is recommended as the force of the key depression stroke.

- Those who type a lot should take regular breaks.

- Learning the touch system helps because the workload is distributed across all fingers.

- Split or individually separable keyboards are something to which you have to get accustomed, but nevertheless are an alternative worth considering. They have been constructed according to the latest ergonomic findings and are already recommended in some standards. They prevent wrist strain to the side.

- The keyboard of a notebook or laptop cannot correspond to the standards because of the crowded keys. A notebook should therefore not be used as workstation equipment unless it is linked to an external keyboard and mouse.

Liberating the Mouse

Due to the advance of graphical user interfaces, users are practically forced to use a mouse. The intensive use of the mouse can cause not only fatigue, but also disorder in the hand-arm-shoulder area. An example of this is RSI. The danger increases when a "bad" mouse is used.

No proper standards yet exist for an ergonomic mouse. Often a PC is sold with the standard mouse. This should certainly be looked at considered closely. Is the mouse really suitable or should it be replaced by a better one? Have the dealer unpack several mice for you to try. The cable is probably too short. Ask the dealer to give you an extension.

Evaluate your own mouse use. Can you be retrained? Professional programs with a lot of interaction do without any mouse clicks. First you have to learn how to use shortcuts to operate programs, but you can work up to four times as fast. Often a combination of mouse and keyboard operation is recommended.

- The ergonomic mouse feels good in your hand. The keys should not be too close or too small. There are even mice for children's hands.

- Your fingers should be able to rest on the keys in a relaxed position.

- The mouse should be next to the keyboard. Left-handed users have an advantage because the keyboard has several function keys and the numerical key block between letter keys and a mouse on the right side. These extend the gripping distance. If you are left-handed, get a mouse for left-handers.

- Learning keyboard codes reduces the workload on the complete arm. An arm-shoulder area strengthened by the appropriate physical training can deal better with overstrain for a short time.

- The cable should be long enough. If necessary, an extension has to be purchased. A wireless mouse is a luxury.

- The mouse needs a proper base to function well. Get a good mouse pad.

- Pay attention to the mouse driver. Good mice have mouse drivers with a multitude of functions. You can, for example, adjust the cursor movement exactly according to your requirements or allocate special instructions to the different mouse keys. The double-click might be placed on the middle key with the mouse driver.

- Make sure you adjust the acceleration and double click adjustment of the mouse to your own preferences. Some people work with the mouse from the hand joint. Others prefer moving their complete forearm.

- An alternative to the mouse is a trackball. Here, you move a ball inside a stationary casing to control the mouse pointer. In contrast to the mouse, the trackball reduces the movements in the hand and arm area.

Links and Literature

A great manual for staff members and superiors with many checklists and questionnaires, taking the mental strain into account:

Burmester, M., Görner, C., Hacker, W., Kärcher, M. and others (1997). The SANUS-manual. Screen work EU-conform (- research - FB 760). Berlin: Series of the Federal Office for Work Protection and Work Medicine. [SANUS: Safety and health protection at terminal work on the basis of international standards]

A clear and well-structured guide for analysis and work protection tasks around the terminal workstation:

Richenhagen, G., Prümper, J. & Wagner, J. (1998, 2nd edition). Handbuch der Bildschirmarbeit (trans: Manual of terminal work). Neuwied: Luchterhand.

An extensive collection for work and health with all important information on the latest German or international standards. Highly recommended, but, unfortunately, only in German: http://europe.osha.eu.int/

Part III

Applications

Word Processing and More with OpenOffice.org

OpenOffice.org is an extensive and powerful office package for Linux. It offers tools for all kinds of office tasks, such as writing texts, working with spreadsheets, creating impressive graphics, or designing complex presentations. Open, edit, and even save files in Microsoft Office formats. This chapter covers the installation and initial steps with OpenOffice.org.

StarOffice Evolves into OpenOffice.org

StarOffice was previously enclosed with SuSE Linux. Recently, the manufacturer *Sun* released version 6.0 of its office package, which is no longer made available free of charge like its predecessors. Those who would like to use the package must pay a fee (which is still low when compared to competing products). To continue to provide StarOffice, SuSE would have needed to raise the price of SuSE Linux by a considerable amount.

However, OpenOffice.org is excellent replacement. It is the result of the concentrated effort of programmers of the Open Source community and Sun over a period of eighteen months since the source code of StarOffice 5.2 was released in October 2000. The package is subject to the LGPL license, which means that it can be downloaded and used free of charge.

> **Note**
>
> Because the name "OpenOffice" is a registered product of *Sun*, the Open Source office package is not permitted to use this name. For this reason, it is called "OpenOffice.org".
>
> **Note**

OpenOffice.org is very similar to StarOffice and there are few new features. The main differences from StarOffice 5.2 are:

- As OpenOffice.org is an Open Source product, the commercial components of StarOffice had to be removed from the package. This affected the database *StarBase*, several import and export filters, graphics, clipart, and templates. The spell checking utility Sun purchased for StarOffice was also removed and replaced by the Open Source utility myspell.

- The scheduler, the e-mail module, the web browser, the *Image* application, and the calendar were also removed. Math, a comfortable tool for generating mathematical formulas, was added.

- The program was modularized, which means that the individual components can be started directly. The desktop, which was formerly the central user interface, was removed by the programmers. The individual applications can now be started in a convenient manner from 'K' → 'Office' → 'OpenOffice.org'.

- A new XML-based standard file format was introduced (see `http://xml.openoffice.org`). Files in StarOffice and Microsoft Office format can be read and created. The filters for Microsoft Office files were improved.

Installation

Before working with OpenOffice.org, install it on your computer Then use the program's graphical installater of the program. The following section provides assistance for the installation.

If you followed the quick installation procedure and did not explicity deselect OpenOffice.org, the program should already be installed on your computer. If this is not the case, install OpenOffice.org, package `OpenOffice_org-en` with YaST2.

The OpenOffice.org Installer

When you start OpenOffice.org for the first time with 'K' → 'Office' → 'OpenOffice.org' → 'Writer', a setup utility is launched. This screen displays some important information, such as the software license. Read it carefully and confirm your acceptance to start the installation of OpenOffice.org.

After you have accepted the conditions, import your personal data and settings from an earlier installation, if available. If a previous version is detected, OpenOffice.org shows it. If not, click 'import personal data'. Then activate the button 'Browse'. A window opens in which to specify the directory.

After you click 'Next', enter personal user data, such as your name, address, and ZIP code. Optionally, leave these fields blank or fill them in later. However, we recommend entering your data to avoid frequent reentries later, for example, in letters.

Note

Do *not* change the default settings for the installation path and the installation type (Standard Workstation Installation). OpenOffice.org offers the possibility to install on the local hard disk, but this is not necessary, as OpenOffice.org has already been installed locally. To repeat the installation, delete the files `.sversionrc` and `.user*.rdb` in your home directory.

Note ⌐

To enable Java and Javascript support in OpenOffice.org. the package `java` must be installed. If you have installed other Java versions, select the "correct" one — the one installed in the directory `/usr/lib/java`. When OpenOffice.org is installed, the user `root` is sent an e-mail message summarizing the installation procedure.

Next, select the installation type: "Standard" or "Standard Workstation" (default). Select "Standard Workstation".

After the installation, start OpenOffice.org from the K menu or with `openoffice`.

Repairing OpenOffice.org

If files are damaged while using OpenOffice.org, repair these at any time. In KDE, press (Alt) + (F2) and enter the following in the entry field:

```
/usr/X11R6/bin/openoffice
```

A dialog window opens in which to choose to remove or repair OpenOffice.org. A damaged installation can be restored with 'Repair'. All steps are performed automatically.

Overview of the Programs

OpenOffice.org consists of several programs that are more or less able to interact:

Writer	Powerful text processing application
Calc	Spreadsheet application with a utility for generating charts
Draw	Drawing application for creating vector graphics
Math	Application for generating mathematical formulas
Impress	Application for creating presentations

Table 9.1: Available Programs in OpenOffice.org

The main focus here is on Writer and Calc. The other applications are only covered briefly. For more information, use the online help (see also Section *Getting Help* on this page).

Getting Help

Get help for OpenOffice.org at any time in the 'Help' menu. To get thoroughly acquainted with a topic, use of 'Help' → 'Contents'. Here, find information about OpenOffice.org components, such as Writer, Calc, and Impress.

The 'Help Agent' attempts to offer help information relevant to your current task. It updates its window when you perform different actions in OpenOffice.org and provides helpful hints. To use it, activate 'Help' → 'Help Agent'. 'Tips' or 'Extended Tips' display a help text when you point to an icon with the mouse. The text displayed by 'Extended Tips' is more detailed. At the outset, 'Tips' and 'Extended Tips' (both located in the 'Help' menu) are very useful. When more familiar with OpenOffice.org, easily deactivate them.

Tip

If you are not sure whether the features are active or not, click the 'Help' menu. Checked menu items are activated.

Tip

Converting Microsoft Office Documents

Easily edit Microsoft Office 97 or 2000 documents in OpenOffice.org by selecting 'File' → 'AutoPilot' → 'Document Converter...'. Choose the file format to convert. Various StarOffice and Microsoft Office formats are available for selection. Then click 'Next' and specify where OpenOffice.org should look for documents to convert and in which directory the converted files should be placed. Also review the other settings on this page.

Note

Documents from a Windows partition are usually in a subdirectory of
`\windows`

Note

Click 'Next' to proceed to a summary. Here, check your entries again. Click 'Convert' to start the conversion procedure.

Making and Changing Settings

All global settings can be accessed under 'Tools' → 'Options'. A window as shown in Figure 9.1 opens.

The left side shows the various settings arranged in a tree structure.

'OpenOffice.org' This structural unit contains various basic settings. Enter user data, such as the address and e-mail, as well as important paths and settings for printers and external programs.

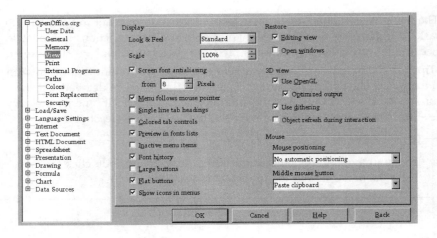

Figure 9.1: The Options Dialog

'Load/Save' In this dialog, determine how files are opened and closed. A number of special parameters affect the handling of other formats.

'Language Settings' This menu contains various settings for the language and linguistics. Country-specific parameters and spell checker settings can also be adapted here. The support of Asian languages, which was improved considerably since StarOffice 5.2, can be activated here.

'Internet' Proxy and search engine settings.

'Text Documents' Global settings for Writer, such as default fonts and layout.

'HTML Document' All parameters that affect the Internet functionality of OpenOffice.org can be set in this menu.

'Spreadsheet' Various settings for Calc, such as sort lists, grid, and input.

'Presentation' Settings for all presentation documents. For example, specify the measurement units used for snapping to the grid.

'Drawing' This menu point allows you to define the scale, grid, print options, and other settings.

'Formula' Print options and formats.

'Chart' Default colors for charts.

'Data Sources'   Settings for access to external data sources.

Note ──

All settings made here apply *globally*, which means settings made in this dialog are used every time you open a new document.

─────────────────────────────────────── **Note** ┘

Text Processing with OpenOffice.org Writer

Creating Texts with the AutoPilot

The AutoPilot is a small utility that uses your entries to create a ready-to-use text from a template. For example, to write a business letter, select 'File' → 'AutoPilot' → 'Letter. . . '. A dialog as shown in Figure 9.2 opens.

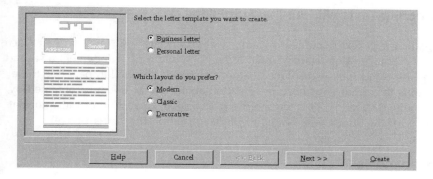

Figure 9.2: The AutoPilot in OpenOffice.org

Click 'Next' to proceed to the next page. To modify previous entries, use 'Back'. Click 'Create' to generate the letter according to your specifications. 'Cancel' exits the dialog. 'Help' displays a help text in the Help Agent.

The following list shows the individual pages and their entries. You do not need to enter all details. Generate your letter at any time with 'Create'.

1. Decide whether to write a business letter or a personal letter. Three styles are offered: modern, classic, or decorative.

2. Add and position graphics.

3. Enter your sender address and specify the position and size of the sender field.

4. Enter the details of the addressee here.

5. Add elements, such as the date, subject line, and page numbers.

6. Define footers and the size of the margins.

7. Enter information for additional pages of your letter.

8. Enter document information and the file name.

9. Select the paper tray and when to print your logo and sender data.

Now all you need to do is to compose the letter text. There are other useful AutoPilots for creating documents like fax messages, agendas, memos, and presentations.

Creating Texts Without the AutoPilot

Create a new text document by simply clicking 'File' → 'New' → 'Text Document'. You can now start writing. When opening a new document a second bar (the object bar) is displayed below the standard function bar. Use these buttons to format your text. Information about the tools can be obtained by activating 'Help' → 'Tips' or 'Help' → 'Extended Tips'. You can also format text with the Stylist (see *Working with the Stylist* on the current page).

Selecting Text

To select text, click the beginning position, keep the mouse button pressed, and run the cursor over the desired text. Selected text appears white on black. After selecting the desired text, release the mouse button. Open a context menu by right-clicking the selection. With the context menu, modify settings, such as the the font and the style.

Working with the Stylist

The Stylist enables you to format texts comfortably and quickly. Open or close it at any time with 'Format' → 'Stylist' or by pressing (F11). Figure 9.3 on the facing page shows the dialog window of the Stylist.

Figure 9.3: The Stylist for Writer

A style is a designated assignment of predefined formatting, such as paragraph indents, text style, text color, and font size.

Tip

If the box in the lower part of the Stylist is set to 'Automatic', OpenOffice.org tries to "guess" which styles could be used for the current context. If 'All' is set, all styles of this group are listed.

Tip

Text can be *hard-formatted* or *soft-formatted*:

Hard formatting A text attribute is *directly* assigned to a text area. It is called hard because it is *hard* work to change. This procedure is only useful for short texts (short letters, articles, and the like), but is a quick and intuitive method.

Soft Formatting The text is not formatted directly, but is assigned a style, which can be modified easily. A change of the style automatically results in an update of the text to which it is assigned. This approach is useful for larger texts (theses, books, and the like). Although not as intuitive, it is very effective and fast if the formatting is changed extensively. It provides a substantial advantage for trying different layouts.

The Stylist offers various styles for diverse formatting needs:

Paragraph Styles   Indents, spacing, hyphenation, tabs, alignment, fonts, initials.

Character Styles   Font, font size, language.

Frame Styles   Position, anchoring, frame.

Page Styles   Header, footer, margins, columns.

Numbering Styles   Bullet or numbering type, structure, graphics, position, options.

Assigning Paragraph Styles with the Stylist

To assign a style to a paragraph, select the name of the style to use in the Stylist. Click the bucket symbol in the Stylist. Assign the selected style by clicking the respective paragraphs with the mouse. To exit this mode, press (Esc) or click the bucket symbol again.

Creating a New Style

Easily create your own styles as follows:

1. Format a paragraph or a character as desired. Use the toolbar or the 'Format' menu.

2. In the Stylist, left-click 'New Style from Selection' (to the right of the bucket symbol) with the left mouse button.

3. Enter a name for your style and click OK.

Use the newly created style for other paragraphs. Easily change details of the style by selecting the name and clicking 'Modify...' with the right mouse button. All modifications can be made in the ensuing dialog.

Inserting a Table

Create a table by clicking the 'Insert' icon in the toolbar and keeping it pressed for a few seconds. Another toolbar appears in which to specify your selection. If you touch the third icon with the mouse, a grid as shown in Figure 9.4 on the next page opens.

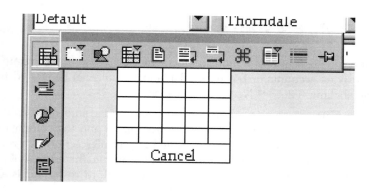

Figure 9.4: Inserting a Table Using the Toolbar

Run the mouse over the grid. The grid automatically turns black when you move over it and shows the current selection of lines and columns. Insert the table in the current text at the current cursor position with a click.

Tip

The 'Insert' icon changes depending on what was last inserted.

Tip

Inserting Graphics

Graphics can be inserted by means of the toolbar (second icon from the left) or by selecting 'Insert' → 'Graphics' → 'From file...'.

A dialog window opens. Select the respective file. If you click 'Preview', the contents of the file are displayed on the right-hand side. This procedure may take some time with larger images. After you confirm your choice, the inserted image appears at the cursor position. Activate the image (shown by the eight squares surrounding the image). Now, select 'Graphics...' in the context menu. The ensuing dialog offers various settings, such as wrapping and borders.

To modify the size of the image, click it to activate it. Click one of the "handles", keep it pressed, and drag in the desired direction. A dashed frame shows the new dimensions. Release to scale the image.

To change the position of the image instead of its size, click the image and keep the mouse button pressed. Move the image to the desired position. Release the mouse button.

Spreadsheets with Calc

Calc is the spreadsheet application in OpenOffice.org. Use this program for your private accounts or business calculations. Calc can be started from Writer by clicking 'File' → 'New' → 'Spreadsheet'.

At start-up, Calc presents an empty spreadsheet divided into rows and columns. The rows are numbered from top to bottom and the columns are lettered from left to right. "Cells" are located at the intersection of a row and a column. Each cell has a unique address. For example, the address B3 refers to the cell located in the second column (B) and the third row. This is also indicated at the top left next to the entry line.

Possible contents for cells include numbers, text, dates, times, currencies, and formulas. A cell may be active or inactive. There can only be one active cell at a time. The active cell has a thick black frame. Move the activation with the cursor keys or by clicking another cell with the mouse. An active cell can be edited.

Changing Cell Attributes

To enter something in a cell, simply write in the cell. By default, texts are aligned to the left and numbers to the right. Confirm your entry with ⏎. To change the formatting of your cells, select the cells to modify then right-click to open a context menu. Select 'Format Cells...' to open a dialog in which to adjust the settings. The dialog, as shown in Figure 9.5 on the facing page, has the tabs 'Numbers', 'Font', 'Font Effects', 'Alignment', 'Borders', 'Background', and 'Cell Protection'.

'Numbers' Choose a category, such as percent, currency, date, or time. The format determines the decimal digits and leading zeros.

'Font' Set the font face and style.

'Font Effects' Set additional font effects including underlining, strikethrough, relief, outline, and shadow.

'Alignment' Determine the horizontal and vertical position of the contents of the cell. The direction of the text can also be set here.

'Borders' Add borders to a cell. All kinds of shadows and line styles can be adjusted here.

'Background' Determines the color of the cell background.

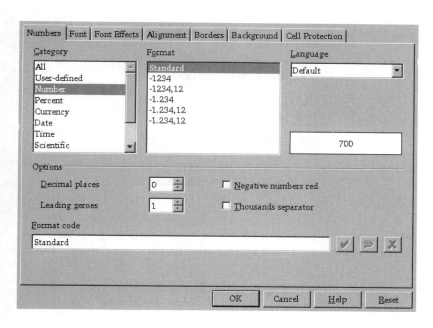

Figure 9.5: Setting Cell Attributes

'Cell Protection' Prevent unintentional or intentional changes of the cell by activating 'Protected'.

A Practical Example: Monthly Expenses

Calculations in OpenOffice.org can be made with formulas. Enter your numbers in the cells. Use formulas and the unique cell coordinates to calculate other values based on the entered values.

For example, you want to check your monthly expenses. You can see the items in the following (simplified) spreadsheet:

The cell B3 contains the phone bill for January and B4 contains the fuel expenses. To add both amounts, enter the formula = B3+B4 in B5. The result is displayed in B5. If you have mistyped the numbers (or estimated your phone bill inaccurately), reenter the amount. The sum is updated automatically.

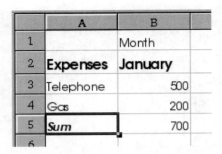

	A	B	
1		Month	
2	**Expenses**	**January**	
3	Telephone	500	
4	Gas	200	
5	**Sum**	700	
6			

Figure 9.6: A Spreadsheet Example for Calc

Calc offers many functions beyond the four basic mathematical operations. An extensive list arranged in categories is available under 'Insert' → 'Function...'.

The spreadsheet can be extended easily. To insert another entry between `Fuel` and `Sum`, right-click the adjacent 5. Select 'Insert Row' from the context menu. A new row is inserted in row 5.

Entering formulas becomes rather burdensome for larger numbers of cells. If you have several items in your A column and want to add them, try the SUM function. To do this, enter = `SUM(B3:B5)` in the field B6. Another possibility is to click the Sigma (Σ) symbol next to the entry line and enter the range manually. This formula adds all numbers from B3 to B5.

You can also specify several ranges. As shown in the above formula, a range is defined by two cell addresses separated by a colon. Several ranges can be separated by semicolons. Accordingly, the formula = `SUM(B3:B5;D3:D5)` adds everything from B3 to B5 *and* from D3 to D5.

Creating Charts

Add some more entries to the spreadsheet. Write a few more months in row 2 so it looks like Figure 9.7. Select the range from A2 to E5. The text appears white on black.

To create a chart, click 'Insert' → 'Chart...'. A dialog window appears. Optionally, modify the selection or use the first row or column as a label. Usually, the offered settings can be accepted. Click 'Next'.

The dialog window has four pages. The most interesting and important page is shown in Figure 9.8 on the next page.

	A	B	C	D	E
1		Month			
2	**Expenses**	**January**	**February**	**March**	**April**
3	Telephone	500	300	430	350
4	Gas	200	80	200	470
5	*Sum*	*700*	*380*	*630*	*820*
6					

Figure 9.7: *Expanded Example Spreadsheet*

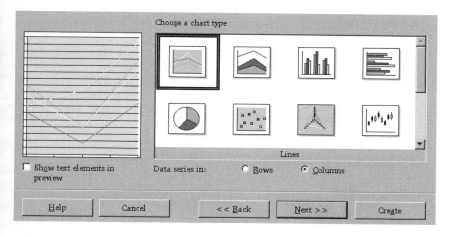

Figure 9.8: *Choice of Chart Types*

The available chart types are displayed in the center. Options include line, area, column, and bar. To the left, see a preview of your data presentation.

The line chart is best suited for our example. Click 'Next' to proceed to different variants of line charts: with or without symbols, stacked, percent, or cubic spline. We chose 'Symbols'. If you activate 'Show text elements in preview', the designations (like `January` and `February`) are displayed on the X axis and the values on the Y axis. A legend is added on the right-hand side.

In the next page, assign a title to the chart and to the X axis and the Y axis. By default, the X axis is deactivated. Nevertheless, you can enter a text here, too. After you click 'Create', the chart appears in your spreadsheet. Figure 9.9 on the following page shows the example chart.

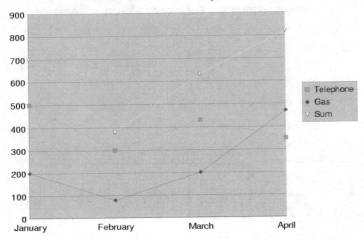

Figure 9.9: A Chart in Calc

Importing Tables

From time to time, you may need to import information in tabular form to a Calc table, such as stock exchange data, phone rates, or lists. There are two ways to import this information to Calc.

Method 1: Importing from the clipboard

Suppose you want to import stock exchange information. To do this, enter the address of your favorite stock exchange page in a web browser. When the table appears, select it with the mouse button. Depending on the browser, you may need to press 'Copy'. The selected range is copied to the clipboard.

In OpenOffice.org, open a new document with 'File' → 'New' → 'Spreadsheet'. Select the cell from which to begin the inserted table. Select 'Edit' → 'Paste'. The table is pasted to the document together with all formatting specifications, hyperlinks, and other information.

Method 2: Importing with a filter

To import an existing HTML file to Calc, select 'File' → 'Open'. A dialog window will open up. Now select 'File type' → 'HTML (OpenOffice.org Calc)'. Use the arrow keys to navigate in the list. Select the file name and click 'Open' to import the table.

Drawing with OpenOffice.org Draw

Draw can be used to create vector graphics. A line can be described in two ways: First, by means of many dots that combine to form a line. This is the "conventional" variant, referred to as bitmap. Common bitmap formats include GIF, JPEG, and PNG. However, this is only a rough approximation that depends on the number of dots.

A line can instead be described by defining the two end points This saves a lot of memory, but it requires a description of the line thickness, color, and other details. Common formats include EPS and AI. This method of representation is referred to as vector graphics. Vector graphics can also be scaled better.

Drawing Graphical Elements

To create a new drawing, start Draw with 'K' → 'Office' →OpenOffice.org → 'Draw'. If OpenOffice.org is already running, instead select 'File' → 'New' → 'Drawing'.

The graphical elements available in Draw can be modified with various operations that affect the line thickness, line type, color, fill, and other parameters. Try to draw a rectangle. The toolbar is displayed on the left-hand side. Click the the filled rectangle icon and keep the mouse button pressed for a few seconds. A small submenu opens with filled and unfilled rectangles and squares, some with rounded corners. Select a filled rectangle. The shape of the mouse pointer will change to a crosshair. Click the document to set a corner and drag the mouse down to the right. A rectangle appears and scales to the mouse movements. Release the mouse button when the desired size is reached.

To change the fill color, activate the rectangle with a mouse click. Green handles, which can be used to modify the size, appear at the four corners and the four edges. If you press the right mouse button, the context menu opens. Select 'Area...' to access a dialog box for various settings. Click 'OK' when satisfied with the result. Alternatively, change the color using the toolbar.

The toolbar contains even more useful graphical elements, such as circles, ellipses, lines, and even 3-D elements. For more information and assistance, use the help function.

Creating Presentations with OpenOffice.org Impress

Creating Presentations with the AutoPilot

If you have difficulties putting your ideas on "virtual paper", try using the AutoPilot. Select 'File' → 'AutoPilot' → 'Presentation...'. With the AutoPilot, define the basic structure of your presentation in three brief steps. Configure backgrounds, the output medium, and various effects. Also import information from an existing presentation with the help of the assistants.

After you have terminated the AutoPilot with 'Create', Impress offers a number of templates for the page layout. Select one that suits your purposes and enter a title for the first page. Click 'OK' to generate the first page of the newly created presentation. To complete your presentation, enter headers and texts.

With 'Presentation' →Slide Show, view the presentation immediately. You can advance page by page by pressing the left mouse button. Exit presentation mode with (Esc).

Turn to the help system of OpenOffice.org for information about the range of modification options.

Adding a Slide

To add a slide to your presentation, use 'Slide' → 'Insert'. A dialog window opens as in Figure 9.10 on the next page.

Enter a name for the slide and determine which AutoLayout to use. Click 'Ok' to insert the slide or 'Cancel' to abort the procedure.

Use templates with 'File' → 'New' → 'From Template...'.

For More Information

To track or support the ongoing development of OpenOffice.org or get more information on this important project, visit the OpenOffice.org home page at http://www.openoffice.org.

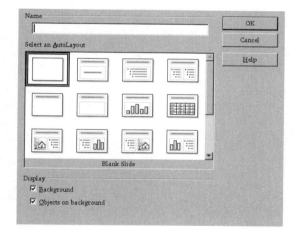

Figure 9.10: *Inserting Slides in Impress*

Adobe Acrobat Reader— The PDF Viewer

Adobe Acrobat Reader is a program for viewing and printing PDF files (portable document format files). Acrobat Reader can be used as a stand-alone viewer or as a Netscape plug-in. The interface makes even complex documents easy to navigate. The package `acroread` can be installed at any time with YaST2.

The developers' goal was to make paperless information management possible for computer users. Electronic documents of a visionary paperless office theoretically have several advantages. These range from easy e-mail sending to space-saving archiving of larger amounts of data.

Viewed globally, the PDF format is only one of the many possible core image formats for text. Acrobat Reader is a viewer for this file format. The program and the file format have several useful features. Figure 10.1 shows the screen displaying the help document.

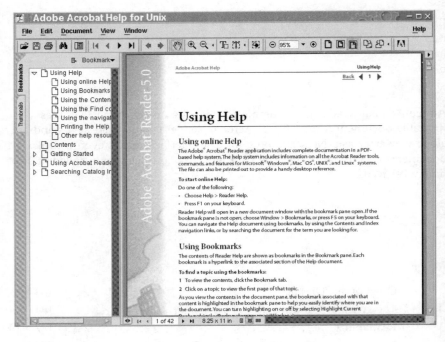

Figure 10.1: Adobe Acrobat Reader

The PDF format has been highly optimized for its intended use and is now regarded as the standard format for portable documents. Adobe Acrobat Reader takes full advantage of all PDF features. It is available for Macintosh and Windows as well as Unix and Linux. This provides users with a standard interface to go with their standard documents, giving standardized viewing and printing.

The PDF format is the most popular standard format for documents. You can find many PDF documents on the Internet, which you can easily view and download. Acrobat Reader can be integrated in Netscape in the form of a plug-in (a special program that performs services for another program). When you click a PDF file on the web, Acrobat Reader is started automatically and the selected document is displayed. The file can be saved locally using the respective icon in the Acrobat Reader toolbar.

PDF documents can contain links and bookmarks pointing to other parts of a document or to other documents. These are displayed in a separate window to the left of the text when the 'Bookmarks' tab is active. They are also shown in the text. Clicking a link immediately opens the appropriate page.

PDF files can also contain preview images, often called thumbnails. These miniature images, which represent one entire page, are also displayed in the left window. Thumbnails provide a quick overview of the document and can be used to locate specific sections or passages.

Note

With Acrobat Reader, PDF documents cannot be created, only viewed. Unfortunately, Adobe currently provides Acrobat (the full text processing application) only for Windows and Macintosh. In SuSE Linux, you can use various programs to create your own PDF documents. For example, ps2pdf is a widely-used utility for generating PDF files from PostScript files.

Note

Opening a PDF File

Start Acrobat Reader with 'SuSE Menu' → 'Office' → 'Viewer' → 'Acrobat Reader'. Alternatively, start Acrobat Reader from a console with `acroread`. Open a file in Acrobat Reader with 'File' → 'Open', Ctrl + O, or the respective icon.

If you click any file with the `.pdf` extension in the KDE file manager and have the basic SuSE Linux system, the file will be opened with KGhostView instead of Acrobat Reader. Because PDF files are based on the PostScript format, KGhostView can display and print them. However, KGhostview lacks the link and search functionality of Acrobat Reader. Manually configure KDE to use Acrobat Reader instead, if desired.

This can be done with the 'File Associations' dialog (Figure 10.1 on the facing page) accessed from 'Settings' → 'Configure Konqeror'. In the tree, look for the extension pdf under 'application'. In 'Application Preference Order', move 'Acrobat Reader' to the top. Following a restart of the file manager, PDF files should automatically be opened with Acrobat Reader.

Figure 10.2: File Type Association in Konqueror

The Acrobat Window

If the default settings are used, Acrobat Reader appears as shown in Figure 10.3 on the next page. The first line with control components is the menu bar. The menus contain all the control commands for Acrobat Reader. Familiarize yourself with the keyboard shortcuts to use the program more efficiently.

The toolbar is under the menu bar. Use the toolbar icons to access the most important functions. The icons are structured in groups that can be arranged according to your own preferences or moved to other sides of the application window. It is even possible to move the icons to a separate application window or hide some of them.

Here a brief explanation of the individual icons from left to right (all icons are visible):

— Opens the Acrobat Reader file manager.

Figure 10.3: The Menu Bar and Toolbar of Acrobat Reader with Bookmarks

— Opens the dialog for saving the currently displayed PDF file.

— Opens a printer dialog with several configuration options.

— Opens the search function.

— Displays or hides the left-hand window containing thumbnails and bookmarks.

— Goes to the first page of the displayed document.

— Goes to the previous page.

— Goes to the next page.

— Goes to the last page of the document.

— The application saves the path on which you moved through the document. This feature is especially useful if you used bookmarks. Use this function to go back in the history list by one step.

— Move forward in the history list.

— Activate this to grab and move the page displayed in the text window with the left mouse button.

⊕ — Enlarge the displayed document. The new view is centered on the clicked spot.

⊖ — Decrease magnification of the document. The new view is centered on the clicked spot.

T — When this icon is active, select text and copy it to the clipboard using the right mouse button or the menu. The text is marked according to lines.

T — Another tool for selecting text. This tool works according to columns. Use the left mouse button to draw a dashed selection frame around the text to copy.

▣ — Use this icon to copy images from the displayed PDF file to the clipboard. However, the copied images will not be available in all applications.

⊖ — Gradually zoom out.

95% ▾ — Directly enter the display size in the percent window. Select common values with the arrow.

▯ — Set the zoom factor to 100%

▣ — Zoom to show an entire page.

▯ — Fit the page to the window width.

A — Open the Adobe web site. If no browser is defined for Acrobat Reader, the respective configuration dialog opens.

The window on the left-hand side below the toolbar contains the links (referred to as bookmarks) or the preview images (thumbnails). If a document does not have these functions, the window is not be shown.

The selected document is displayed on the right-hand side. Normally, this window takes up most of the space in the program window. The status bar below the document includes more information and additional tools (Figure 10.4 on the facing page). Use the tools for navigating in the document and toggling the page display modes 'Single Page', 'Continuous', and 'Continuous – Facing'.

the document. You can turn highlighting on

1 of 42   8.25 × 11 in

Figure 10.4: *Acrobat Reader Status Bar*

Displaying Documents

Sometimes the document text is shown too small to read. Acrobat Reader has several ways to enlarge the text. The easiest way is to click the paper icons in the toolbar. This way, change the size of presentation to '100%', 'Full page', or 'Width of page'. Click the magnifying glass in the toolbar to activate its function. A left-click in the document enlarges. (Ctrl)-click reduces the display size. Alternatively, click the percent display and directly enter your own zoom factor.

Navigating Documents

To change pages, use the mouse or the keyboard. The mouse allows you to easily control the vertical and horizontal scroll bars. Alternatively, click the arrow icons in the toolbar or status bar. To move to a specific page, click the page number in the status bar and type in the page number. The arrow keys of the keyboard move the page up or down in small steps. (PgUp) and (PgDn) change to the previous or next page.

┌─ **Tip** ───

(F6) turns the link window off and on. (F7) and (F8) respectively deactivate and activate the menu and toolbar. (Ctrl) + (F) activates the search function.

─────────────────────────────────────── **Tip** ─┘

Finding Specific Information

Acrobat Reader has a search function for easily locating text. Use the icon with the binoculars or select 'Edit' → 'Find'. Enter the desired keyword. Acrobat Reader will find the first reference. To continue the search, use 'Edit' → 'Find Again'.

Adobe Acrobat Reader—The PDF Viewer

10

Printing

In the printer menu, the following options are important:

Printer selection: With 'Printer command', specify the print queue. `lpr` is the default.

Selection of pages: Print all or only a few pages.

Reverse printing: Use this to print the document last page first.

Enlargement of the pages: Use 'Fit to page' if the page size of the document is larger or smaller than the paper.

Help

Clicking 'Help' opens a PDF file with a detailed help text. Use Acrobat's search, link, and scrolling functions to find the information needed.

Opening PDF Files in Netscape

If PDF documents cannot be opened automatically, it may be due to an incorrect Netscape configuration. Netscape must be instructed what to do with a PDF file. To access these settings, open 'Edit' → 'Preferences' → 'Navigator' → 'Applications'. The MIME type is `application/pdf` and the file extension is `pdf`. If you have an entry for this MIME type, click 'Edit'. Otherwise, click New. `nppdf.so` should be available for selection (see Figure 10.5 on the next page).

If, for some reason, the plug-in module is not available, enter `acroread %s` under the 'Application' column. In this case, Acrobat Reader will not be opened in Netscape as a plug-in, but instead started as an independent application in its own window. Acrobat Reader must be installed on your system first.

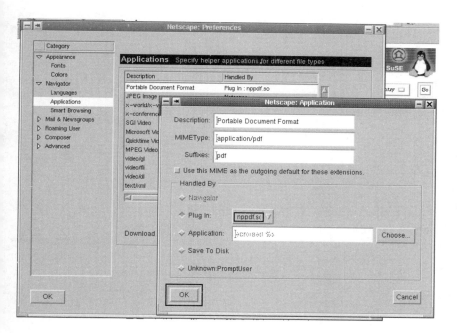

Figure 10.5: *Netscape Settings*

Konqueror — The KDE File Manager and Web Browser

Konqueror is a combined web browser, file manager, and document viewer designed for the KDE desktop. It provides a powerful multipurpose tool to its users. Despite the range of uses, it is still user-friendly. Users only need to familiarize themselves with one interface to perform a number of varied tasks.

Starting Konqueror

Konqueror can be started in several ways. In KDE, an icon in the panel depicts a house. Left-click this icon to start Konqueror or press (Alt) + (F2) and enter konqueror. A Konqueror window is shown in Figure 11.1. Konqueror can be started from other desktops with the command konqueror.

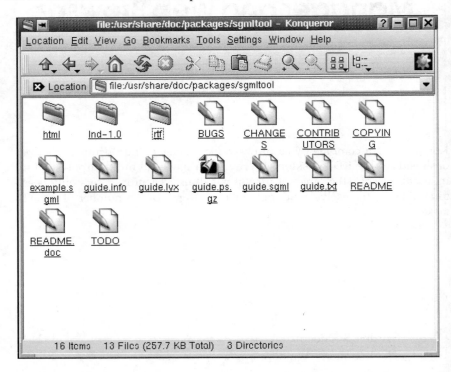

Figure 11.1: *The Konqueror Window*

The Konqueror Window

The Konqueror window is divided into several parts. The title bar is the strip at the top of the window. It displays the path of the current directory, document, or web page.

Underneath the title bar is the menu bar. Depending on whether Konqueror is running as a web browser or as a file manager, you can only select certain items. The toolbar shows icons frequently needed for navigation in Konqueror. If you leave the mouse cursor over an icon for a few seconds, a small help text appears. A right-click opens a pop-up menu. Here, set justification, text position, and icon size.

Beneath the toolbar is an entry line in which to enter URLs. A URL is a general address for one of many different objects. These locations can be on the Internet or a local hard disk. Enter a URL and press ⏎.

A URL consists of a transmission protocol and an address. The most common protocols are:

`http`	web pages
`file`	local files
`ftp`	files on an ftp server
`smb`	shares on a Samba computer
`man`	man pages
`info`	info pages
`tar`	compressed files in tar format
`audiocd`	audio CDs in Konqueror
`floppy`	browse floppies

There are a number of other protocols. Valid URLs are, for example, `http://www.suse.de` and `file://localhost/opt/kde2` or, in abbreviated form, `file:/opt/kde2`.

┌─ **Tip** ──

  Delete the entire line with the × icon to the left of the entry line.

─────────────────────────────────────── **Tip** ─┘

To return to previous entries, click the arrow pointing down on the right edge of the screen. This opens a list of previous entries. Select the desired entry. You can also have a bookmark panel displayed. Under 'Settings' → 'Display bookmark toolbar', activate or deactivate this.

Beneath the URL line is the main window. It shows the contents of directories, web pages, or documents. You can divide the window into different views and look at a document in one section and a web page in the other.

The status bar at the bottom of the window provides a general summary. If the mouse cursor hovers over a link for a few seconds, it will show the Internet address. If the mouse rests over a directory, it will show the folder name. Over files, the name, size, and type of file will be shown. If the window is divided (see Section *Different Display Modes*), a status line is available for each view and, on the left-hand side, a small icon shows which view is currently active.

The Basics of Konqueror

The Help

There are many ways of getting help in Konqueror. Normally, select 'Konqueror manual' in the 'Help' menu. The KDE help system starts, showing documentation for Konqueror with numerous additional references. Sometimes, this help is too extensive, such as when you just want information about a small icon. Normally, a small help text appears when the mouse hovers over an icon for a few seconds. For more information, press ⇧ Shift + F1 or choose 'Help' → 'What's This?' then click the icon. A small window opens giving more detailed information. A left-click closes it again.

Different Display Modes

In 'View' → 'View Mode', select icon view, multicolumn view (the file name appears on the left of the icon), tree view, detailed list view, or text view. Figure 11.2 shows, from left to right, icon view, tree view, multicolumn view. At first glance, the tree view and the detailed list view both look the same. You can, however, examine the directories more closely by enabling the tree view — several directories can be opened at the same time. The tree view is denoted by a '+' or '−' in front of the folder name. The detailed list view does not provide this option. It is used to change to a directory.

Dividing Windows and Saving this Configuration

You are probably familiar with the dilemma of going to a directory and losing sight of the overall structure in the process. One solution is to have different displays as in Figure 11.2 on the facing page.

Konqueror can divide the window horizontally or vertically. To do this, just click, in the 'Window' menu, on 'Split View Left/Right' or 'Split View Top/Bottom'. The active display shows a green dot in the status bar.

You can even activate a terminal window. If the check mark in front of 'Show Terminal Emulator' is activated, a terminal window is opened in

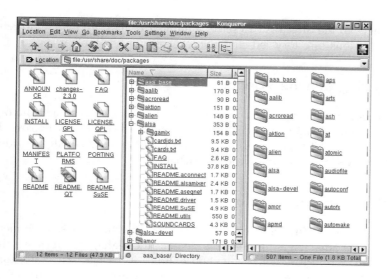

Figure 11.2: Konqueror Window with Various Views

which you can enter and run commands as usual. This makes it easy to combine both preferences — graphical and command-line oriented — in one window.

Once you have "assembled" a display, save it under 'Window' → 'Configure View Profiles...'. Give your profile a name and load it again in the future. In addition, decide if the window size should be saved. If the space is too small, move your Konqueror window to its own desktop and choose 'Fullscreen Mode'.

Konqueror as a File Manager

Navigating in Konqueror

As a file manager, Konqueror enables navigation through various directory levels with ease. Enter your home directory in the URL entry line, for example (or click the icon with the house). Switch directories or open files with the mouse as usual. A single-click is usually sufficient for changing directories or opening files. You can also move around in Konqueror using the arrow keys. Use any of the arrow keys to highlight an item (the background of the selected icon is shown in a different color). Pressing ⏎ opens the file

or changes to the directory. To select a number of files, press (Alt). To return
to the previous directory, left-click the left arrow in the toolbar.

Navigating with the Sidebar

Konqueror provides a sidebar. This is a window that you can activate or deactivate inside Konqueror, giving several options: display your bookmarks,
recently visited URLs, home directory, and much more. Activate the sidebar
via 'Windows' → 'Display extended sidebar'.

Deleting Files and Directories

In KDE, there are three methods to delete files and directories. Each method
has different advantages. In the first method, the highlighted files are moved
to the Trash directory when you choose 'Edit' → 'Delete'. They are stored
there and can be retrieved until the trash can is emptied. Of all the deleting
methods, this is the safest. Delete the contents of the trash by right-clicking
the trash icon on the desktop. In the pop-up menu that appears, choose
'Empty Trash Bin'.

The second method deletes the file by marking the the file system objects as
"free". These deleted files can only be restored with special tools, if at all.
The third method *really* deletes the file: 'Edit' → 'Shred'.

Caution

Be extremely careful with 'Shred'. After this treatment, files really are
deleted, because the space they occupied is overwritten with random
data. If you have sensitive data, which should not fall into the wrong
hands, use this method.

Caution

Selecting Several Files

To select several files in Konqueror, drag a frame around the files required.
Click a free area in the window, hold the mouse button down, and move the
mouse. A dotted frame surrounds the selected files. When the background
color changes, release the mouse button and carry out the desired action,
such as copying or deleting.

For a more exact selection, such as all PNG files, choose 'Edit' → 'Select'. In
the dialog box that appears, enter an expression, for example, *.png. Now

all PNG files in the directory currently displayed will be selected. To add additional files to your selection, open the dialog box again and repeat the individual steps.

Finding Files

To find files, go to 'Extras' → 'Find file...'. Specify the name or pattern along with a path and click 'Find'. Konqueror will search the directory specified and show the results below. Conduct a more precise search by selecting 'Date Range' (from when to when) or 'Advanced' (type, text, or size). The program can be run separately from the K menu by clicking 'Find files'.

Renaming Files

To rename files, right-click the respective file. A pop-up window will open. Select 'Rename'. Give your file a new name and complete this action with
⏎.

Using Filters

If your directories show more files than desired, try using filters. Filters can limit the display to just the files needed. To do this, select 'Extras' → 'View Filter'. It lists the currently recognized file types. If you click an entry, only this type of file will be displayed in the Konqueror window. Via the menu item 'Use multiple filters', designate several filters. View all files again with 'Reset'.

Browsing Compressed Files

Konqueror has another interesting feature: it can browse compressed files. If you have a tar.gz file, click it and Konqueror will show the contents as if it were a directory.

You can also copy individual files from it. Copying files *into* an archive is not yet supported, but this feature may be included in one of the next versions. `tar:/` at the beginning of the entry line in the URL window shows that you are browsing inside a compressed file.

Reading Audio CDs

Using `audiocd:/`, Konqueror can be used to convert the contents of audio CDs to various formats and save them to the hard disk. The exact procedure is described in *Reading Audio CDs* on page 244.

Creating an Image Gallery

Konqueror can help with managing directories full of images by generating an HTML file with the image in miniature. Open the respective directory in Konqueror and select 'Extras' → 'Create Image Gallery'. A window opens in which to specify the background and foreground colors, the title, and where to save it. Start by clicking 'Ok'. By default, a file called `index.html` is created. Open it with Konqueror to see your images displayed in a minimized, clear format.

Pop-Up Menus with the Right Mouse Button

If you have a directory displayed in an open Konqueror window, open a pop-up menu with the right mouse button at any time. Depending on the file type, you can start various actions here. If you click a file or directory, entries appear as in the 'Edit' menu.

Konqueror as a Web Browser

Konqueror is more than a file manager. It is also an effective web browser.

Opening Web Pages

Simply enter a web address in the URL line, for example, `www.suse.de`. Konqueror will attempt to display the address. You do not even need to write the protocol (`http://`) at the beginning, as it is recognized automatically by the program. This feature only works properly with web addresses, however. For FTP servers, you must enter `ftp://` at the beginning of the entry line.

Saving Web Pages and Graphics — Web Archives

To save a web page, select 'Address' → 'Save as...' and give your HTML file a name. Images will not be saved along with it. To archive an entire web page — both text and graphics — select 'Extras' → 'Archive Web Page'. Konqueror suggests a file name to accept or edit. The file name ends with `.war`, the ending for web archives. To view the saved web archive at a later point, click the corresponding file and the web page will then be displayed in Konqueror along with its images.

Extended Web Browsing (Internet Keywords)

Searching the web using Konqueror is very practical. Konqueror defines a number of search engines for you, all with a specific abbreviation. To search for a certain topic on the Internet, enter the abbreviation and the keyword, separated by a colon. The relevant page containing the search results will be displayed.

To define your own abbreviations, click 'Settings' → 'Configure Konqueror' and choose 'Advanced Web Browsing'. A dialog appears in which to define your own abbreviations.

Translating Web Pages

Konqueror cannot translate web pages directly, but requires an external Internet source. To translate a web page, enter the address then select 'Tools' → 'Translate Web Page'. A dialog opens in which to choose the source language and the target language. After the selection has been made, it will take a few seconds until the translated page appears.

Your Bookmark Collection

If you frequently visit certain pages, it is often a hassle to type in the same address repeatedly. Konqueror helps you set up a bookmark list. For this, use the 'Bookmark' menu. Here, save all your bookmarks, from web pages to directory links, on your local hard disk.

To create a new bookmark in Konqueror, click 'Bookmarks' → 'Add Bookmark'. If you have already added some bookmarks, you will also see them in this menu. It is recommended to arrange your collection by subjects, grouped hierarchically. 'New Directory' creates folders in which bookmarks can be grouped. Open the bookmark editor by selecting 'Bookmarks' → 'Edit Book-marks...'. Using this program, organize, rearrange, add, and delete book-marks.

If you are using Netscape or Mozilla as additional browsers, you do not need to set up your bookmark folders again. The bookmark editor includes 'File' → 'Import Netscape Bookmarks' where you can integrate your Netscape and Mozilla bookmarks into your most current collection. The reverse is also pos-sible via 'Export as Netscape Bookmark'.

Change your bookmarks by right-clicking the entry. A pop-up menu ap-pears in which to select the desired action (cut, copy, delete, etc.) When you achieve the desired results, save it ('File' → 'Save').

To save your bookmark list and have instant access to it, make your book-marks visible in Konqueror. Select 'Settings' → 'Show Bookmark Toolbar' and a bookmark panel will automatically be displayed in the current Kon-queror window.

Java and JavaScript

Do not confuse these two languages. Java is an object-oriented, platform-independent programming language from Sun Microsystems. It is frequently used for small programs (applets), which are sent over the Internet for things like online banking, chatting, and electronic shopping systems. JavaScript is an interpreted scripting language mainly used for the dynamic structuring of web pages.

Konqueror allows you to enable or disable these two languages, even on a domain-specific level. You can allow some hosts access while denying access for other hosts.

┌─ **Note** ───

For applets to run correctly, at least a "Java Runtime Environment" must be installed. The minimum solution can be found in the package `javarunt` package. If you need to compile Java source code, install the Java Development Kit (package `java`) instead.

─── **Note** ─

If you have high system security requirements, completely deactivate Java and JavaScript. Unfortunately, some web pages require JavaScript.

Proxies

If access to a proxy server is allowed by your provider, enter this for KDE. The advantage is that your pages may be available more quickly if multiple users have access to them at the same time.

In 'Settings' → 'Configure Konqueror...', select 'Proxy Server'. Enter the proxy for HTTP and FTP along with their respective ports. Under 'No proxy for:', exclude specific servers. Normally, enter `localhost` here or the name of your Linux computer.

Konqueror as a File Viewer

In Konqueror, view different files as well as directories and web pages. If you click a text file, for example, the program belonging to this will not be started. Instead, the text will be "embedded" into the Konqueror window. The displayed documents cannot be edited. To do this, right-click the file. Use 'Open with' to select a program in which to open the file.

For More Information

The following links provide further information.

`http://www.kde.org`	All about KDE
`http://bugs.kde.org`	Known KDE bugs
`http://www.konqueror.org`	All about Konqueror

The Web Browser Galeon

Recently, the widely-used web browser has been transformed into a real "jack of all trades". The fact that today's Internet applications feature such depth in integration and are heavily integrated into their corresponding desktop environments is almost taken for granted. Users of outdated machines soon feel the effects of this development. All-around browsers are often memory-eaters, sluggish in their operation, and occupy thirty megabytes on the hard disk.

That is why the idea behind Galeon is to devote itself just to one assignment: the web and only the web. Galeon implements the speedy "Gecko" engine of the Mozilla browser and integrates this into a slick, extremely functional user interface. The application loads quicky and is one of the fastest browsers available.

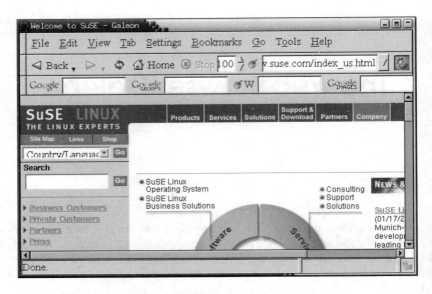

Figure 12.1: The Main Window in Galeon

With Galeon on the Internet

Galeon's most essential navigation tools can be found in the first toolbar. 'Next' and 'Back' offer the feature of flipping through Internet sites, just as in other browsers. To the the right of those buttons is 'Reload', which updates the contents of a site. 'Cancel', which stops a connection or transfer from taking place, follows. A useful function is zoom, usually scaled to 100% — a 1:1 display of the document. To the right of it, both the up and the down arrows can be used to set the zoom levels in intervals of ten. Enter Internet (URLs) addresses in the following entry box. To the far right is the GNOME foot, which shows Galeon's progress. If the icon is animated, Galeon is working and transferring data.

Optimized for the Web

Galeon is primarily designed to make surfing the Internet as convenient as possible. In the default configuration, Galeon presents a second toolbar, enabling quick access to the popular Google search engine as well as its news and image search function. It can also offer access to an online dictionary and use the "bookmarklets". This is made possible by small JavaScript functions built into Galeon. You can, for example, find out how current a page you is, or allow the Internet site to slowly scroll down the screen. This provides a lot of practical functionality.

Efficient Surfing with Tabs

Galeon can display multiple WWW documents in a single application window. Such a procedure is often more practical than opening a new window for each Internet document. To open a link in a web site in the form of a new tab, right-click that link. Select 'Open in new tab' in the emerging pop-up menu. Now, Galeon will divide its application window into "index cards", so you can maintain easy access to the documents. Create a fresh Galeon tab by clicking 'File' → 'Open New Tab'.

Settings and Controls

All settings characteristic of other web browsers can be also be accessed here via 'Settings' → 'Preferences'. With this dialog's user-friendly layout, the key selection options are quite self-explanatory. Galeon's appearance can also be changed with these options.

Galeon features built-in password management and cookie controls. It also has options that specify the web sites from which images may be downloaded. All these options can be accessed through a single dialog via 'Tools' → 'Cookies' → 'View Cookies'.

After the brief period of initial adjustment, you will find that Galeon is optimized for its single important task. The breathtaking speed of the Mozilla HTML engine does its part as well. Have fun!

For More Information

http://galeon.sourceforge.net   The Galeon home page
http://www.gnome.org   All about GNOME

Opera—
The Commercial Alternative

The web browser Opera is becoming increasingly popular. Its excellent technical properties as well as the many useful features make it highly attractive. This chapter introduces this browser and draws your attention to some of the obvious features as well as the more concealed possibilities. Install package opera with YaST2.

Philosophy of Opera

It is compact, fast, and comfortable — a fact that users especially appreciate about Opera, the alternative web browser from Oslo, Norway. While Netscape and Microsoft were engaged in a furious battle for browser market shares by flooding the market with faster, bigger browsers with an increasing load of technical features, Opera developed from its initial niche position into a viable alternative among the display programs for Internet contents.

In contrast to the two main competitors, who integrated a bulging number of features into their products at the expense of stability and speed, the development of Opera was guided in another direction. Instead of crowding the browser with features, the developers endeavored to improve the speed and correct the display of web pages. Despite their enhanced functionality, new versions often turned out to be smaller in size than their predecessors and the display speed continued to improve steadily.

However, this focus on the bare essentials also poses some disadvantages: no e-mail client is included (at least not in the Linux version), full Java support is only available as a download, and Opera is not quite comfortable with some plug-ins. In contrast to Internet Explorer, Netscape Navigator, Konqueror, and similar products that can be used free of charge and without any restrictions, users of Opera have to pay $39 or put up with the advertising banner at the top right. For many users, the advantages seem to outweigh the disadvantages. About five percent of Internet users use of Opera and several million users have downloaded the one or two megabyte Opera file in recent years.

Structure

One of the differences from other programs becomes obvious when the browser is started: after you have accepted the license conditions, you can choose whether you want web pages displayed outside or inside the browser window.

In desktop mode, only one Opera instance is seen by your window manager. To select an Opera window, use the window bar in Opera. If you do not want to be ask at each start-up, check 'Do not ask me again'.

Toolbars

As you can see in Figure 13.1 on the facing page, the user interface of the program resembles other web browsers in many respects. The main navigation toolbar is located at the top. The advertising banner is on the right.

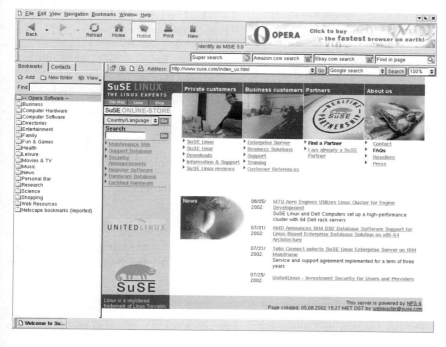

Figure 13.1: *Opera with Default Settings*

The toolbar includes the usual 'Back', 'Forward' , 'Reload', and 'Home' buttons. The 'Hotlist' button activates or deactivates the bookmark list in the left part of the main window. More information on this user-friendly bookmark tool is provided in Section *The Bookmark Manager* on the next page.

Below the main bar, the 'Personal bar' is displayed. Frequently-used bookmarks can be filed here. Go to these pages with one mouse click.

In the right frame, search in search engines or at Internet traders comfortably. Simply enter the search string in the respective field and press ⏎. This saves the effort of explicitly opening the Internet page then filling in the search form.

The status bar is located below the Personal Bar. If you move your mouse over the Opera icons without clicking them, a brief description is displayed in the left part of this bar.

The right part shows which browser Opera claims to be to Internet servers. The advantage of this feature is that you can "camouflage" Opera when you visit pages only available for specific browsers. Click this field to introduce Opera to other servers as Netscape ("Mozilla"), Internet Explorer, or simply as Opera.

If you decided to display all windows inside Opera when the program started, an overview of all web pages currently open is displayed at the bottom of the window in the 'window bar'. If pages are displayed outside Opera, a similar bar – the 'page bar' – is displayed below the status Bar.

The Main Window

Having acquired some general information on the possibilities of the various bars in Opera, we now want to turn our attention to the main window, which covers a major portion of the Opera user interface.

The Bookmark Manager

Opera provides a convenient bookmark manager in the left part of the main window. If you previously used Netscape in Linux, the Netscape bookmarks are automatically imported to Opera.

Tip

The bookmarks of Konqueror or Internet Explorer can also be imported. For more information, see 'File' → 'Preferences...' → 'Applications' → 'Bookmarks'. The bookmark file can even be exported with 'File' → 'Export'.

Tip

Use the drag and drop functionality to arrange bookmarks and folders by simply clicking and dragging them. Deactivate the bookmark manager using 'Hotlist' in the main toolbar. The bookmarks will still be available under 'Bookmarks'.

The Display Window

The display window is the large window in which Internet pages are displayed. It has a number of buttons and input fields along upper border.

 This icon to the far left shows if the current connection is encrypted. This stands for (insecure) unencrypted connections.

⊞ indicates that the current connection is protected against sniffing and data manipulation. If you click this button, a configuration window for encrypted connections opens.

⊙ If this icon is shown, images on web pages are displayed normally.

⊙ displays only existing images.

⊠ images are not displayed at all. This can be useful for very complex pages, as not all images may be necessary to use a web page.

◻ "Author mode", which displays a page as designed by the author, is used.

⊞ "User mode" shows a page according to your preferences. Configure both modes under 'Document' → 'Page layout'.

⊟ Using this button, view how the current page would be printed on the printer.

Next to these four buttons is a field for entering the desired Internet address. When entering an address visited recently, Opera completes the URL after a few characters have been entered. If Opera's suggestion matches the desired address, simply press ⏎.

┌─ **Tip** ─────────────────────────────

The current page can be bookmarked very quickly by clicking 'Address:', keeping the mouse button pressed, and moving the mouse pointer towards the bookmark manager. Release the button at a location of your choice to set a new bookmark.

──────────────────────────────── **Tip** ┘

The double arrow next to the address field unfolds a list of pages previously visited by entering the address. This feature is especially useful if the desired page was recently visited by entering the address (and not by means of a bookmark or by clicking a link).

The 'Go!' button next to the arrow has the same effect as ⏎. When you click this button, the address entered will be loaded.

A much more interesting feature is the entry field designated as 'Google search' on the right side. Similar to the four search buttons of the "Personal bar", you can send search queries to various web pages directly from here. However, the difference from the other fields is that a click on the double arrow symbol produces a selection of about twenty searchable pages. Extensions for Opera, which you can use to send search queries to countless other pages directly from the browser, are available on the Internet.

Tip

This quick-search functionality can also be used in the actual address bar. Type a letter and a space in front of the search string. The respective abbreviations are listed under 'File' → 'Preferences...' → 'Network' → 'Search'. For example, if you enter g Linux in the address field, Opera automatically sends a search query for the keyword Linux to the Google search engine.

Tip

At the top right border of the display window, find a field designated as '100%' for setting the zoom factor. This is especially useful if the fonts on Internet pages are very small and difficult to read.

Special Features

Opera offers a number of special features. Many of the features described in the following paragraphs can be accessed under 'File' → 'Preferences...' or by pressing the (Alt) + (P).

Adjusting the Appearance and Structure

Do not be deterred by the structure of Opera, which looks somewhat complicated at the first start-up. The various bars, buttons, and entry fields can be useful for your daily work. If, however, you do not like the appearance of the browser, adjust it according to your own preferences.

Move toolbars by simply clicking the left border of the respective bar and dragging it while keeping the left mouse button pressed or right-click to assign the new position. With 'Menu', see and configure all bars in the drop-down menu.

Use 'Preferences...' → 'General' → 'Look' for additional modification. http://my.opera.com also provides a wide range of button designs and backgrounds for the browser.

Data Protection

Opera can be adapted to the data protection requirements of the user in a very flexible manner. 'Preferences...' → 'Security' provides a number of configuration options. The number of pages to store can also be set in the same menu under 'Network' → 'History and cache'.

Opera for Linux has a utility for managing existing cookies. Under 'Edit' → 'Cookies', find a detailed list of all "data cookies", which can be deleted individually or entirely.

⌐ Note

Cookies are text fragments that store identification data. When the page is revisited, you are spared the effort of entering the password or e-mail address, as these are extracted from the cookies. While this is quite convenient, it also makes the user transparent for others. Although this does not necessarily constitute a security risk, certain data might be transferred without your consent.

Note ⌐

To erase all traces of your activity, use 'File' → 'Delete private data...'.

Keyboard Shortcuts

A large number of key combinations enables you to use Opera fully and efficiently even without a mouse. For example, (F8) takes you to the address bar and (F9) takes you to the content window. Move up and down page by page with (Page ↑) and (Page ↓). (A) and (Q) move from link to link. (F12) displays a brief overview of the most important settings on the screen.

A complete list of shortcuts for Opera can be accessed under 'Help' → 'Keyboard'. The list provided under 'Edit' → 'Shortcuts...' is more complex, but offers the additional possibility of defining new shortcuts and editing or deleting existing shortcuts.

Mouse Gestures

With a little practice, "mouse gestures" can be used just as effectively as keyboard shortcuts. The principle is easy: a mouse button is pressed and the mouse is moved in a certain direction to execute a specific operation. For example, if you press the right mouse button and, at the same time, move it downwards, a new window is opened. If the mouse is moved up and down while the button is pressed, the current page is reloaded. 'Help' → 'Mouse' provides an overview of the "mouse gestures" and the general use of the mouse in Opera.

Double-Click Functionality

Double-click a word to search for it in a search engine, check it in an encyclopedia, translate it to another language, or even send it by e-mail. If you click three or four times, a sentence section or the entire paragraph is marked.

Registration

If you like Opera, consider registering the browser. For $39, receive a key consisting of numbers and letters that removes the advertising banner in the top right corner and makes you eligible for priority support.

KMail — The KDE Mail Application

KMail is the KDE mail application. In addition to the usual features, like sending and receiving e-mail and multiple mail protocols, it offers several custom-definable filters for sorting e-mails into individual folders. This is useful for separating important business correspondence from less important e-mails from mailing lists, for example. Mails can be either read at leisure or skimmed over briefly and safely deleted.

The First Steps

When first starting KMail, a `Mail` folder will be added to your home directory. This folder contains the initial mail directories (inbox, outbox, sent, and trash). Use 'Settings' → 'Configure KMail...' to enter the first information needed for KMail to send and receive your messages.

Defining Your User Identity

The settings in 'Identity' are organized into three tabs: 'General', 'Advanced', and 'Signature'. Under 'General', enter your full name in 'Name' and, optionally, the relevant information in the 'Organization' field. Enter your e-mail address in 'Email address'.

Under 'Advanced', enter a 'Reply-To Address' (if applicable). To send encrypted or signed messages, select a key under 'OpenPGP keys' (if you already have a public key) (see also *Mail Encryption with PGP or GnuPG* on page 224). Select 'Sent message folder' and 'Draft folder'. 'Special sending method' is not usually needed.

Finally, choose to add a special message at the bottom of each e-mail by selecting 'Enable signature' under the 'Signature' tab. This is a common way to add personal information or expression to e-mails.

Add additional user identities with the 'New' button.

Configuring Mail Boxes

The settings in the 'Network' icon panel tell KMail how to receive and send e-mails. Here, find two tabs — one for sending and one for receiving e-mails.

Many of these settings vary depending on the system and network where your mail server is located. If you are unsure about the settings or which items to select, consult your Internet service provider or system administrator.

Sending Create outgoing mail boxes under the 'Sent' tab. 'Add' gives the choice of either SMTP or sendmail. For most purposes, select SMTP here. After making this selection, a window appears in which to enter SMTP server data, such as 'Name', 'Server', and, if needed, the required authorization.

Security settings are under the 'Security' tab. Specify your preferred encryption method here. If uncertain, click 'Test server capacity'. The corresponding settings will then be tested and applied.

Receiving Find all you need for receiving e-mails under the 'Receiving' tab. Using 'Add', select from various options: local (Mbox format), POP3, IMAP, or local (maildir format). Normally, POP3 is sufficient.

After making your selection, a window appears in which to enter the POP3 server data. Give the server a unique name. As all additional data should have been given to you by your Internet Service Provider or your system administrator, you will only need to enter the values in the corresponding fields. The fields that need to be filled out here are 'User', 'Server', and 'Password'.

Under the 'Extras' tab, find several methods of encryption and authorization. If you are uncertain of which options your server provides, try 'Test server capabilities'.

Using KMail

Main Window

The main window appears when KMail is started. It is divided into three sections.

Figure 14.1: Main Window in KMail after Start-Up

- Folder area (left)
  This section contains a list of your mail folders or mail boxes. The number next to the folder indicates that it contains unread mail. Select folders by simply clicking them. The messages they contain then

appear in the upper right window panel. A status bar shows the number of unread mails and the total number of messages in the selected folder. The folders can be displayed either in short form (which only takes up a small portion of the left window margin) or in a detailed display (which takes up the entire left portion of the screen, but displays more folders).

- Header area (right)

  In this window panel, the header information (message status, sender, subject, and date) is listed for messages in the currently selected folder. Clicking the header to select the message and display it in the message window. Select several messages at once by clicking one message then, holding (⇧ Shift), clicking another. Both of these messages, as well as all the ones in between, will be selected. By holding down (Ctrl), select any number of messages without highlighting the ones in between. Sort messages by clicking the column by which to sort. If you click more than once on a column, the sort direction switches between ascending and descending order. Sort according to subject, sender, or date.

- Message area (below)

  Here, the header and contents of the currently selected message are opened and displayed. Attachments are depicted in the lower message margin as icons, based on the attachment's MIME type. Use (PgUp) and (PgDn) to scroll through the pages of the message or use (↑) and (↓) to scroll line-by-line. Find the shortcut keys in the main window.

Messages can be labeled with several different kinds of status flags. Change them under 'Message' → 'Highlight as'.

'New' (red dot, header in red print): The message is new and has not yet been read.

'Unread' (green dot, header in blue print): a message changes its status from 'New' to 'Unread' after the folder containing it is reopened.

'Read' (–): The message has been read.

'Replied' (blue, U-shaped arrow): The message has been answered.

'Waiting' (envelope): The message has been placed in the outbox to send later.

'Sent' (slanted envelope): The message was sent.

'Important' Label for important messages.

Creating a New Message

The window 'Create Message' is used for writing new messages. It can be opened either using the document icon in the button panel inside the main window or with 'Message' → 'New Message'.

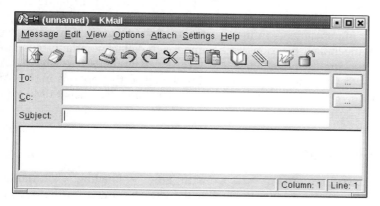

Figure 14.2: Creating a Message

Creating a Message

Fill out the corresponding fields in the 'New Message' window. There are a number of key shortcuts that can help in writing your message. To send e-mails using various e-mail accounts, select your identity, already configured in *Defining Your User Identity*. The buttons next to 'To:', 'CC:', and 'blind copy (Bcc):', if applicable, open the address book for address selection. If you have already entered the beginning of the address, press (Ctrl) + (T) to obtain a list of possible completions. After writing your message, click 'Send'. Use 'View' to set up different headers.

Attachments

Attach files to your messages using one of the following methods:

- Click the paper clip icon and choose the file to attach.

- Drag a file from the desktop or from another folder into the 'New Message' window.

- Select one of the options in the 'Attach' menu.

'Attachment Properties' appears, which will ask for information about the attachment. Normally, the file's MIME type is properly recognized, but, if not, select it from a list. Enter a short descriptive text in the description field. Next, select a code for your file from the options list (the default values usually work well). If a file is attached to your message, it will appear in the list of attachments in the lower part of the window. Save, remove, or open an attachment by choosing a name for the attachment and by subsequently clicking 'Remove', 'Save', or 'Properties' in the 'Attach' menu. Attach PGP keys to your messages by choosing the respective options in the 'Attach' menu. PGP keys are treated like file attachments. Their MIME type is `application/pgp-keys`.

Check Message for Spelling Errors

Check the spelling of your message with 'Edit' → 'Spelling...'. KMail uses KSpell to check the spelling. KSpell is the KDE front-end for the ispell and aspell spell check programs. The spell checker must be configured via 'Settings' → 'Spellchecker...'.

Message Folders

Message folders serve as an organizing tool for your messages. By default, all the message folders are stored in the `Mail` folder in your home directory. When first starting KMail, the `Inbox`, `Outbox`, `SentMessages`, and `Trash` folders will be added. These folders have the following functions:

- Inbox: New messages are stored here (unless a filter has been defined).

- Outbox: Messages to send are stored here.

- Sent: Copies of all e-mails sent are stored here.

- Trash: Stores deleted e-mails.

Although the default folders most likely serve your needs, you may require additional folders to organize your e-mails. Select 'Folder' → 'Create' to add a new folder. A dialog will ask what to name the folder (see Figure 14.3 on the next page). If it should be a subfolder, select the folder above it (a pull-down menu labeled 'Belongs to:'). Specify the folder type, any mailing lists belonging to it, and an expiration date (after a certain amount of time, the e-mails will be marked for deletion) inside this window. You still have the option of choosing another user identity or displaying a given sender or receiver.

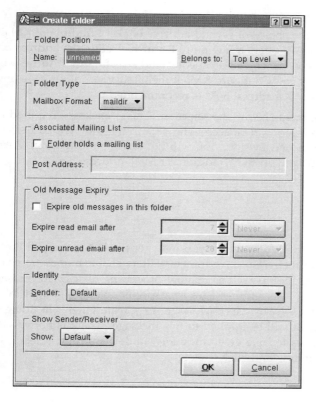

Figure 14.3: Creating New Folders

To move messages from one folder to another, highlight the message to move then press (M) or click 'Message' → 'Move to...'. A list of folders will appear. Select the folder to which to move your messages. Messages can also be moved from the upper window into the left window panel by dragging and dropping the message into the appropriate folder.

To remove all the messages from a folder, click 'Folder' → 'Empty'. All the messages located in the folder will, at this point, be moved to Trash. The messages will not be permanently deleted until you actually empty the trash.

The Address Book

Save frequently used e-mail addresses in the address book. Open the address book under the 'File' menu, from the open book icon in the main window, or in the 'New Message' window.

KMail offers the choice of several address books. 'Traditional KMail' is very simple and 'KAB' offers a few more features. Define the address book by clicking the icon panel 'Miscellaneous' and selecting the 'Address Book' tab in the 'Settings' → 'Configure KMail' menu. If you do not have any previous address books, 'KAddressbook' is recommended.

Note the comments below the selection. There, packages required by the enhanced alternatives can be seen. The data in the different address books are independent of one another. You will not see the addresses in 'KAB' that are entered exclusively in the 'Traditional KMail' address book.

Filters

After using KMail for a while, you may get tired of sorting all the new inbox messages into their respective folders. Filters enable automatic processing of incoming messages as well as manual processing of selected messages in a folder. To filter selected messages to a specific folder, highlight the messages and enter (Ctrl) + (J) or select 'Message' → 'Create Filter'. In doing so, *all* of your filter rules will be applied to this message. There is no way to just use particular filters for one given message. To delete a filter, select it in the 'Filter Rules' window and click 'Delete'.

Filter Rules

A filter consists of criteria and actions. One filter criterion, for example, selects messages according to the sender, contents, or recipient. The filter action that corresponds to this criterion could, for example, move, delete, highlight, or forward these messages.

Examples of Filters

If you are subscribed to the KDE user list, create a folder for this list (we will call it KDE Users). Create a filter to automatically transfer new messages from your inbox to the KDE User folder, as described in the following:

1. Add a new folder as described in *Message Folders* on page 220. Call it kde-user, for example.

2. First, think about the most concise way to identify messages to filter. The messages in the KDE user list described in our example are specified by their `kde-user@kde.org` address, found in the 'To': or 'Cc': field.

3. Click 'Settings' → 'Configure Filters'. A window opens. The left side displays the available filters. The right side of the window is composed of two panels: filter rules and filter actions.

4. Click the 'New' icon to create an empty filter. It appears as `unknown`.

5. Select 'To:' or 'Cc': from the first drop-down menu and 'contains' from the second drop-down menu. Enter `kde-user@kde.org` in the text field.

6. In the field 'Filter actions', pick the option 'Move to Folder' from the first drop-down menu. A second drop-down menu appears from which to select the folder. Choose the folder to which the filtered messages should be moved if they meet the desired criteria. In this case, choose `kde-user` from the drop-down menu.

You might need complex criteria to filter your messages. You may want to only save the messages from the KDE user list written by your friend Fred Johnson (`fj@anywhere.com`). Here, the remaining filter criteria come into play:

1. Click 'Settings' → 'Configure Filters' and highlight the filter just added.

2. To filter all messages containing `kde-user@kde.org` in the 'To': or 'Cc': fields *and* originating from Fred, define a second filter under 'Filter Criteria' using the second row of drop-down menus. Select 'From' in the first menu and 'contains' in the second. Then enter the e-mail address to filter.

   Select the second pop-up menu inside the filter criteria from the drop-down menu and select 'From'. Next to it, select 'contains'. Enter your friend's e-mail address: (`fj@anywhere.com`). 'Applies to all' is activated here.

3. Now you have created a filter that transfers all mails from Fred Johnson on the KDE user list.

Mail Encryption with PGP or GnuPG

You can encrypt your e-mails (those you send using KMail). This does not mean that the attachments will be encrypted, so you must take care of that in advance with a shell command or one of the other tools. Before you can implement PGP or GnuPG in KMail, install and configure it correctly. For details, refer to the man page for gpg (man gpg) or the man page for pgp (man pgp).

Requirements for PGP and GnuPG

KMail requires that you name your PGP binary file pgp. If you are using GnuPG, KMail will expect a binary file named gpg. First, generate a key pair for your identity. This can be done at the command line (use pgp -kg or gpg --gen-key). The identity (usually your name followed by your e-mail address in angle brackets, as in JohnDoe<john@example.com>) and your password are required by KMail to interpret PGP.

KMail Settings

Open the KMail settings dialog with 'Settings' → 'Configure KMail'. Click 'Security' → 'OpenPGP'. Specify the application to use for this purpose in 'Select encryption program'. The option 'Automatic recognition' is usually chosen.

Once you have made your decision, click 'Identity'. Here, find the item 'OpenPGP key'. A click on 'Change' shows you a dialog box from which to select the required key.

Under the 'OpenPGP' tab, there are the following additional options:

- 'Keep passphrase in memory': If this option is disabled, KMail will always ask for your password when you sign a message (before sending it) or when you decode a message received. If you enable this option, KMail will only ask you twice for your password before storing it in memory. Thus it is stored in memory, but not written to your hard disk. However, be aware that a user with the right privileges (e.g., root) might be able to read your password from memory.

- 'Always encrypt to self': If this option is disabled and you want to send an encrypted e-mail, you will not be able to read this message yourself once it has been created and encrypted. Enable this option when you still want to be able to read your encrypted messages yourself. You can read the pure text of the message in the `Sent` folder.

- 'Show ciphered/signed text after composing': Enable this option if you want to have the text displayed after it is encrypted or signed.

- 'Always verify the encryption key': If you click this option, you will be asked each time which key to use for signing and encoding.

Under 'Composer', click the check box next to 'Automatically sign messages with OpenPGP'. At this point, all messages will be signed before they are sent. To send encrypted messages and have the recipient verify your signature, give him your public key. To send encrypted e-mails to others or to review your signed messages, you will need your public key. Public keys can be stored on a public PGP key server, such as `www.pgp.net`.

Signing Messages

Create your messages as usual. Before sending the message, click the second-to-last icon in the tool panel of the window. Then send the message. To sign it, KMail must know your PGP password. However, if you have already given the password, KMail will sign the message without requesting any further information. Review the results of the PGP signing process in the `Sent Messages` folder (or in the outbox if you did not use 'Send now'). There, your e-mail should be marked with the label that it was signed by you.

Sending Public Keys

Create a message for the person who should receive your public key. Choose 'Attach Public Key' in the 'Attach' menu. The mail can now be sent. There is no guarantee that the recipient of a signed message will get the correct key. It can happen that the mail is intercepted on the way to the recipient and signed with another key. Therefore, the recipient should check the attached key by comparing the finger print with a previously received value. Further information on this can be found in the PGP and GnuPG documentation.

Decoding Encrypted Messages

In KMail, you only need to click the message. Enter your password when prompted. KMail will attempt to decode the message, if it was encoded with your public key, and display it in clear text. If not, you will not be able to read the e-mail. KMail saves the e-mails as encrypted messages to prevent anyone from reading them without your password.

Receiving a Public Key

You can receive a public key as attachment, over FTP, or on a floppy disk. Before using it to encrypt an e-mail going to the person who has the key, check the key (look over the fingerprint or look for a reliable signature). Add the key to your public key ring by entering the command `pgp -ka ⟨filename⟩` or `gpg --import ⟨filename⟩` in a command line. If the key does not have a reliable signature, you will not be able to use it to encode in KMail (use `pgp -ks ⟨identity⟩`).

Using Other People's Public Keys — Encoding your Own Messages

To send an encoded message to a recipient for whom you have a public key, write the message in the 'Create Message' window. Before sending the message, click the red key icon in the toolbar in the Create Message window. Now, the message can be sent. If KMail cannot find a single key for the recipient, a list will appear with all the available keys. Select the appropriate one from the list or cancel the action. KMail will also inform you if errors occur during the encryption process. As already mentioned, you will not be able to read encrypted mails if you did not click 'Always encrypt to self' in the 'Security' tab.

Evolution: An E-Mail and Calendar Program

Evolution is a groupware suite created by Ximian. It offers regular e-mail features along with extended features like task lists and a calendar. Use Evolution to make appointments with other users through the calendar features or just to check and sort your e-mail. It also provides a complete address book, including the ability to send your contact information as a vCard to others.

Starting Evolution

Evolution is not included in the default SuSE installations. To install Evolution, use YaST2 to install package `evolution` and all dependent packages automatically selected by YaST2.

Evolution is a GNOME application. However, with the required libraries installed, it can be used from any window manager. To start Evolution from GNOME, select 'Programs' → 'Applications' → 'Evolution'. It can also be started from the SuSE menu under 'Internet' → 'Tools' → 'Evolution'. From a terminal, Evolution can be started with `evolution &`.

Evolution Setup Assistant

When started for the first time, Evolution opens a configuration tool to assist in initial setup. If it does not open automatically, access it from the Inbox view with 'Tools' → 'Mail Settings...' then clicking 'Add' in the 'Accounts' tab. Click 'Next' to use the assistant. Enter your name and e-mail address in the appropriate fields. If you have multiple e-mail addresses, use your preferred address here. Additional addresses can be configured later. Click 'Next'.

Select the appropriate incoming mail format for this address from the 'Server Type' drop-down box. 'POP' is the most common format for downloading mail from a remote server. 'IMAP' works with mail folders on a special server. Obtain this information from your ISP or server administrator. Complete the other relevant fields displayed when the server type is selected. Click 'Next' when finished.

The next set of information to enter is about mail delivery. This will be used for all the e-mail addresses configured. To use outgoing mail on the local system, select 'Sendmail'. For a remote server, select 'SMTP'. Get the details from your ISP or server administrator. For SMTP, complete the other fields displayed after selection. Click 'Next' when finished.

By default, the e-mail address is used as the name to identify the account. Enter another name if desired. The field 'Make this my default account' determines whether the account should be used as the default. The default account is the e-mail address initially selected for sending mail. Another account can be selected in the message composition window if desired. Click 'Next'.

The time zone information from the next window is used for the calendar functions. It is important to select the correct time zone for using the appointment scheduling functions. Click the dot on the map for a city in your time zone. Selection zooms the display to that area and a change can be made if desired. When the correct time zone is displayed under 'Selection', click 'Next'. In the next window, click 'Finish' to save the data entered. Use 'Back' to make changes.

Importing from Other Mail Programs

Evolution can import mail from other mail programs, such as Netscape or KMail. To import, select 'File' → 'Import'. For KMail or mutt, use 'Import a single file'. For Netscape, select 'Import data and settings from older programs'. More information is available in the internal help.

The Evolution Window

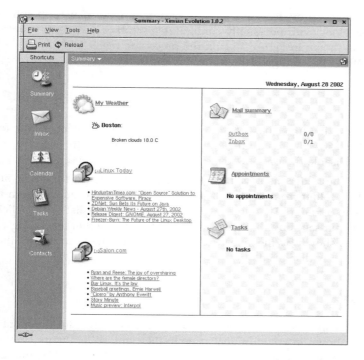

Figure 15.1: *The Evolution Window with Shortcuts and Summary*

The default window view is shown in Figure 15.1 on the page before. The menus and menu items available and the icons in the toolbar vary from window to window. Use the 'Shortcuts' pane to the left to select the information to display in the right pane. Adjust the size of any panes by dragging the dividing bars.

Tip

Right-clicking an item, such as a mail message or contact, opens a menu of actions relevant to that item.

Tip

Use 'View' to remove the 'Shortcuts Bar' or add a 'Folder Bar' at any time. The different items listed in the 'Shortcuts' are described in the following.

Summary

The 'Summary' provides some basic information about mail, appointments, and tasks along with personally configurable weather and news sources. This window is shown in Figure 15.1 on the preceding page. Use 'Tools' → 'Summary Settings' to configure the information displayed.

Inbox

In this view, the upper half of the window shows the contents of the folder Inbox. The lower half is a preview pane used to display the selected mail message. Disable the preview pane with 'View' → 'Preview Pane'.

To change the folder displayed, click the down arrow next to 'Inbox' and select another folder from the list. The search bar can be used to search the messages in a folder. The table headers for the message list can be clicked to sort the messages by that header. The sort can be either ascending or descending as shown by the arrow to the right. Click the header until the correct direction is displayed.

Calendar

The initial display shows a day view of the current day with the month and a task list shown in an additional pane to the right. Week, work week, and month views are also available from the toolbar or the 'View' menu. Use the search bar to find an entered appointment. Add appointments and tasks using the buttons in the toolbar. Also use the toolbar to page through the calendar or jump to a specific date.

Tasks

'Tasks' provides a list of tasks. Use the toolbar to add tasks. Search the tasks with the search bar.

Contacts

This view shows all the addresses in your address book. To locate a particular address, use the search bar or click the button to the right displaying the first letter of the contact's last name. Add contacts or lists with the toolbar.

Mail

To configure the mail settings in Evolution, switch to the 'Inbox' view with the 'Shortcuts'. Select 'Tools' → 'Mail Settings...'.

Configuring Accounts

Evolution is capable of fetching mail from multiple mail accounts. The account from which to send can be selected when composing a message. To edit a current account, select the account and click 'Edit'. To add a new account, click 'Add'. This opens the configuration assistant described under *Evolution Setup Assistant* on page 228. Delete a current account by selecting it then clicking 'Delete'

To make an account the default account used when sending mail, select the desired account then hit 'Default'. To disable fetching mail from an account, select the account then click 'Disable'. A disabled account can still be used as the address for sending, but that account will not be checked for incoming mail. Reactivate the account with 'Enable'.

Other Settings

Use 'Display' to select or disable the quote highlight color or after how long a message is marked as read after opening. Also make settings regarding how images in HTML mail messages are treated.

Use 'Composer' to make settings for your mail composer. 'Other' contains settings for PGP, character encoding, and other functions.

Writing Mail

Click 'New Message' to compose a new message. Replying or forwarding a message opens the same basic message editor. Next to 'From', select from which account to send the message. In the recipient fields, enter an e-mail address or part of a name or address in your address book. If Evolution can match what you enter to something in the address book, Evolution displays a list from which to select. Click the desired contact or continue entry if none match. To select directly from the address book, click 'To' or 'CC' instead.

Evolution can send regular text e-mail or HTML e-mail. Use the format tool-bar to format HTML mail. Click 'Attach' or 'Insert' → 'Attachment' to send a file along with the message. To protect your e-mail with PGP, make appropriate selections from the 'Security' menu.

To send your message, click 'Send'. If not ready to send it immediately, make another selection under 'File'. For example, save the message as a draft or send it later.

Folders

It is often convenient to sort e-mail messages into a variety of folders. Evolution also offers folders. To view your folder tree, select 'View' → 'Folder Bar'. If you are accessing mail over IMAP, the IMAP folders will also be shown in this folder bar. For POP and most other formats, your folders are stored locally, sorted under 'Local Folders'. Your 'Contacts', 'Calendar', and 'Tasks' are also treated as folders in this view, but should not be used for filing mail.

Several folders are included by default. 'Inbox' is where new messages fetched from a server are initially placed. 'Sent' is used for saving copies of mail you send. 'Outbox' is temporary storage for mail that has not yet been sent. It is useful for working offline or if the outgoing mail server is temporarily unreachable. 'Drafts' is used for saving unfinished e-mail messages. 'Trash' is temporary storage for deleted items. Configure automatic emptying of that folder under 'Tools' → 'Mail Settings...'.

New folders can be created under 'Local Folders' or as subfolders of existing folders. Create as complex a folder hierarchy as desired. To create a new folder while in 'Inbox' view, select 'File' → 'Folder' → 'New Folder'. In the dialog that opens, enter a name. Also select the folder for which the new folder will be a subfolder. Leave the 'Folder Type' as 'Mail' for a new mail storage folder. Click 'OK' to create the new folder.

To move a message into a folder, select the message to move. Right-click to open the context menu. Select 'Move to Folder...' and, in the dialog that opens, the destination folder. Click 'OK' to move the message. The message header in the original folder will be shown with a line through it, meaning it is marked for deletion in that folder. The message is stored in the new folder. Messages can be copied in a similar manner.

Manually moving a number of messages into different folders can be time-consuming. Filters can be used to automate this procedure.

Filters

Evolution has a number of options available for filtering. Filters can be used to move a message into a specific folder or to delete a message. Messages can also be moved directly to the trash with a filter. There are two options for creating a new filter: creating a filter from scratch or creating a filter based on a message to filter. The latter is extremely useful for filtering messages sent to a mailing list.

Creating a Filter from Scratch

Select 'Tools' → 'Filters'. This dialog lists your existing filters, which can be edited, and allows for deletion or addition. Click 'Add' to create a new filter.

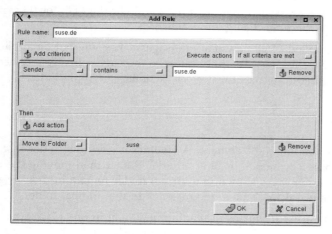

Figure 15.2: Creating a Filter

Enter a name for the new filter in 'Rule Name'. Select the criteria to use for the filter. Options include sender, recipients, source account, subject, date, and status. The drop-box showing 'Contains' provides a variety of options, such as "contains," "is," and "is not." Select the appropriate condition. Enter the text for which to search. Click 'Add criterion' to add more filter criteria. Use 'Execute actions' to determine if all or only some of the criteria must be met to apply the filter.

In the lower part of the window, determine the action to be taken when the filter criteria are met. Messages can, for example, be moved or copied to a folder or assigned a special color. When moving or copying, select the destination folder by clicking. In the folder list that appears, select the folder. Use 'New' to create a new folder. Click 'OK' when the correct folder is selected. When finished creating the filter, click 'OK'.

Creating a Filter from a Message

Select the message on which to base the filter. Right-click and select 'Create Rule From Message'. Select the filter option desired. This opens the filter creation dialog with the correct criteria already selected. Add additional criteria if desired. Select the appropriate filter action. Click 'OK' when finished.

Applying Filters

Filters are applied in the order listed in the dialog under 'Tools' → 'Filters'. Change the order by highlighting a filter and clicking 'Up' or 'Down'. Click 'OK' to close the filter dialog when finished.

Filters are applied to all new mail messages. They will not be applied to mail already in your folders. To apply filters to messages already received, highlight the desired messages then select 'Actions' → 'Apply Filters'.

VFolders

Evolution offers unique VFolders. A VFolder is a virtual folder that displays messages based on search or filter criteria. Rather than moving the messages into a folder, messages shown in a virtual folder remain in their original folder. Actions taken occur to the message in the original folder.

VFolders are a useful means of reading new mail in one place after it has been sorted into a number of different directories with filters. For example, a VFolder could be created to search all your folders for unread mail.

To create a new VFolder, select 'Tools' → 'Virtual Folder Editor...'. In the dialog, click 'Add'. VFolders can also be created from a message as with filters. Right-click, select 'Create Rule from Message', then select the correct VFolder criteria.

Enter a 'Rule Name'. For the new mail example mentioned above, set the criterion to 'Status' 'is not' 'Read'. Set the sources as desired. Other VFolder searches can be set similarly. Click 'OK' when finished. This returns to the virtual folder list. The order can be changed if desired. Click 'OK' to close it.

The new VFolder will be shown in the folder list under 'VFolders'. You can read, answer, and delete mail with the VFolder. However, deleting the message deletes it from the real folder in which it is stored, not just the VFolder.

Calendar

Adding Appointments

To add a new appointment to your calendar, click 'New Appointment'. Under the 'Appointment' tab, enter the details for the appointment. Select a category, if desired, to ease searching and sorting later. Optionally set for Evolution to provide a reminder before your appointment under the 'Reminder' tab. If the appointment occurs regularly, set that under 'Recurrence'. Click 'Save and Close' after all settings are made. The new appointment will be shown in your calendar.

Scheduling a Meeting

To schedule a meeting with other people, click 'New Appointment' then select 'Actions' → 'Schedule Meeting'. Enter information like for an appointment. Under 'Meeting', add attendees. For those in your 'Contacts', click 'Invite Others...' and select attendees from the dialog. When finished, click 'Save and Close'. The attendees will be sent an e-mail about the scheduled meeting.

This system can also be used to schedule a time that fits all attendees or to reserve resources. For more information about using the scheduling functions, refer to the internal help.

Adding Tasks

Evolution can be used to keep track of a list of things to do. To add a new task to your list, click 'New Task'. Enter summary information, your due and start dates, and a description. Enter task status and other information under 'Details'. Click 'Save and Close' to add the task to your list. Double-click the task to reopen the dialog and make changes or mark it completed.

Contacts

Adding Contacts

Along with the name and e-mail address, Evolution can store other address and contact information about a person. To quickly add the name and e-mail address of someone who has sent you an e-mail, right-click the underlined address in the message preview. Select 'Add to Contacts'. To enter more information, click 'Edit Full'. Otherwise, click 'OK'. If you have selected 'Edit Full', click 'Save and Close' when finished.

To enter a completely new contact, click 'New Contact' in the 'Contacts' view. Enter all desired contact information. Click 'Save and Close' when finished.

Making a List

If you frequently send messages to the same group of people, make this easier by creating a list. Click 'New List' when in 'Contacts' view. Enter a name for the list. Add addresses by typing the address in the box then clicking 'Add' or by dragging contacts from the Evolution Contacts view and dropping them in the box. Toggle 'Hide addresses' to select whether or not the recipients can see who else has recieved the mail. Click 'Save and Close' when finished. The list is now one of your contacts and will appear in the composition window after the first few letters are typed.

Sharing Contacts

To send contact information from your address book to another Evolution user, right-click the contact to forward. Select 'Forward Contact'. This sends the contact "card" as an attachment in an e-mail. Compose and send this message as usual.

To add a contact you have been sent, view the contact inline. Click 'Save in addressbook' to add the complete contact card to your address book.

For More Information

Evolution includes extensive internal help. Use the 'Help' menu to access this information. For more information about Evolution, refer to Ximian's web site at http://www.ximian.com.

Sound Applications in Linux

Linux offers a wide range of sound applications in various states of development. Because of the variety of applications and their unusual names, it can be difficult to determine what an application does and to find the application that suits a particular purpose. The following is an introduction to some of the more useful or interesting sound applications included in the SuSE Linux distribution.

Many of these applications are not included in the default installation. Use YaST2 to install the corresponding packages.

Note

Unless otherwise specified, applications can be started from the 'SuSE
Menus' under 'Multimedia' → 'Sound'.

Note

Mixers

Mixers are a convenient way of controlling the volume and balance of the
computer's sound output and input. The main differences in the various
mixers are the interfaces. Select one that meets your needs with which you
are comfortable working. Other mixers are available. Most programs in the
'Multimedia' → 'Sound' menu with "mix" in the name are mixer applications.

Tip

Generally, it is advisable to open a mixer application prior to opening
other sound applications. Use the mixer to test and adjust the control
settings for the input and output of the sound card. Some sound cards
may not allow simultaneous access from multiple applications. If a
sound application freezes, this may be the cause.

Tip

gamix

If you have multiple sound cards, gamix provides a set of controllers for each
card. Slide the control sliders to set the levels as desired.

alsamixer

The alsamixer is a text-based mixer that can be run from the command line
outside the X environment. Enter alsamixer to start it. Use the left and
right arrows to select the level to adjust. Use up and down arrows to control the level evenly. Ⓠ, Ⓦ, Ⓔ, Ⓨ, Ⓧ, and Ⓒ can be used to make different settings for the left and right channels. Use Ⓜ to mute a channel. Press
Ⓔsc to exit. More information is available in the man page for alsamixer
(man alsamixer).

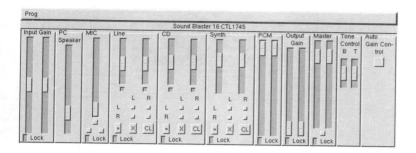

Figure 16.1: *The Mixer gamix*

KMix

KMix is the KDE mixer. It provides a convenient and familiar interface for KDE users. It can also be integrated into the KDE panel.

Players

Linux offers a variety of programs for playing audio CDs and the various music formats available, including MP3, OGG, and WAV files. Where possible, the supported formats of the players are listed.

kscd — Audio CD Player

kscd is an easy-to-use audio CD player. Access it from the 'SuSE menus' under 'Multimedia' → 'Multimedia' → 'CD' → 'KsCD'. Access the configuration menu by clicking the button with the tools. kscd can be configured to search an online CDDB server for the name and track names of a CD.

WorkMan — Audio CD Player

For those who prefer a CD player without a KDE feel, WorkMan offers a very basic interface without sacrificing function or convenience.

Figure 16.2: kscd

GNOME CD Player Applet

This is a simple applet that can be added to a GNOME panel. Add it by right-clicking the panel and selecting 'Panel' → 'Add to Panel' → 'Applet' → 'Multimedia' → 'CD Player'.

XMMS — MP3, WAV, OGG, and Stream Player

XMMS is one of the most popular players for Linux. It offers GNOME and KDE applets, allowing integration in the panel in those desktop environments. It also offers a range of visualization and effects plug-ins. Use the eject button to open files. The playlist editor, accessible with the 'PL' indicator under the title display, can be used to select and sort a number of files for playing. Playlists can be saved for future use. Click the button in the upper left corner to open the complete menu. More information and documentation is available at http://www.xmms.org.

FreeAmp — MP3, OGG, and Stream Player

FreeAmp is another popular player, available for several platforms. Use 'MyMusic' to arrange your collection and create playlists. FreeAmp offers a number of themes that can be used to completely change the appearance of the player.

GDAM — An Application for DJs

GDAM is a complicated application providing several features, including simultaneous playback of multiple files, playback on multiple sound cards, and the ability to add a range of special effects. The package includes extensive documentation located in the /usr/share/doc/packages/gdam directory.

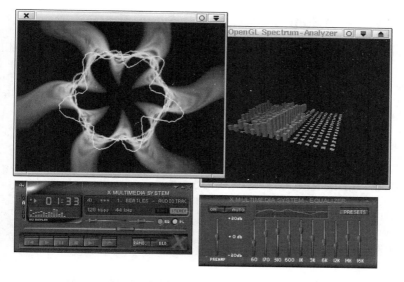

Figure 16.3: xmms *with Equalizer and the "OpenGL Spectrum-Analyzer" and "Infinity" Plug-Ins*

terminatorX — Another Application for DJs

terminatorX is another application for DJs with special effects. Documentation is in the directory `/usr/share/doc/packages/terminatorX`.

MIDI Programs

Many sound cards have an external MIDI port for connecting MIDI devices, such as synthesizers, keyboards, or sound modules. If your card's MIDI port is supported by ALSA, record and play back MIDI files over this port using a sequencer application like jazz. On the command line, view the available MIDI devices and internal ALSA port numbers with `pmidi -l`. With a command such as `pmidi -p 73:0 mysong.mid`, play a MIDI file over one of the ports listed. Replace `73:0` with the desired port number from the list.

TiMidity++ — A Software WaveTable Synthesizer

If your sound card does not have a WaveTable synthesizer with which MIDI files can be played according to a loaded sound font or instrument patch, use TiMidity++ to emulate this. Information about configuration can be found in the man page for `timidity.cfg` (`man timidity.cfg`). Instrument patches can be found at `http://www.stardate.bc.ca/eawpatches/html/default.htm`. timidity++ offers a range of interfaces and a server mode. Information is available in the man page for `timidity` (`man timidity`).

vkeybd — The Virtual MIDI Keyboard

vkeybd provides a virtual keyboard for those who do not have an external MIDI one. For information, refer to the man page for `vkeybd` (`man vkeybd`) or `vkeybd --help`.

aconnect and kaconnect — Connecting MIDI Ports

aconnect and the KDE version kaconnect can be used to connect MIDI ports and devices. kaconnect provides a simple graphical interface for making the connections. aconnect depends on commands, described in the man page for `aconnect` (`man aconnect`).

KMid — The KDE MIDI Player

KMid can be used to play MIDI files. Access online help by pressing (F1). Files in KAR format include lyrics. The lyrics can be scrolled and highlighted while the song is played, enabling KMid to function as a karaoke machine.

jazz — A MIDI Sequencer

jazz is a powerful and sophisticated sequencer. It includes jazz harmonies under 'Misc' → 'Harmony Browser'. jazz can be used with either timidity++ or a sound card with WaveTable synthesis. The program includes extensive internal help as well as documentation in `/usr/share/doc/packages/jazz`.

Synthesizers

Not everyone can afford fancy equipment like a synthesizer or a drum machine. The following programs allow you to emulate these devices with your computer.

SpiralSynth — The Software Analog Synthesizer

SpiralSynth provides a complete analog synthesizer. The interface is similar to early analog synthesizers. It can be controlled with the keyboard or vkeybd. Information is available in `/usr/share/doc/packages/SpiralSynth` or from `http://www.pawfal.org/Software/SpiralSynth/Manual.html`.

RTSynth — Software Physical Modeling in Real-Time

Input and output for RTSynth should be specified when starting the program from the command line. The command is something like `RTSynth -i /dev/snd/midiC1D0 -o /dev/dsp`. Obtain information about command-line parameters with `RTSynth --help`. Other documentation is in `/usr/share/doc/packages/rtsynth`.

tk707 — A Drum Machine

tk707 is based on the TR-707 drum machine by Roland. Configure the desired MIDI ports in the initial dialog. Documentation is available in `/usr/share/doc/packages/tk707/tk707.html`

trommler — A Drum Computer Including Samples

trommler, unlike tk707, does not need access to MIDI ports to play sounds. Drum samples are included in `/usr/share/sounds/trommler`. Use the number buttons at the beginning of lines to load samples. For more information, refer to the documentation and sample in `/usr/share/doc/packages/trommler`.

Composition and Scores

Although graphical composition programs are not as advanced or capable as might be desired, it is still possible to use Linux to create and edit musical scores.

LilyPond

LilyPond does not include a graphical interface. A score is created from a text file containing the specification of notes, key, and layout. Although it may be slightly more difficult to use than a graphical program, LilyPond is stable, extensive, and produces excellent output. A detailed manual for using LilyPond is available at `http://lilypond.org/stable/`. LilyPond is sometimes available as an output option from other programs.

NoteEdit

NoteEdit is probably the most complete score editing software with a graphical interface for Linux. With it, it is possible to create scores with a full range of musical symbols. Notes are entered by right-clicking and rests by middle-clicking. Internal documentation is available in the 'Help' menu. After creating the score here, it can be exported in LilyPond format for printing.

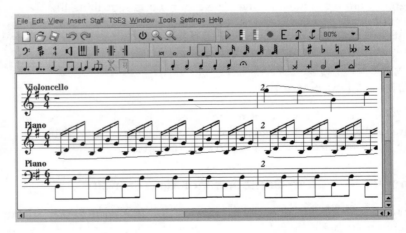

Figure 16.4: *The Composition Editor* noteedit

Reading Audio CDs

Konqueror can easily convert audio CDs to audio files. Insert a CD into the drive and enter `audiocd:/` in the URL window. After a few seconds, the contents of this CD are displayed. If you receive an error message, check to make sure you are a member of the group `disk` (use `id`). Add yourself to this group with YaST2 if needed. Log out of KDE, log back in, and try again.

If you have an open Internet connection, even the title of the audio CD is shown. This is automatically queried from a CDDB server. Entries are made there by many different users. It is quite likely that your CD title can be found. Copying audio tracks from the CD to your hard disk is also possible. Even convert them to ogg-vorbis (a nonpatented music format similar to MP3).

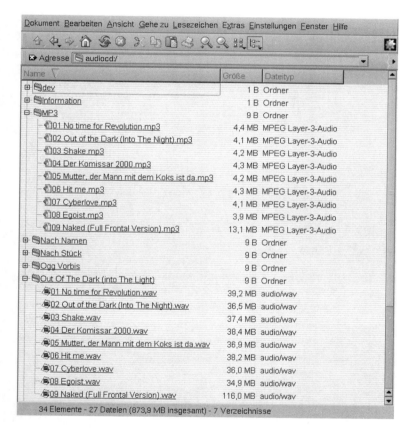

Figure 16.5: *Ripping CDs with* konqueror

TV, Video, Radio, and Webcam

This chapter introduces applications with which to watch TV, listen to the radio, and access your webcam in Linux. As not all the applications described in this section are included in a basic installation with YaST2, install them manually with YaST2.

Required Packages

Package	Series	Description
motv	xap	TV application with OpenMotif interface
xawtv	xap	TV application with Athena interface
alevt	gra	Video text decoder
nxtvepg	xap	The TV magazine for your PC
kradio	kde	Radio application
bttv	doc	bttv module documentation

The configuration of TV cards is integrated in the configuration tool YaST2. If your card has been correctly identified, it can be autoconfigured. Otherwise, enter the card settings by hand.

The following sections focus on the motv application, created by the author of the BTTV driver. Another TV application is KWinTV. If you prefer KWinTV, it should be easy to use after reading this chapter.

Watching TV with motv

motv is an improved successor to xawtv. It incorporates all essential functions into the user interface. Start the application with 'SuSE' → 'Multimedia' → 'Video'. Start it at the command line with motv. Initially, only a TV window appears after the application starts. Open a menu window by right-clicking it.

Video Source and Network Search

In the 'Settings' → 'Input' menu, select the video source. If you select 'Television' here, set up the broadcasting network before starting the application. This automatically takes place with the network search, also found under the 'Settings' menu. If you click 'Save settings', the network found is entered into the .xawtv file in your home directory and will be available the next time you start the application.

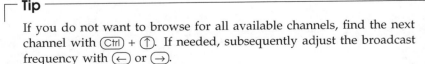

Tip

If you do not want to browse for all available channels, find the next channel with (Ctrl) + (↑). If needed, subsequently adjust the broadcast frequency with (←) or (→).

Tip —

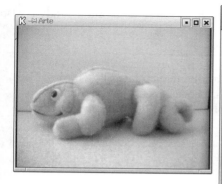

Figure 17.1: *The TV Application* motv

From Silent Film to Sound Film

The audio output of the TV card is connected to the line input of your sound card, to the speakers, or to an amplifier. In the case of some TV cards, the volume of the audio output can be changed. Set the volume in the slider that appears if you select 'Settings' → 'Slider'. Also find sliders for brightness, contrast, and color here.

To use your sound card for audio playback, check the mixer settings using gamix. For sound cards meeting AC97 specifications, set 'Input-MUX' to 'Line'. The volume can then be adjusted with the 'Master' and 'Line' sliders.

Screen Proportions and Full-Screen Mode

Most television images have a height and width ratio of four to three. With 'Tools' → 'Screen Dimensions', set these proportions. If '4:3' is selected here (this is the default setting), the screen dimensions are retained automatically, even when the display size is changed.

With Ⓕ or 'Tools' → 'Fullscreen', switch to full-screen mode. If the TV image in full-screen mode is not scaled to the full monitor size, some fine-tuning is required. Many graphics cards can scale the full-screen mode television image to the full monitor size without changing the graphical mode. If your card does not support this function, the graphics mode needs to be switched to 640x480 pixels for the full-screen mode. Create the related configuration in

'Settings' → 'Configuration'. After restarting motv, the monitor mode is also changed if you have switched to full-screen mode.

Tip

The .xawtv file is created automatically and updated by clicking 'Settings' → 'Save settings'. Here, the broadcasters are saved along with the configuration. More information pertaining to the configuration file can be found in the man page on xawtvrc.

Tip

The Launcher Menu

Use the launcher menu to start other applications to use with motv. Start the audio mixer gamix and the video text application alevt, for example, using a keyboard shortcut. Applications to launch from motv must be entered in the .xawtv file. The entries should look like this:

```
[launch] Gamix = Ctrl+G, gamix AleVT = Ctrl+A, alevt
```

The shortcut then the command used to start the application should follow the application name itself. Start the applications entered under [launch] via the 'Tool' menu.

Video Text with alevt

Use alevt to browse video text pages. Either start the application via 'SuSE' → 'Multimedia' → 'Video' → 'alevt' or at the command line with alevt. The application saves all the pages of the broadcasting network just activated with motv. Browse these sites by either entering the page number to view or by clicking a page number with the mouse. Move forward or backward through the pages by clicking '«' or '»', located in the lower window margin.

Webcams and motv

If your webcam is already supported by Linux, access it with motv. Find a summary of the supported USB devices at http://www.linux-usb.org. I you have already used motv to access the TV card prior to accessing the webcam, the bttv driver is loaded. The webcam driver is loaded automatically when your webcam is connected to the USB. Start motv at the command line with the parameter `-c /dev/video1` to access the webcam. Access the TV card with `motv -c /dev/video0`.

Note

When connecting the webcam to the USB before the bttv driver has been automatically loaded (this normally occurs when you call up a TV application), `/dev/video0` is reserved for the webcam. In this case, if you start motv with the `-c /dev/video1` parameter to access the TV card, you might get an error message, because the bttv driver will not be automatically loaded. Deal with this problem by loading the driver separately with `modprobe bttv` as the user `root`. An overview of the configurable video devices on your system can be viewed with `motv -hwscan`.

Note

Listening to the Radio with kradio

The kradio application can be found in the 'SuSE' → 'Multimedia' menu. To start the channel search, click the buttons with the double arrows. Use the buttons with the single arrows to change the frequency in 50 kHz intervals. Engage the six broadcasting network buttons by right-clicking them then enter the name of the network. This will be saved, along with the frequency just set, to the `~/.kde2/share/config/kradiorc` file.

Figure 17.2: The Radio Application kradio

The volume cannot be changed for every TV card. If you have connected the TV card's audio output with the line in input of your sound card, set your volume with the mixer gamix.

K3b — The KDE Burning Application

K3b is a very comprehensive program for writing data and audio CDs. Along with the usual features, the program offers some additional options that facilitate work, especially in the field of multimedia. Access the program under 'Multimedia' → 'CD' in the KDE or SuSE menu. The following section describes the main program functions.

The First Launch

Following the first program launch, the K3b setup assistant appears. Root permission is required to set up the program, so enter the `root` password. Follow the procedure of the setup assistant, which usually makes all settings automatically. In the fourth point of the setup assistant, you can manually assign the mount point and the entries in the file `/etc/fstab`. If you do not know anything about this file, do not modify anything. In step five, define the users authorized to create their own CDs. Enter at least one user. Step six completes the setup. The program is now ready for use.

Creating a Data CD

Creating a data CD is easy. Select 'File' → 'New Project' → 'New Data project'. As shown in Figure 18.1, a tab displaying a folder for your new data project appears at the bottom left side. Drag and drop the desired directories or individual files to the project folder. Select 'Burn' from the toolbar. A dialog appears with four tabs offering various options for writing the CD (Figure 18.2 on page 256).

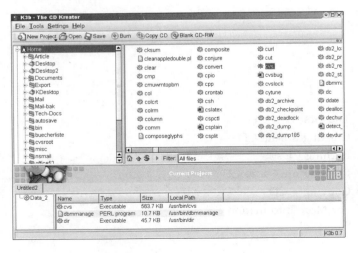

Figure 18.1: *Creating a New Data CD*

Burning CDs

The detected writer is displayed under 'Device' in the burning dialog. Set the
burning speed in 'Burning Speed'. The following options are offered here:

- 'Simulate writing' — This function can be used to check if your system
  is able to keep pace with the requirements of the current writing speed.
  The writing is performed with the laser deactivated to test the system.

- 'Writing on the fly' — Burns the desired data without first creating an
  image file. Do not use this function if the system performance of your
  computer is limited.

> **Note**
>
> An image file — also known as ISO image — is a file containing
> the entire CD contents that is subsequently written to the CD
> exactly as it is.
>
> **Note**

- 'Only create image' — Initially only writes an image file. You can write
  it to a CD later. For this purpose, use 'Tools' → 'Write Iso Image'.

- 'Delete image' — The image file is deleted after the CD is written.

- 'Disc at once' — The CD is burned without interruption. This is recommended for audio CDs (see below).

- use BURN-PROOF — If your writer supports this function, activate it
  to prevent interruptions of the data flow. The button is deactivated if
  this function is not supported.

Under the 'Settings' tab, enter information about the CD, such as a name.
However, this is optional. 'Multisession' displays several options required for
writing CDs with multiple data or audio tracks. The 'Advanced' tab is used
for the file name conventions. To achieve a high level of compatibility, make
sure 'Generate joliet entries' is marked.

Creating an Audio CD

Basically, there are no significant differences between creating an audio CD
and creating a data CD. Select 'File' → 'New Audio project'. Copy the individual audio tracks to the project folder with drag and drop. The audio data

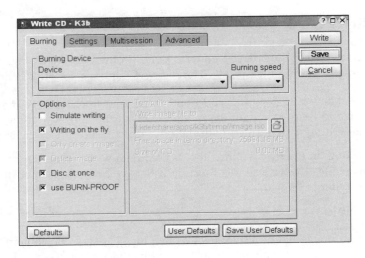

Figure 18.2: Burning CDs with K3b

must be in MP3, WAV, or Ogg Vorbis format. Set the sequence of the tracks in the project folder by shifting them with drag and drop.

The dialog for burning is not very different from the dialog for burning a data CD. However, the option 'DiscAtOnce' or, in case this option is not activated, the 'TrackAtOnce' mode bears greater importance. The 'TrackAtOnce' modes inserts a silent break of two seconds after each track.

Copying a CD

Select 'Copy CD' from the toolbar. In the following dialog, make settings for the reading and burning device (Figure 18.3 on the facing page). The options introduced above are also available here. An additional function enables you to create several copies of the CD.

For More Information

Apart from the two main functions described above, K3b offers other functions that are not described here. This includes the creation of DVD copies, reading audio data in WAV format, rewriting CDs, or the integrated autdio

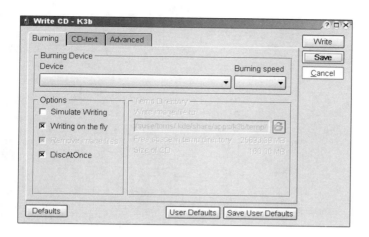

Figure 18.3: Copying CDs with K3b

player. A detailed description of all available program features is available at
`/usr/share/doc/packages/k3b/README`.

Digital Cameras and Linux

A wide range of digital cameras can currently be used with Linux. One of the best programs supporting these devices is gphoto2. gPhoto 2.0 is a command line program, called a "back-end library". It is compatible with several graphical interfaces (the "front-ends"), including gtKam, Konqueror, Kamera, and GnoCam. The use of gtKam and Konqueror is discussed in this chapter.

Connecting to the Camera

The fastest and most convenient connection between the digital camera and the computer is USB. This requires USB support both in the camera and in the computer. The default SuSE kernel provides this support, provided your computer has a USB port. An appropriate connecting cable is also required.

Note

Using the USB connection can quickly drain your camera's batteries. Consider using a power adapter.

Note

To use it, simply connect the camera to the USB port. Turn the camera on.

Installation and Preparation

Use YaST2 to install the gtkam package. The other required packages will be selected automatically. For more information on installing packages with YaST2, refer to *Install/Remove Software* on page 48.

Using Konqueror

For KDE users, accessing a digital camera through Konqueror provides a familiar interface and easy access. Connect your camera to the USB port. A camera icon should appear on the desktop. Double-click this icon to open the camera in Konqueror. The camera can also be accessed by entering the URL `camera:/` in Konqueror. Navigate through the camera's directory structure until the files are shown. Use the usual Konqueror file management features to copy the files as desired. More information about using Konqueror is available in *Konqueror — The KDE File Manager and Web Browser* on page 191.

Using gtKam

gtKam is compatible with all window managers. It is a fast and simple graphical interface for downloading and deleting pictures from the digital camera. To adjust or edit your pictures, use The GIMP as described in *Graphics with The GIMP* on page 275.

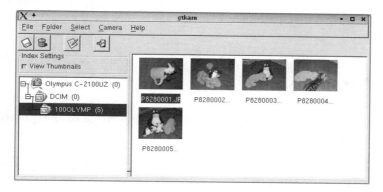

Figure 19.1: *The Main Window of gtKam*

Connect your camera to the appropriate port and turn it on. Start gtKam with the command `gtkam &`. From the menus, select 'Camera' → 'Select Camera...'. In the dialog, select the camera model or use 'Detect'. Select the appropriate port if not detected.

The main gtKam window is divided into three sections — the menu and toolbars, the left pane with index settings and camera and directory selection, and the right pane for displaying an index listing with or without thumbnails. The icons in the toolbar provide the main functions needed. The disk icon saves the selected images. The trash icon deletes them. The icon with the arrows reloads the image index displayed in the right pane. The icon with the paper and pencil opens the camera configuration options. The door icon exits the program.

Your camera should be listed in the left pane. Use the plus sign ('+') to the left to expand the tree display of the directory structure. Your exact directory stucture depends on the camera make and model. Continue expanding until you reach the entries that cannot be expanded. Those are the index listings of the actual pictures. Click an item to select it. If 'View Thumbnails' is activated, the picture names and thumbnails will be displayed in the right window pane. Otherwise, the names and an icon are displayed.

Images in the right pane can be selected or deselected by clicking them. Select all images with 'Select' → 'All' or $\boxed{\text{⇧ Shift}}$ + $\boxed{\text{A}}$. Use the disk icon in the toolbar, 'File' → 'Save Selected Photos...', or $\boxed{\text{Ctrl}}$ + $\boxed{\text{S}}$ to save the selected images. The 'Save' dialog, shown in Figure 19.2 on the facing page, has a number of options. Under 'What to Save', select whether to save the thumbnails, the images, or both. With 'Open image(s) with:', you can both save the image and open it in another program. To open the images in The GIMP immediately, enter `gimp`. Using the file names provided by the camera is recommended.

For More Information

For more information about using digital cameras with Linux, refer to the following web sites.

- `http://www.gphoto.org` — Information about gPhoto, gPhoto2, and gPhoto2-compatible GUIs

- `http://www.thekompany.com/projects/gphoto/` — Information about Kamera, a KDE front-end for gPhoto2

- `http://www.stud.uni-karlsruhe.de/~urc8/GnoCam/` — GnoCam information

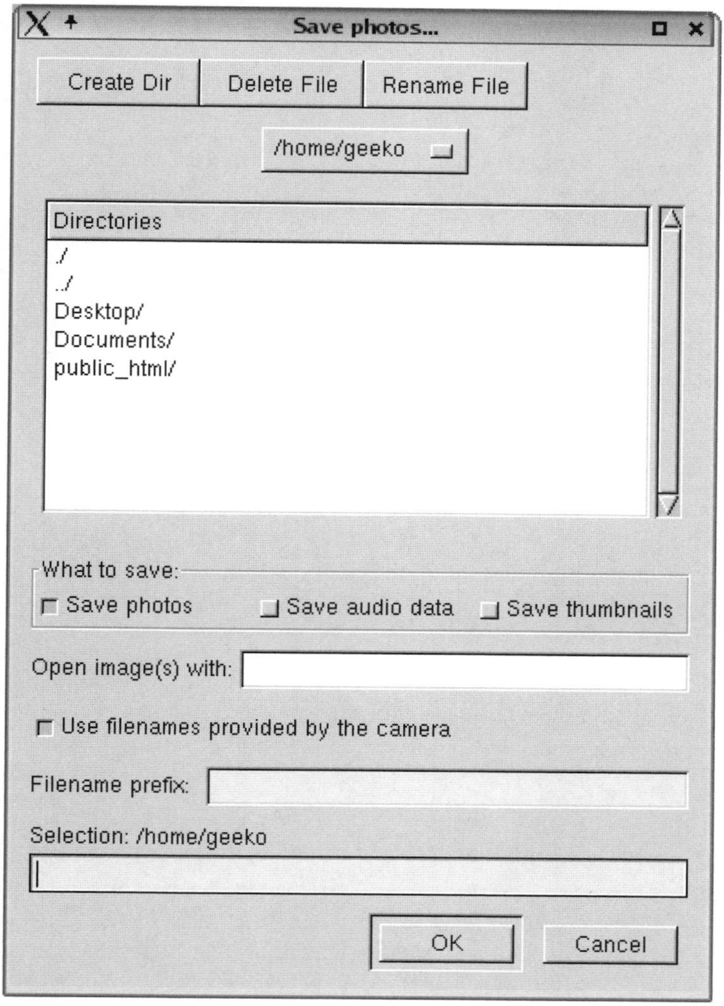

Figure 19.2: *Saving Images*

Kooka — The Scanning Application

Kooka is a graphical scanning application combining the simplicity of operating xscanimage with the functional breadth of XSane, incorporating the easy and user-friendly operation common in KDE applications. Kooka is a KDE application with integrated SANE system libraries. The SANE package must be installed to use Kooka. This chapter consists of two parts. The first part includes a short description of the Kooka application. The second part outlines some general scanning tips.

The web site http://www.mostang.com/sane has information about which scanners are supported in Linux and the development status of their drivers. If possible, review this information before purchasing a scanner.

Start Window

Start Kooka from a console with the command kooka. If desired, create a link to the application on your KDE desktop. When Kooka starts, it first opens a two-frame window with a menu bar and a toolbar. Optionally, include an additional window with a thumbnail view of an image directory. Use the mouse to enlarge or reduce the windows as needed. If desired, separate an individual window entirely from the Kooka window and move it to a location of your choice on the desktop. To move the windows, click the thin double line above the respective window and drag it with the mouse. You can place all windows (except for the main window) at the left, right, top, bottom, or center of any other window. When placed centrally, both windows have the same size, are superimposed, and can be brought to the foreground with tabs.

Change between the various windows in the two frames of the user interface with the tabs. The image directory view (gallery) is a small file browser that allows you to store scanned images easily.

Use the scanner-dependent part of your window to modify certain scanner-specific settings. At the bottom, see the two buttons for generating a preview and for starting the final scan. The scanned image appears in the large window to the right ('Image'), which is the only window that cannot be moved.

The Preview

For the sake of better understanding, these sections assume the gallery and the preview window are located at the top left and the scanner settings at the bottom left. The image viewer and thumbnail view are to the right.

At the top left, see the preview window and, next to it, the settings for the size and orientation. By pressing 'Preview Scan' (bottom left), the image in the scanner is test scanned and appears in the preview window. This preview scan does not generate a file. 'Final Scan' activates the actual scanning process to create a file, but only use it after making the appropriate settings.

Find information regarding the size and memory requirements of your image in the upper left section under the document's size and orientation information. Use preview window to define the scanning range and for adjusting the gamma value, brightness, and contrast. Do not assume that the printout will look exactly like the preview display. Correctly adjusting the monitor, scanner, and printer is a difficult procedure.

Scanning the Preview

Before scanning a preview, set the mode for generating the preview in the window containing the scanner settings (bottom left in our example). 'Color' and 'Gray' are self-explanatory. 'Binary' means that only black and white are used, without any gray tones. This option only makes sense for the preview if only pure text or black-and-white graphics are involved. It is necessary if you are performing a final scan of an image or text for the purpose of text recognition (see *The Final Scan* on the current page). The resolution and other settings in the window below especially affect the final scan.

Scan size and orientation can also be defined in the upper left section, if 'Preview' is selected. The size is given below in both mm and KB or MB. If you select 'User defined' as your scan size, you cannot choose the orientation. Mark the display window after the preview scan to define the area to scan. This is usually the most sensible mode. After all settings are adjusted, press 'Preview Scan' to scan the image preview. A miniature of the image then appears in the preview window.

The Final Scan

If you selected 'User defined' for the scanning size, use the mouse to highlight the rectangular area to scan. The selected area is marked with dotted borders. Select the scanning mode and resolution. You will be presented with further options, such as gamma values, contrast, and brightness. These options are specified by the scanner model itself. After configuring all your settings, click 'Final Scan' to scan the actual image.

Select the format in which to create the image. To generate future scans in the same format without confirmation, mark 'Don't ask again' then click 'OK'. Reconfigure this under 'Settings' → 'Configure Kooka' → 'Image Saving'.

The image appears in full size in the image window to the right. The size shown varies depending on the scanning area and resolution selected. If you selected a higher resolution, you will probably only see part of the image displayed to the right. In the right-hand window, scale the displayed area to your preferences.

The Menus

The toolbar functions can be found under the 'File' and 'Image' menus. Modify Kooka settings under 'Settings' → 'Configure Kooka'. Under 'Tool Views', display or hide the individual windows.

Under 'File', find 'Print...', which opens a print assistant, and 'Quit'. The option 'Open image in graphic application' is located under 'Image'. A description of these menu items follows.

Open image in graphic application
Choose an application for viewing the scanned image using a file browser or a command line. The GIMP is very useful for this purpose, but it is not included in the default installation.

Character Recognition (OCR) image...
Open a window for optical character recognition (OCR). If you have gocr installed, the application should be located at /usr/bin/gocr. This application then allows you to start the character recognition for the preview image or for the selection highlighted in the preview image.

OCR on selection...
Opens the character recognition window only for the area already marked in the final scan (see Section *Character Recognition with gocr*).

Scale to Width
Use this option to scale the image in the main image display to fit the width of the window.

Scale to Height
Scale the image to the full height of the image display.

Original Size
Reset the image in the display to its original scanned size.

> **Note**
>
> Access more possibilities for scaling the image display by right-clicking the image. The options include the three options previously mentioned along with options for enlarging it to your own specifications. You can also do the same in the preview window.
>
> **Note**

Create from selection

If you did not accurately select the area for the image, use this tool crop your image permanently by marking the large image display to the right then clicking this option. See the results to the right. You may already be familiar with this functionality from the crop tool in The GIMP.

Mirror image vertically

Flips the image vertically.

Mirror image horizontally

Flips the image horizontally.

Mirror image both directions

Flips the image horizontally and vertically at the same time.

Rotate image clockwise

Rotates the image ninety degrees clockwise.

Rotate image counter-clockwise:

Rotates the image ninety degrees counter-clockwise.

Rotate 180 degrees

Rotates the image 180 degrees.

Save

Saving images in Kooka is somewhat different from methods to which you may be accustomed. After clicking the 'Gallery' tab in the upper left window, see a small file browser depicting the `~/.kde/share/apps/ScanImages/` directory.

This is where all scanned images are initially saved as files. `ScanImages` is the only directory that exists when you first start Kooka. Subfolders can be created by right-clicking this main folder. The selected folder (highlighted in blue) is the first location to which scanned images are saved. The images will be named `kscan_0001`, `kscan_0002`, and so on, and be assigned consecutive numbers.

To save the image, click the name. Now, give it a new name and assign the correct file ending — the format in which the image was scanned. If you specify the wrong ending, receive an error message notifying you that the ending does not correspond to the format in which the image was scanned. Currently Kooka does not support "on-the-fly" conversion.

If you do not want to manage your images under `~/.kde/share/apps/ScanImages/`, save your images to another location. To do this, right-click the image and select 'Save'. Then enter the path.

You can also close or permanently delete the image here. Add external images to the gallery using Konqueror's drag and drop feature. Start Konqueror (the earth symbol in your KDE bar), go to the directory containing the images to add to your gallery, then simply drag them with the mouse and drop them in the Kooka gallery directory.

Character Recognition with gocr

gocr must be installed for this. Scan a preview of your document using either gray or color mode. You can also scan in binary mode. In the preview window, mark the area of the text to recognize. Choose binary mode for the final scan then scan with 'Final Scan'.

Click the second icon from the left inside the toolbar, 'Character recognition image...', or select this menu item from the 'Image' menu. Leave the default settings in the OCR window that opens unchanged, at least for the first trial run (Figure 20.1 on the facing page). These settings suit most users' needs. Now click 'Start character recognition'. A window, like that in Figure 20.2 on page 272, shows the results of the character recognition. The quality largely depends on that of the document itself. Open the text by clicking 'Open in Kate'.

If you only want to submit part of the text or image after the final scan in binary mode, mark your selection in the image display to the right. Then click the third button from the right in the toolbar or select 'Image' → 'Character recognition on selection'. Proceed as described in the previous paragraph.

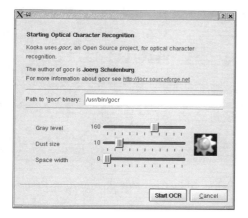

Figure 20.1: The gocr Window

Some Scanning Tips

Although Kooka is very easy to use, scanning can be very tricky, especially with scanners featuring numerous setting options or when using poor copies of documents. As a beginner, expect to do some experimenting until the results meet your satisfaction. Keep this in mind: a perfect color printout of your favorite pictures takes time and practice.

Hardware

Your scanning equipment and PC are probably far removed from those of a professional graphic design agency. Unfortunately, price is also a factor in the performance of these devices.

Good hardware is required for successful and convenient scanning. 36-bit scanners provide richer colors and gray scales than 24-bit scanners. SCSI scanners and, more recently, an increasing number of USB scanners are supported by SANE in Linux. Because of their overall better quality, purchasing a SCSI device is recommended. Some companies also offer Linux drivers for parallel port scanners. However, we cannot offer information about their quality and functionality. You may need a basic SCSI card for a SCSI scanner, because the card supplied with the scanner only offers minimal features.

Take a look at the SANE project Internet pages if you are considering buying a scanner. Consider the developmental phase of the drivers available when

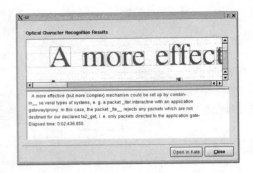

Figure 20.2: Character Recognition Results

selecting a scanner. YaST2 has simplified configuring USB scanners via plug-and-play.

Large images — manipulated or in their original format — may, under certain circumstances, require extensive memory space. Therefore, your computer should have at least 64 MB RAM, preferably 128 MB or more. The faster the CPU, the quicker your data can be processed. However, you do not need a high-end device. A middle-of-the-road one should do for household use. For an adequate display of the images on your desktop, you will also need a graphics card capable of depicting the right color depth in high resolutions.

Resolutions

Note

The printer resolution is usually stated in dpi ("dots per inch"), the halftone resolution of the printer in lpi ("lines per inch"), and the scanner resolution in ppi ("pixels per inch").

Note

A scanner resolution of 75 to 100 ppi is sufficient for scanning a simple photograph and viewing it on your desktop. Desktops typically have a default resolution of 75 dpi. A higher ppi value for scanning only uses more storage space without enhancing the screen display.

If you are not yet sure how you want to use your image later or if you simply want to create an image file, scan with a resolution of 150 ppi. A higher resolution most often leads to immense memory consumption. There may be times when you would want to scan a section of an image with a higher resolution, but this is not needed for normal photographs. Most graphics applications can save an image with lower resolution if needed.

To scan an image to a ratio of 1:1 for a printout, setting the scanning resolution to 1.6–2 times the printer resolution is generally recommended. A normal laser printer usually produces 75 lpi. If you have a printer of this type, you should set 120 to 150 ppi for scanning according to this multiplication factor. To generate images for display on the Internet, the default resolution of 75 dpi is sufficient.

If you want to use your printer to enlarge pictures, you will need an extremely high dpi setting. When making the enlargement, the scanner resolution should be multiplied by the magnification factor. Doing this, you will quickly approach the interpolated resolution range. Using the example above, a 5-fold magnification would require ppi settings of 750 or more. As scanners usually cannot reach such high physical dpi values, the values are calculated by the software.

Adjusting Brightness and Contrast

Keep in mind that the desktop display does not necessarily reflect the actual print results, but is only an approximation. It is generally recommended to set slightly higher brightness and contrast values for a black-and-white or color printout. You do not have to specify these values when scanning unless you want to print the scanned image directly. Otherwise, wait to make these settings later in The GIMP.

Strange Patterns in the Image

When scanning documents from print (books, magazines, newspapers), the individual pixels that comprise the image may produce a "Moiré pattern". Kooka cannot remove this pattern. In The GIMP, find a filter for removing the Moiré pattern under 'Filter' → 'Enhance' → 'Despeckle'. It works at the cost of a certain degree of clarity.

— Tip

If your scan produces in a repeating pattern, try rotating the document five to ten degrees and scanning it again. Later, reset the image to its original orientation in The GIMP. Often, this gives better results than using the enhancement filter to despeckle.

Tip ⌐

For More Information

More information on kooka is available on the KDE pages at `http://kooka.kde.org`.

Graphics with The GIMP

The GIMP (GNU Image Manipulation Program) is a very powerful program for the processing of pixel graphics. The GIMP is the first choice for retouching or modifying photographs and other image files. Once you are familiar enough with the program, you will even be able to create entire images from scratch. An average user, however, will not need all of the powerful functions of The GIMP. It can even be used for free-style painting. All tools, such as brush, pencil, or airbrush, are available (see Figure 21.1 on the following page). Frequent users of these features should definitely consider acquiring a graphics tablet.

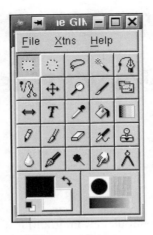

Figure 21.1: The GIMP Toolbox — The Default Window

Taking into account the power and performance of The GIMP and the prices for commercial 'professional' graphics programs, it soon becomes evident that the GNU Image Manipulation Program is a phenomenal gift to the Linux community. As with so many Linux programs, The GIMP is under constant development.

This introduction cannot cover the whole range of features. The "official GIMP manual" has 924 pages and is available on the Internet at `http://manual.gimp.org`. Unfortunately, some of its descriptions and illustrations are outdated, because The GIMP has undergone extensive development since the manual was written. The internal help system, still under development, also provides valuable assistance to the new user.

Note

The version included in this distribution and discussed in this manual is the most recent release of the stable 1.2 series. The unstable GIMP 1.3 series is not intended for regular users. It is only intended for those involved in developing The GIMP itself.

Note

Image Processing and Graphics Formats

Pixel Images

The GIMP has been designed for processing pixel graphics. These images consist of small blocks of color that together create the entire image. A full-screen image on a monitor of 800 × 600 resolution has exactly that number of pixels. It contains 480,000 individual pixels. Considering this, it is not surprising that image files are generally quite bulky. In addition to the co-ordinates of each pixel, the color information is stored. With an image of 800 × 600 pixels, it is easy to get more than one MB of data. From the outset, therefore, much time and energy has been invested in developing compression procedures that squeeze the amount of information together. Some well-known graphics file formats for pixel images include:

XCF The native GIMP format. It supports the layer technique discussed later and other specific GIMP functions. If you have created an image using the GIMP-specific settings and save it in a different file format, information is lost.

BMP A format without compression used by Microsoft Windows. An advantage of this format is that graphics can be loaded and saved very quickly, but this positive aspect is outweighed by the file size.

GIF The "Graphics Interchange Format" has been specially developed for data transfer on the Internet and has special features to support this. For licensing reasons, many programs are no longer able to support this format. One special feature of GIF is the animated Gif, a GIF file in which several images are stored. In an Internet browser, these individual images are displayed so quickly one after the other that the impression of a moving image is created. GIF, despite its limitations, is popular predominantly because it allows transparency.

PNG The "Portable Network Graphics" is a popular replacement for the GIF format. It can generate the same quality of compressed files without loss of information and is freely available. It allows a better form of transparency, but is not yet fully supported by all Internet browsers.

PSD This format is used by the professional Adobe Photoshop application and supports the multilayer technique.

TIFF The "Tagged Image File Format" is yet another method of saving files in the professional arena. It is particularly popular in the printing business.

JPEG The compression method of the "Joint Photographic Experts Group" allows a highly efficient reduction of image files. Depending on the compression factor, image information is lost. Nevertheless, it is an ideal file format for images on the Internet.

┌─ **Tip** ──

Always save an XCF version of images you create. This makes future modifications much easier.

─── **Tip** ─┘

Vector Graphics

Unlike pixel graphics, vector graphics do not store information on all individual pixels. Instead they store information on how image points, lines, or areas are grouped together. A line that runs horizontally across the screen, representing a total of 800 pixels, only needs four information units: the coordinates of the starting point, the coordinates of the end point, the information that these two points are connected by a line, and, possibly, the color of the line. With four coordinates and four lines connecting them, you can easily create a rectangle. The fact that this rectangle is filled with a specific color basically requires just one more information unit. In this way, even complex images can be represented with relatively little basic information. The drawing application of OpenOffice.org, for example, uses this format.

Using The GIMP

Starting The GIMP

By default, The GIMP is included in the standard installation of SuSE Linux Start The GIMP with 'SuSE' → 'Multimedia' → 'Graphics' → 'GIMP' or by typing gimp in a command line. When The GIMP is newly installed, some postinstallation procedures are conducted when it is first started for a user. The left button in the bottom part of dialog box that opens is the 'Install' button. Click this button then, in the following dialog box, click 'Continue'. The GIMP is then correctly installed and set up.

Since many files need to be loaded when it first starts, The GIMP takes some time to load. By default, a window is displayed after each start showing the 'Tip of the Day'. If desired, deactivate it by unchecking the 'Show tip next time' box on the left.

The Toolbox

Initially, The GIMP appears on screen in a rather unspectacular way. It opens a relatively small window containing the toolbox. The buttons of this window are the main functions needed for powerful image manipulation. The following is a description of the icons and their functions.

The GIMP toolbox window can be subdivided into three parts: the menu bar with the 'File', 'Xtns' (Extensions), and 'Help' menus; the tool icons; the color, pattern, and brush selection icons.

The Menu Bar

The menu bar can be been in Figure 21.1 on page 276. Use 'File' for creating a new graphics file, loading an existing image with the file manager, creating screenshots (screenshots are images of sections of your screen), setting basic options, and accessing the most recently processed files. The main items under the 'Xtns' menu are Modules, Plug-ins — additional programs linked into The GIMP that implement a specific graphical functionality, Scripts, and The GIMP web pages. The 'Help' menu contains various ways of accessing help information.

The Tool Icons

Each graphic in the toolbox represents a specific function. The toolbox can be resized both in width and height. Overall, a distinction can be made between three or four function areas.

Selection Tools

In image processing, you will want to process either the whole image or only a specific section of it. The GIMP needs know to which area the following actions should be applied. Several selection tools will help define a specific area. Once a selection has been made, it can be processed without affecting other parts of the image. Selection areas can also be increased or decreased in size with the aid of (⇧ Shift) (additive selection) and (Ctrl) (subtractive selection). The cursor changes to show a plus or a minus sign.

Transform Tools

These functions are used to modify selections. Many functions are available, including crop, flip, and transform.

Paint Tools

The paint tools represent pencil, paintbrush, airbrush, pen, and finger (smudge) and try to emulate their real-world properties on the PC.

A fourth functional area to be classed with these three areas might include the color, fill, and brush options, which specify the paint color or the tip of the painting tool.

┌─ **Tip** ──

One click on a tool icon activates the tool. A double-click opens an additional window with the option settings for the specific tool.
─── **Tip** ─

The Selection Tools

Rectangular select is the simplest selection tool. By keeping the left mouse button pressed and dragging the mouse at the same time, a rectangular area is marked. When you release the mouse button, a frame indicates the selected area. If you press (⇧ Shift) after you begin drawing the selection, only perfect squares can be selected.

This tool works like rectangular select, except it selects a circular or elliptical area. It is used in the same way, except pressing (⇧ Shift) after you begin selecting limits the selection to perfect circles.

This is the first usable selection tool for photographs. The lasso allows a free-hand selection of an irregular shape. Press the left mouse button and follow the shape as required. When you release the mouse button, the start point and end point are joined with a straight line. An accurate selection is difficult, so working with an enlarged image is recommended.

The magic wand fuzzy selection tool selects an image area through color similarity of adjacent pixels. If the default settings are not suitable, either change the threshold value in the option box or combine several selections using (⇧ Shift). The magic wand is ideal for selecting irregular areas of similar color.

With a bit of effort, the Bezier Curves tool allows you to capture specific areas or objects of an image. With the aid of anchor points set with mouse clicks, draw clean, curved lines. One advantage of this technique is that you can change the selection with the aid of control points. Once you have marked the area required, just click inside it and it will be selected. This tool requires some practice to master, but is invaluable for more advanced work. Selections made with this tool can also be saved and manipulated with the 'Paths' tab of the Layers, Channels, and Paths dialog.

As you click, Intelligent Scissors tries to draw a selection along color or brightness edges. Sometimes it works quite well. Modify the settings in the option box.

Transformation Tools

When Move is activated, grab and move your selection with the mouse.

The magnifier is not a true transformation tool because it only zooms the screen representation in or out. The image itself is not changed. To use the zoom out function, which reduces the image on the screen by a certain percentage, press and hold (Ctrl) while clicking with the mouse.

For a true enlargement of your image, open the context menu with a right-click in your image and select 'Image' → 'Scale Image'. In the dialog box that opens, change the height and width of the image by percentages or by pixel values.

Crop and resize your image. For an aesthetically pleasant impression for landscape photographs, for example, it is recommended to assign the sky one-third and the landscape two-thirds of the image height. Using the mouse, click and drag to open a rectangle. A click inside this rectangle crops the surrounding area. You can always undo this immediately by (Ctrl) + (Z). Take your time to experiment with this tool. You can also change the size of this rectangle. Resize the section by grabbing and moving the top left or bottom right corners. The whole rectangle can be moved by grabbing and moving the bottom left or top right corners.

This icon hides a multitude of functionalities that might confuse a beginner. Either process the whole image by clicking the tool icon first then the image or a portion by first making a selection then clicking the tool icon.

Four functions are available: rotate the image or the selection around an arbitrary rotation point, enlarge or reduce (Scaling), convert a rectangle into a trapezoid (Shearing), or distort the perspective of an area. The default setting is Rotation. Other functions can be specified in the option box opened by double-clicking the tool icon.

↔ A simple tool that flips (mirrors) the selected area horizontally or vertically.

Once you have modified your whole image or a selection with the aid of a transformation tool, reconnect this floating selection to the image. Prior to this integration, you can still modify the result of your transformations. There are several possibilities for integrating the changes into the image. Use the anchor layer keyboard shortcut ((Ctrl) + (H)), click in the image somewhere outside the selection, or choose a different selection tool and apply it.

Paint Tools

The first few tools in the following list are somewhat different from the other paint tools. They are included in this section, however, because they are used to add colors or text rather than modify it. The main paint tools provided by The GIMP have particular properties in the real world that are emulated by the program. Set the appropriate options to simulate various pencils or to adjust the paintbrush to your personal requirements. In the option boxes of the paint tools, find the slider 'Opacity'. This is used to set the opacity of the color employed. With the 'Mode' drop-down box, specify how painted lines or surfaces should be integrated into the image. Depending on the tool, the different modes have different effects.

T The T stands for text input. In The GIMP, text input is done in two ways and many options are available. Double-click the tool to open the option box. By activating or deactivating the 'Use Dynamic Text' button, select multiline text input with alignment or single line text input. A click in the image with the T tool activated opens the corresponding dialog box in which to enter text and select font, size, and other parameters.

Caution

If you do not save the text in a separate layer, you will later be unable to modify it because it is integrated into your image in pixel form. See Section *Layers* on page 289 for more information.

Caution

The GIMP provides a relatively simple text tool. Many text effects, such as shadows or gradients, must theoretically be input by hand. In practice, however, 'Script-Fu' and the 'Filters' submenu provide many automatic modification procedures, which have, in part, been specifically designed for use with text.

The color picker allows a controlled selection of a color from your image and transfers it to the color selection box. When you click a specific color in the image with the color picker tool, this color is selected. With it, quickly find, for example, a specific skin tone needed to retouch a photograph.

With the paint bucket, fill a selected area with color. Instead of a color, it can also fill with a pattern. Prior to the filling action, activate 'Pattern Fill'. Everything in the selection is then painted over with the selected settings.

The icon represents a color or grayscale gradient. The GIMP has several predefined gradients to use to fill the selected area. This tool is relatively complicated and requires some practice, especially if you want to overlay an image with transparent color gradients.

The pencil is a painting tool with which every user is familiar. With the virtual pencil — as with a real pencil — draw free-hand lines. The type of line — the width and shape of the pencil point — is selected with the brush dialog. Either double-click the brush icon in the bottom right corner of the toolbox or select 'File' → 'Dialogs' → 'Brushes'. Pencil points are available that do not actually exist in the real world. Make your pencil point extra-fine or extra-thick or select one of the special shapes.

The paintbrush draws with a softer, more liquid effect than the pencil. In the appropriate option box, set a fade out (the color intensity slowly diminishes while painting) or a gradient (selection via the gradient setting options). When the fade out option is activated, release the paintbrush and begin again to apply more color.

The eraser erases. It also unerases. The brush selection also sets the shape of the eraser.

The airbrush allows you to work in the same way as with a real airbrush. Change the 'Pressure' and use the many different brush settings. This tool is ideal for use with a pressure-sensitive graphics tablet.

 The clone tool (the icon represents a rubber stamp) is the ultimate instrument for photo retouching. It can be used to specify parts of images that are then cloned. In practice, this means that you specify very precisely which part of the image to copy where and in what form. This has relatively little to do with the 'Cut' and 'Paste' functions. It uses the paint functionality, allowing you to set shape and opacity of your imaginary rubber stamp.

Things become interesting, for example, if you have an old photograph with white stains. Activate the Clone tool and, if needed, its option box. Keep (⇧ Shift) held down and click the image area to use for the copy. Then release the mouse button and place the cursor on the damaged image area. If you now press the left mouse button and move the mouse, the image area marked in the first step of the procedure is inserted. When you move the mouse upwards, the area being copied moves upwards, too. The point is marked by a crosshair. Depending on the brush settings, a small or a large radius is copied and, depending on the tool settings, copying is carried out in a translucent or opaque manner. You will need this quite frequently to retouch photographs. You can, for example, eliminate unwanted text from scanned images or even skin blemishes from portraits.

 The Convolver tool (the icon shows a drop of water) is used for precise manual blurring or sharpening of image parts. Which of the two actions is active is set in the option box. The brush selection determines size and borders of the manipulation area. Blurring lays a kind of haze over the image or, as when using a drop of water on a water color painting, blurs the "painted" areas. Sharpening is the opposite. Here the program attempts to increase the contrast and make a neater separation of edges. Sharpening works very well if you later look at your image from a distance. It also means a loss of information, however. Seen from very close up, the images look extremely pixellated.

 The pen can be used not only for drawing, but also for calligraphy. Writing well, however, can only be achieved with the aid of a graphics tablet. In the tool settings, adapt the shape of the pen to your own requirements.

The tool icon that looks like a pin is, in reality, a thin wooden stick with a glued-on opaque cardboard circle. Such an instrument is needed in a photographic laboratory for the perfect exposure of a manual paper copy. Since only a small part of the negatives (or positives) is exposed perfectly, this instrument is moved over the areas that would otherwise become too dark while the paper is being exposed. Thus, the exposure of specific problem areas can be adjusted individually. The opposite is a piece of cardboard with a little hole in it for postexposure. Both functions are fulfilled by this GIMP tool. Dodge (make lighter) individual image areas or burn (make darker) them. To create soft transitional borders, use a diffuse brush shape.

The finger shown in this tool icon moves over the color just applied to the paper and smudges it. This can be used to create very interesting effects.

With the calipers, measure distances and angles. In the associated option box, activate the 'Use Info Window' button.

Color, Brush, Pattern, and Gradient Selection

The selected colors, brush, pattern, and gradient are shown in your toolbox. The color selection functions are on the left. On the right are the currently active brush shape, the active pattern, and the active gradient. A click on each of these opens a dialog window for individual configuration.

Working with The GIMP

Opening Images

You have, for example, stored a scanned image or an image from the Internet on your hard disk and want to work on it with The GIMP. Click 'File' → 'Open' or $\boxed{\text{Ctrl}}$ + $\boxed{\text{O}}$ to open The GIMP file manager dialog, shown in Figure 21.2 on the next page).

On the left-hand side, change to a different directory by double-clicking. On the right-hand side, the files are listed. The file list is sorted alphabetically. Individual sorting by file type or date is not possible. A handy feature is the small integrated preview window. If The GIMP recognizes the file format, see

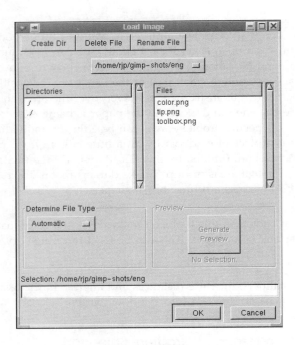

Figure 21.2: Load Images

a thumbnail picture of the currently selected file. Double-click the file name or click 'OK' to open the image.

For convenience, The GIMP works with an image in a separate image window completely independent from the window containing the tool icons. You can move the image window around on your screen and, if needed, change its size and zoom settings independently.

Creating a New Image

To create a new image, select 'File' → 'New' or press ⟨Ctrl⟩ + ⟨N⟩. A dialog box opens in which to specify several image attributes (see Figure 21.3 on the facing page). The most important ones are width and height, usually represented in pixels, image type, and fill type. If you specify a width of 800 and a height of 600 pixels and your screen resolution has the same value, you can use your painted image later as a full-size background image. In the 'Fill Type' selection area, select the type of fill to use in the new image: the current foreground or background color, white, or transparent. By default, transparent areas are rendered with gray checks.

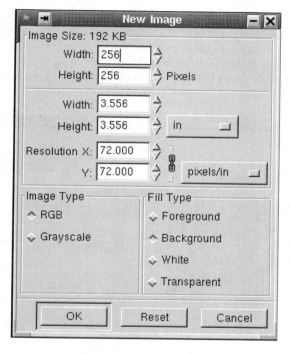

Figure 21.3: Creating a New Image

Saving Images

Save with the mouse or (Ctrl) + (S). When using the mouse, right-click inside the image to open the context menu of the image. To save your image, activate 'File' → 'Save'. If you have already assigned a name to the image, it is saved under that name. If not, The GIMP file manager opens and lets you specify the required file name and path. With 'Determine file type', specify which image format The GIMP should use for saving. Use a correct file extension. In theory, it is no problem to save a GIF file with a .TIF extension. If the file type is set to 'By Extension', The GIMP saves in the file type identified by the file extension in the file name.

Printing Images

To print your images, open the context menu with the right mouse button. With 'File' → 'Print', open the print dialog. Select the correct print queue (printer), media size (default setting "Letter"), orientation (auto, portrait, landscape), and output type (black-and-white or color). Use a `raw` queue because GIMP-Print produces printer-specific data. Scale the image and specify its position on the page. With the 'Print' button, send the print job to the printer.

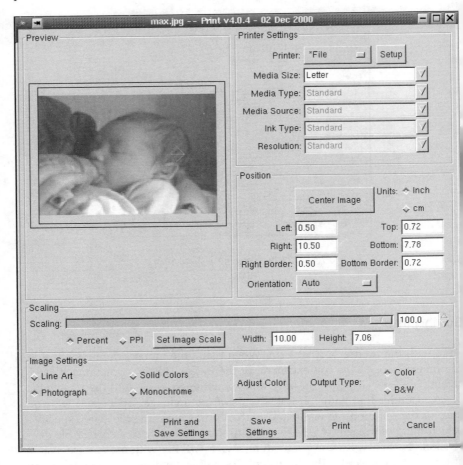

Figure 21.4: Printing Dialog in GIMP

Configuring The GIMP

The GIMP provides some simple setting options for fast and efficient work. Explore 'File' → 'Preferences' to see the range of options available. Once you are more familiar with The GIMP, experiment with the various settings. Refer to the internal help system for advice.

An important setting is the multilevel Undo, used to undo your last actions. To use it, select 'Edit' → 'Undo' in the context menu or press (Ctrl) + (Z). It is important to set how many levels of changes The GIMP should save. Set this in the 'Environment' category of the 'Preferences' dialog mentioned previously.

If you memorize the keyboard shortcuts, The GIMP is much easier to work with. Change the shortcuts to your individual requirements. Right-click the required menu item and keep the mouse button pressed. Then type the required key combination — it is immediately assigned. Avoid repeating shortcuts, as that is possible and will confuse the program.

Tip

Many functions or tool settings have their own windows that you can open and close as needed. On a larger screen, leave frequently needed dialog windows open without any problem.

Tip

Tear-off menus are another outstanding feature of The GIMP. Whenever a menu shows a dotted line on top, click this line, detaching the menu from the larger context menu. The menu is then displayed on your desktop in its own window.

Layers

Layers are crucial to using The GIMP effectively. They allow you to arrange image contents and more easily edit and modify your image. To store layer information when saving a file, save in GIMP's native format, .XCF. As well as preserving layer information, it also saves The GIMP features such as the location of guides.

To understand how layers work, imagine an image created from a stack of transparent sheets. Different parts of the image are drawn on different sheets. The stack can be rearranged, changing which pieces are on top. Individual or groups of layers can shift position, moving sections of the image to other locations. New sheets can be added and others set aside. This is very much how the layers work in The GIMP.

By drawing parts of your image on separate layers, you can manipulate, change, or delete those parts without damaging the other parts of the image. Using separate layers for text is the most common usage, but the possibilities are much more extensive.

The GIMP includes a layer manager. Access it via 'Layers' → 'Layers, Channels & Paths...' in the context menu then under the 'Layers' tab in the dialog that opens (see Figure 21.5). Here you can create, copy, and delete layers or anchor a layer in the background image. In addition, the eye icon in the layer manager can be used to make layers invisible without losing their information. The icon with four arrows indicates linked layers. Layers showing this icon will be moved as a group.

Under the 'Channels' tab, view the three color channels — red, green, and blue — individually or in any combination. The 'Paths' tab provides information about paths which have been drawn with the Bezier selection tool.

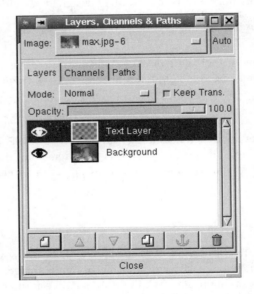

Figure 21.5: Layers, Channels, and Paths Dialog

Image Modes

The GIMP has three basic image modes — RGB, grayscale, and indexed. RGB is the main color mode usually used in The GIMP. Grayscale is for black, white, and gray images. Indexed is used almost exclusively for converting images to the GIF file format. There are a few things to remember when working with image modes:

- Only RGB mode has all the filters available. Most, however, are available in grayscale mode. To run filters on an indexed image, convert to RGB first.

- Convert to indexed only right before saving to image formats that require it, such as GIF. Never work with an image in indexed mode.

- Regardless of any color used on a grayscale image, the color will be desaturated and applied in a shade of gray.

- Study the internal help system for more information about image modes.

Introduction to Image Manipulation

The following sections provide tips for working with your own images. This only introduces a small part of the things possible in The GIMP.

Preparing Photographs for Printing

You have, for example, an image of your kids and want to produce a perfect printout on your color printer. Unfortunately, the first printout was not what you expected. The colors were quite bleak and there is a point in the image which is quite dark.

There is a fundamental problem when printing color images. Color and contrast of the image as seen on screen do not correspond to what comes out of your printer. The images on screen are often richer in contrast and more brilliant. Only in professional systems are all components adjusted in such a way that screen representation and future print output match to a high degree. To improve an image, the following manipulations are recommended.

Before you start, create a backup copy of your image. Once you have saved your manipulation, you can no longer recreate the original state. Although these corrections can be made using 'Image' → 'Colors' → 'Brightness-Contrast', better results are obtained through the Levels dialog found in the context menu under 'Image' → 'Colors' → 'Levels'.

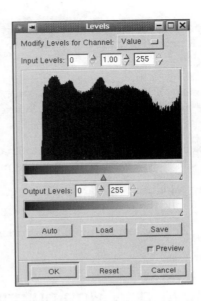

Figure 21.6: The Levels Dialog

The Levels Dialog shows how the color values and colors are spread throughout the image (see Figure 21.6). By adjusting the end sliders to where the black areas begin and end, you redistribute them over the entire range of values. This means that somewhere in the image will become completely black, somewhere will be completely white, and the rest of the range will be spread accordingly. Usually, clicking 'Auto' gives acceptable results, but sometimes manual adjustment is needed. To adjust manually, drag the end sliders to where the black area in the graph begins and ends. Do this in each of the channels (select from the drop-down box showing Value as default). This should correct both brightness and contrast problems.

Occasionally, you may need to to sharpen the whole image to obtain a good quality printout. During sharpening, edges and color transitions are emphasized. Right-click and, in the context menu, select 'Filters' → 'Enhance' → 'Sharpen'. Watch the effect in the small preview window and even undo it with (Ctrl) + (Z).

To make individual image areas brighter or darker, use the 'Dodge or Burn' tool from the toolbox. For the best results, select a brush tip with a diffuse border in the brush selection dialog.

Finally, cut the image to size with the 'Crop or resize' tool and print it out.

Special Effects

In the context menu, many different manipulation tools are available under 'Filter' or 'Script-Fu'. These include some easy-to-apply effects. Usually, clicking the filter in the menu opens an option box with which to control the effects of such filters. Refer to the internal help system for descriptions of the filters.

Inserting Text

You can easily integrate text into your images with The GIMP. First determine the text color with the aid of the color selection icon in the toolbox. Then activate text input with the T icon and click the image. A dialog box as in Figure 21.7 opens in which to specify your text and the font settings. Depending on which fonts are available on your system, specify a font family in the first selection column. The second column determines style and weight (medium, bold, or italic) and the third column sets the type size. Click 'OK' to add the text to your image. As long as dotted lines surround your lettering, you can move the text. However, once the text is anchored in your image, you can only remove it with 'Undo' — as long as you have not saved the image. Put text on its own layer for easy modifications later.

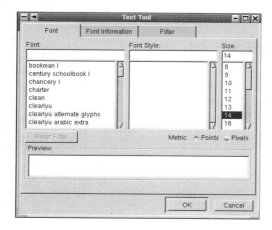

Figure 21.7: Entering Text

In the option box of the text tool, select between a single line of text and a text window with several lines and text alignment. When you activate the

'Use Dynamic Text' button, a click inside the image opens an option box in which to enter and align multiline text.

Retouching Images

The most suitable tool for this purpose is the clone tool. It is represented by a rubber stamp in the tool window. Since we have already explained earlier how this tool functions, some brief hints are sufficient here:

- Set the brush to a medium size with a diffuse border area.

- Work on an enlarged representation of your image.

- Open a second view of the image with 'View' → 'New View' and zoom to 1:1 to see how the changes look.

- Save your work from time to time under a different file name. If you do not like one of your modifications, revert to a previous stage.

Retouching may take some time because you often need to change brushes and redefine the image section to copy. Working with the clone tool requires some experience.

For More Information

There is a very good The GIMP web site at `http://www.gimp.org`. There, find and download documentation, plug-ins, and more. Also, 'Important Links' offers an impressive collection of links for The GIMP.

Working with the Shell

Graphical user interfaces are becoming more and more important for Linux, but using the mouse is not always the best way to perform daily tasks. Command-line tools may prove much more efficient and flexible. In the first part of this chapter, read an introduction to the bash shell. This is followed by a section about the basic concepts of user permissions on Linux and another section about the most important commands available. The chapter closes with a primer on the vi editor.

Text-based applications can be an interesting option, especially if Linux is installed on older machines that do not have the resources for more "hardware hungry" user interfaces. In those cases, control the system from a virtual console in text mode. A total of six consoles are available. Switch between them with the key combinations (Alt) + (F1) through (Alt) + (F6). The seventh console is reserved for X11.

Introduction to Bash

In the KDE taskbar, there is an icon depicting a monitor with a seashell. When you click this icon with the mouse, a console window opens in which to enter commands. The console will normally run Bash (which stands for "Bourne again shell"), a program developed as part of the GNU project. It is by far the most widely used derivative of the Bourne shell (sh). Once you have opened the shell, see the prompt on the first line, which usually consists of the user and the host name along with the current path. The prompt can be configured individually, however. When the cursor is next to this prompt, send commands directly to your computer system.

```
newbie@earth:~ >
```

Commands

A command consists of several elements. The first one is always the name of the command, which is followed by parameters or options. Commands are executed when you press (↵). Before doing so, easily edit the command line, add options, or correct typing errors.

One of the most frequently used commands is ls, which can be used with or without arguments. Entering the plain ls command in the console shows the contents of the current directory. Options are prefixed with a hyphen. The command ls -l, for instance, shows the contents of the same directory in full detail. Next to each file name, also see the date when the file was created, the file size in bytes, and further details discussed below. One very important option that exists for many commands is the --help option. By entering ls --help, see all the options for the ls command.

You can also use the ls command to view the contents of other directories. To do so, the directory must be specified as a parameter. For example, to see the contents of Desktop, enter ls -l Desktop.

Files and Directories

To use the shell efficiently, it is really useful to have some knowledge about the file and directory structures of a Linux system. You can think of directories as electronic folders where files, programs, and subdirectories are stored. The top level directory in the hierarchy is the root directory, referred to as /. This is the place from which all other directories can be accessed. The /home directory contains the home directories of different users, where they can put their personal files.

Figure 22.1 shows the standard directory tree in Linux, with the home directories of users xyz, linux, and tux. The directory tree of a Linux system has a certain functional structure to follow — the "File System Standard". Table 22.1 on the following page provides a short description of these standard directories.

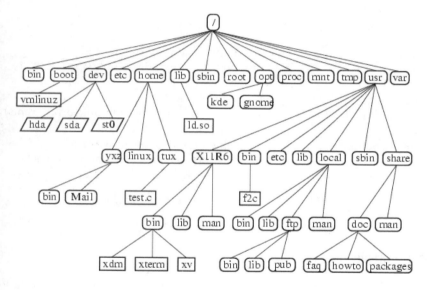

Figure 22.1: Excerpt from a Standard Directory Tree

/	root directory, starting point of the directory tree
/home	(private) directories of users
/dev	device files that represent hardware components

Table 22.1: continued overleaf...

`/etc`	important files for system configuration
`/etc/init.d`	boot scripts
`/usr/bin`	generally accessible programs
`/bin`	programs needed early in the boot process
`/usr/sbin`	programs reserved for the system administrator
`/sbin`	programs reserved for the system administrator and needed for booting
`/sbin/init.d`	boot scripts
`/usr/include`	header files for the C compiler
`/usr/include/g++`	header files for the C++ compiler
`/usr/share/doc`	various documentation files
`/usr/man`	system manual pages (man pages)
`/usr/src`	source code of system software
`/usr/src/linux`	kernel source code
`/tmp`	temporary files
`/var/tmp`	large temporary files
`/usr`	contains all application programs
`/var`	configuration files (e.g., those linked from `/usr`)
`/var/log`	system log files
`/var/adm`	system administration data
`/lib`	shared libraries (for dynamically linked programs)
`/proc`	process file system
`/usr/local`	local, distribution-independent extensions
`/opt`	optional software, larger add-on program packages (such as KDE, GNOME, Netscape)

Table 22.1: Overview of Important Directories

Bash Functions

There are two important functions of the shell that can make your work a lot easier:

- The history function — To repeat a command that has been entered before, press (↑) until the previous command appears at the prompt. Move forward through the list of previously entered commands by pressing (↓). To edit the command line, just move the cursor to the desired position using the arrow keys and start typing. Use (Ctrl) + (R) to search in the history.

- The expansion function — Expand a file name to its full length after typing its first letters until it can be uniquely identified. To do so, type the first letters then hit (Tab). If there are several file names starting with the same letters, obtain a list of them by hitting (Tab) twice.

First Example: Managing Files

Now that you know what a command looks like, which directories exist in SuSE Linux, and how to speed up things when using Bash, put this knowledge into practice with a small exercise.

1. Open a console from the KDE desktop by clicking the shell icon.

2. Enter the ls command to see the contents of your home directory.

3. Use the command mkdir (which stands for "make directory") to create a new subdirectory named test by entering mkdir test.

4. Now launch the KEdit editor by pressing (Alt) + (F2) and entering "kedit" in the input field. Type a few letters in the editor then save the file as Testfile in your home directory. Linux distinguishes between uppercase and lowercase. For this example, use an uppercase T.

5. View the contents of your home directory again. Instead of typing ls again, just press (↑) twice and the ls command should reappear at the prompt. To execute the command, hit (↵). The newly created directory test should appear in blue letters and Testfile in black. This is how directories and files can be distinguished in a console.

6. Move Testfile into the subdirectory test with the command mv. To speed this up, use the expansion function: just enter mv T and press (Tab). As long as there is no other file beginning with this letter in the directory, the shell will expand the file name and add the string "estfile". Otherwise, add a letter or two yourself and test with (Tab) each time whether the shell can now expand the name. Finally, type a space then test after the expanded file name and press (↵) to execute the command.

7. At this point, Testfile should no longer be in the directory. Check this by entering ls again.

8. To see whether the file has been successfully moved, change into the directory test with the command cd test. Now enter ls again. You should see Testfile in the listing. Change back to your home directory at any point by entering only cd (which stands for "change directory").

9. To make a copy of a file, use cp. For instance, enter
cp Testfile Testbackup to copy Testfile to Testbackup. Once
again, the command ls can be used to see whether both files are in the
directory.

Specifying Paths

When working with files and directories, it is important to use the correct
path leading to their actual location. To do so, however, does not require
specification of the complete (or absolute) path to the corresponding file. You
can also start from the current directory.

A ~ represents your home directory. There are several ways to list the file
Testfile in the directory test: either by typing the relative path as in
ls test/* or by specifying the absolute path as in ls ~/test/*. To list
the contents of home directories of other users, enter ls ~username. In the
directory tree shown above, one of the sample users is tux. Thus, the command ls ~tux would list the contents of the home directory of tux.

The current directory can always be referred to by putting a dot. The next
higher level in the tree is represented by two dots. By entering ls .., see
the contents of the parent directory of the current directory. The command
ls ../.. shows the contents of the directory two levels higher in the hierarchy.

Second Example: Working with Paths

Here is another example to illustrate how you can move around in the directories of your SuSE Linux system.

- Change into your home directory with the command cd. Then create a
  directory in it with the name test2 by entering mkdir test2.

- Change into the new directory with cd test2 and create a subdirectory in it with the name subdirectory. To change into it, you can
  use the expansion function: enter cd su then press (Tab). The shell will
  expand the rest of the directory name.

- Now try to move the previously created file Testbackup into the
  current directory (which is subdirectory) without changing the directory again. To achieve this, specify the relative path to that file:
  mv ../../test/Testbackup ..

The dot at the end of this command is required to tell the shell that the current directory is the destination to which the file will be moved. Two dots (..), on the other hand, take you one level up in the directory tree. In our example, ../../ refers to your home directory.

Wild Cards

Another convenience offered by the shell is that it allows the use of wild cards. There are four different types of these in Bash:

Matches exactly one arbitrary character

Matches an arbitrary number of characters

set]   Matches one of the characters from the group specified inside the square brackets, which is represented here by the string "set"

!set]   Matches one character other than those identified by "set"

Assuming that your test directory contains the files Testfile, Testfile1, Testfile2, and datafile, the command ls Testfile? will list the files Testfile1 and Testfile2. With ls Test*, the list will also include Testfile. The command ls *fil* shows *all* the sample files mentioned above. Finally, use the set wild card to address all files whose last character is a number: ls Testfile[1-9].

Among the four types of wild cards, the most inclusive one is the asterisk. It could be used to copy all files contained in one directory to another one or to delete all files with one command. The command rm *fil*, for instance, would delete all files in your test directory whose name includes the string "fil".

More or Less

Linux includes two small programs that enable you to view text files directly in the shell. Rather than starting an editor to read a file like Readme.txt, for example, simply enter less Readme.txt and the text will be shown in the console window. With (Space), scroll down one page. You can also use (Page ↑) and (Page ↓) to move forward or backward in the text. To exit from less, press (Q).

The program less can also be used to view the output of commands in a more convenient way. To see how this works, read Section *Redirection* on the next page.

Apart from less, you can also use the older program more, although it is less convenient because it does not allow you to scroll backwards. One could say you get more with less.

Redirection

Normally, the standard output of the shell is your monitor or — to be more precise — the console window. The standard input device is your keyboard. To redirect the output of a command to a program like less, use a "pipe".

To view the list of files in test, try the command ls test | less. On your console, you can now see the contents of the directory test, as displayed by less. In general, this only makes sense if the output of ls is longer than one screen page. For instance, if you try to list the contents of /dev with a simple ls /dev, only a small part of the list fits into the window. With ls /dev | less, on the other hand, scroll through the entire list of files without any problem.

The shell also allows you to save the output of a command to a file. As a variation of the above sample command, enter ls test > listing. This creates a new file with the name listing that contains a list of files and directories in test. The command less listing lets you view the contents of this file.

Conversely, you can take a file and use it as the input of a command. For example, to sort the lines in the previously created test file in alphabetical order, enter sort < Testfile. The command sort will send its output to the screen — you are shown the contents of that file with the lines sorted according to their first letter. A command like this may come in very handy to arrange the entries of a name list or similar data.

To create a file containing the sorted list, the output of the sort command needs to be redirected into a file. To try this yourself, create an unsorted list of names in an editor and save it under the name unsortedlist in the test directory. Then change into test and enter the command sort < unsortedlist > sortedlist. Finally, view the sorted list with less.

Just like the standard output, the standard error output is sent to the console as well. However, to redirect the standard error output to a file named errors, you need to append 2> errors to the corresponding command. On the other hand, both standard output and standard error will be saved to one and the same file named alloutput if you append >& alloutput. Finally, to append the output of a command to an already existing file, the command must be followed by >> instead of a single >.

Archives and Data Compression

Now that you have already created some files and directories, consider archives and data compression. Suppose you want to have the whole test directory packed in one file so you can save it on a floppy disk as a backup copy or send it by e-mail. To do so, you need the program tar (for "tape archiver"). With tar --help, view all the options for the tar command, the most important of which are explained here:

-c (for create) Create a new archive

-t (for table) Display the contents of an archive

-x (for extract) Unpack the archive

-v (for verbose) Show all files on screen while creating the archive

-f (for file) Allows you to choose a file name for the archive file. When creating an archive, this option must always be given as the last one.

To pack the test directory with all its files and subdirectories into an archive named testarchive.tar, you definitely need the options -c and -f. For the testing purposes of this example, you should also add -v to follow the progress of the archiving, though this option is not mandatory. After using cd to change to your home directory where the test directory is located, enter tar -cvf testarchive.tar test. After that, view the contents of the archive file with tar -tf testarchive.tar. The test directory with all its files and directories has remained unchanged on your hard disk. To unpack the archive, enter tar -xvf testarchive.tar, but do not do so yet, as we first want to compress the archive file to save some disk space.

When it comes to file compression, the obvious choice on Linux is the popular gzip program. Just enter gzip testarchive.tar. With ls, now see that the file testarchive.tar is no longer there and that the file testarchive.tar.gz has been created instead. This file is much smaller and therefore much better suited for transfer via e-mail or storage on a floppy.

Now, unpack this file in the test2 directory created earlier. To do so, enter cp testarchive.tar.gz test2 to copy the file to that directory. Change to the directory with cd test2. A compressed archive with the .tar.gz extension can be "unzipped" with the gunzip command. So just enter gunzip testarchive.tar.gz , which will result in the file testarchive.tar, which then needs to be extracted or "untarred" with tar -xvf testarchive.tar.

You can also "unzip" and extract a compressed archive in one step by adding the -z option. The complete command would be `tar -xvzf testarchive.tar.gz`. With `ls`, see that the `test` directory has now been restored with the same contents as the original one in your home directory.

mtools

The `mtools` are a set of commands you can use to work with MS-DOS file systems. This is useful, especially when dealing with floppy disks. The commands included in `mtools` allow you to address the first floppy drive as a:, just like under MS-DOS, and the commands are like MS-DOS commands except they are prefixed with an 'm':

`mdir a:`   displays the contents of the floppy disk in drive `a:`

`mcopy Testfile a:`   copies the file `Testfile` to the floppy disk.

`mdel a:Testfile`   deletes `Testfile` in `a:`

`mformat a:`   formats the floppy disk in MS-DOS format (using on the `fdformat` command).

`mcd a:`   makes `a:` your current directory

`mmd a:test`   creates the subdirectory `test` on the floppy disk.

`mrd a:test`   deletes the subdirectory `test` from the floppy disk.

Cleaning Up

After this crash course, you should be familiar with the basics of the Linux shell or command line. You may want to clean up your home directory by deleting the various test files and directories using the `rm` and `rmdir` commands.

User Permissions

Introduction

Since its inception in the early 1990s, Linux has been developed as a multiuser system. Any number of users can work on it simultaneously. This resulted in some notable distinctions from the Microsoft end-user operating systems Windows.

The most important distinguishing feature is the necessity for users to log in to the system before starting a session at their workstation. Each user has his own user name with corresponding password. This differentiation of users guarantees that unauthorized users cannot see files for which they have no permission. Larger changes to the system, such as installing new programs, are also usually impossible or restricted for normal users. Only the ☞*root*, or "superuser", has the unrestricted capacity to make changes to the system and has unlimited access to all files.

Those who use this concept wisely, only logging in with full `root` access when necessary, can cut back the risk of unintentional loss of data. Since under normal circumstances only the super user can delete system files or format hard disks, the threat from the "Trojan horse effect" or from accidentally entering destructive commands can be significantly reduced.

File System Permissions

Basically, every file in a Linux file system belongs to a user and a group. Both of these proprietary groups, along with "alien users", can be authorized to write, read, or execute these files.

A group, in this case, can be defined as a set of connected users with certain collective rights. For example, call a group working on a certain project `project3`. Every user in a Linux system is a member of at least one proprietary group, normally `users`. There can be as many groups added to a system as needed, but only `root` is able to add groups. Every user can find out, with the command `groups`, of which groups he is a member.

File Access

Take a closer look at the access structure in the file system. We can start with the files.

The output of `ls -l` can read like this:

```
-rw-r-----  1 tux    project3  14197 Jun 21 15:03 Roadmap
```

Output 1: *Sample Output Showing File Permissions*

As shown in the third column, this file belongs to user `tux`. It is assigned to the group `project3`. To discover the user permissions of the `Roadmap` file, the first column must be examined more closely.

–	rw–	r––	–––
Type	User permissions	Group permissions	Authorization for other users

This column is comprised of one leading character followed by nine characters grouped in threes. The first of the ten letters stands for the type of listed file system components. The dash (–) shows that this is a file. Here a directory (d), a link (l), and a block device (b), as well as a character device, could also be indicated.

The next three blocks follow a standard pattern: The first three characters refer to whether the file is readable (r) or not (–). A w in the middle portion symbolizes that the corresponding object can be edited and a dash (–) means it is not possible to write to the file. An x in the third position denotes that the object can be executed. Since the file in this example is a text file and not one that is executable, executable access for this particular file is not needed.

In our example, tux has, as owner of the file Roadmap, read (r) and write access (w) to it, but cannot execute it (x). The members of the group project3 can read the file, but not change it or execute it. Other users do not have any access to this file.

With these security options, user tux can make sure that only authorized people (members of the working group) can read the file and that only he can change it, since he is the only member that has write access to it.

Directory Permissions

Look at access permissions for directories (those objects that have the type d). Here, the significance of each type of access is a little bit different than the above example.

```
drwxrwxr-x  1 tux  project3  35 Jun 21 15:15 ProjectDat
```

Output 2: Sample Output Showing Directory Permissions

Here, the owner (tux) and the owner group (project3) of the directory ProjectData is easy to recognize. In contrast to the file access permissions from *File System Permissions* on the preceding page, the set reading permissions (r) means that the contents of the directory can be shown. The write permission (w) means new files can be created. The executable permission (x) means that the user can change to this directory. In the above example, this consequently means that the user tux as well as the members of the group project3 can change to the ProjectData directory (x), view the contents (r) and add new files to it (w). The rest of the users, on the other hand, are given less access. They may enter the directory (x) and browse through it (r), but not insert any new files (w).

Modifying File Permissions

Changing Access Permissions

The access permissions of a file or a directory can be altered by the owner (and by `root`, of course) with the command `chmod`, which needs to be entered along with the parameters for the access permissions and the names of the files to modify.

Both parameters are comprised of

1. the categories concerned
   - u (*user*) — owner of the file
   - g (*group*) — group that owns the file
   - o (*others*) — additional users (if no parameter is given, the changes apply to all categories)
2. a character for deletion (−), setting (=), or insertion (+)
3. the abbreviations
   - r — *read*
   - w — *write*
   - x — *execute*
4. file name or names separated by empty characters

If, for example, the user `tux` in Output 2 on the preceding page also wants to grant other users write (w) access to the directory `ProjectData`, he can do this using the command:

```
newbie@earth:~ >  chmod o+w ProjectData
```

If, however, he wants to deny all users other than himself write permissions, he can do this by entering the command

```
newbie@earth:~ >  chmod go-w ProjectData
```

To prohibit all users from adding a new file to the folder `ProjectData`, enter

```
newbie@earth:~ >  chmod -w ProjectData
```

Now, not even the owner can write to the file without first reestablishing write permissions.

Changing Ownership Permissions

Additional commands in this context are `chown` (CHange OWNner) and `chgrp` (CHange GRouP), which control the ownership of individual file system components.

The command `chown` serves to change the ownership of a given file. Only `root` can initiate these changes.

Suppose that the file `Roadmap` from Output 2 on page 306 should not belong to `tux`, but to the user `geeko` instead. The appropriate command would be entered as user `root` as follows:

```
earth:~ #  chown geeko Roadmap
```

`chgrp` is also fairly self-explanatory — it changes the group ownership of the file. You should remember, however, that the owner of the file must be a member of the new group.

In this way, the user `tux` from Output 1 on page 305 can switch the group owning the file `ProjectData` to `project4`, as long as he is a member of this new group, by entering

```
newbie@earth:~ >  chgrp project4 ProjectData
```

These limitations do not present a problem for `root`.

The Most Important Linux Commands

This section gives insight into the most important commands of your SuSE Linux system. Along with the individual commands, parameters are listed and, where appropriate, a typical sample application is introduced. To get more information on commands, use `man`. Enter `man` followed by the command as in `man ls`.

In these ☞*manual pages*, move up and down with (PgUp) and (PgDn) and move between the beginning and the end of a document with (Home) and (End). End this viewing mode by pressing (Q). Learn more about the `man` command itself with `man`.

There are many more commands than listed in this chapter. For information about other commands or more detailed information, we recommend the O'Reilly publication *Linux in a Nutshell*.

In the following overview, the individual command elements are written in different typefaces.

- The actual command is always printed as `command`. Without this, nothing can function.

- Options without which the respective program cannot function are printed in *italics*.

- Further details, like file names, which must be passed to a command for correct functioning, are written in the `Courier` font.

- Specifications or parameters that are not required are placed in `[brackets]`.

Adjust possible specifications to your needs. It makes no sense to write `ls file(s)`, if no file named `file(s)` actually exists. You can usually combine several parameters simply by writing `ls -la` instead of `ls -l -a`.

File Commands

File Administration

`ls [option(s)] [file(s)]`
> When `ls` is called without further specifications and parameters, the contents of the current directory are listed in a short form.

> **Options:**
> `-l` detailed list
> `-a` displays hidden files

`cp [option(s)] sourcefile targetfile`
> Creates a copy of `sourcefile` in `targetfile`.

> **Options:**
> `-i` Waits for confirmation, if necessary, before an existing `targetfile` is overwritten
> `-r` Copies recursively (includes subdirectories)

`mv [option(s)] sourcefile targetfile`
> Places a copy of the `sourcefile` in `targetfile` then deletes the original file.

> **Options:**
> `-b` Creates a backup copy of the `sourcefile` before moving

-i Waits for confirmation, if necessary, before an existing
targetfile is overwritten

rm [option(s)] *file(s)*

Removes the specified file(s) from the file system. Directories will not be deleted by rm except when explicitly specified with the parameter *-r*.

Options:

-r Also delete existing subdirectories

-i Waits for confirmation before deleting each file

ln [option(s)] *sourcefile targetfile*

Places an internal ☞*link* to the sourcefile under a different name. This reference normally points directly to the position of the sourcefile within the file system. However, if ln is called with the -s option, a symbolic link is created that only points to the path of the sourcefile and therefore also works across file system borders.

Options:

-s Creates a symbolic link

cd [options(s)] [directory]

Changes the current directory. If only cd is entered without parameters, the command carries out a change to the user's ☞*home directory*. Usually, however, the destination directory is specified. cd .. changes to the next higher directory (parent directory).

mkdir [option(s)] *directoryname*

Creates a new directory.

rmdir [option(s)] directoryname

Deletes the specified directory, but only if already empty. To delete directories still containing files, the rm -r command should be used.

chown [option(s)] username.group file(s)

Changes the owner of a file to the specified username and group.

Options:

-R Changes files and directories in all subdirectories.

`chgrp [option(s)] groupname file(s)`

Changes the name of the group that owns a given `file` to `groupname`. The file owner may only change this value if they are a member of both the previous and new owner group.

`chmod [options] mode file(s)`

Changes access permissions.

The `mode` parameter has three parts: `group`, `access`, and `access type`. `group` accepts the following characters:

group options:

u   user

g   group

o   others

For `access`, access is granted by the + symbol and denied by the – symbol.

The `access type` is controlled by the following options:

Access type:

r   read

w   write

x   eXecute — for executing files or changing to the directory.

s   Set uid bit — the application or program is started as if it were being started by the owner of the file.

`gzip [parameters] file(s)`

This program compresses the contents of files through complicated mathematical procedures without loss of data. The names of the compressed files end in `.gz` and must be uncompressed before being used again. To compress multiple files or entire directories, also use `tar`.

Options:

`-d` decompresses the packed gzip files so they return to their original size and can be processed normally (like the command `gunzip`).

`tar options archive file(s)`

`tar` normally combines one or more files together in one archive, which can then, for example, be compressed. `tar` is a quite complex command that makes a number of options available. The most frequently used options are:

Options:

- -f Writes the output to a file and not to the screen as is usually the case
- -c Creates a new tar archive
- -r Adds files to an existing archive
- -t Outputs the contents of an archive
- -u Adds files, but only if they are newer than the files already contained in the archive
- -x Unpacks files from an archive ("extraction")
- -z Packs the resulting archive with gzip
- -j Compress the resulting archive with bzip2
- -v List files processed

The archive files created by tar end with .tar. If the tar archive was also compressed using gzip, the ending is .tgz or .tar.gz. If it was compressed using bzip2, .tar.bz2.

Sample applications can be found in Section *Archives and Data Compression* on page 303.

locate *pattern(s)*

With locate, find in which directory a specific file is located. You can also use ☞*wild cards*. The program works very quickly as it is not searching slowly through the file system itself, but through a database specifically created for this purpose. This is also the main problem with this very fast command. No files created after the last update of this database can be listed. The database can be generated by root with updatedb.

updatedb [options(s)]

This command allows the database needed by locate to be easily brought up-to-date. To register the largest possible number of files, the program should be run by root. It also makes sense to place it into the background by appending an ampersand ('&'), so you can immediately continue working (updatedb &).

find [option(s)]

With the find command, look for a file in a certain directory. The first argument represents the directory from which the search starts. The option -name uses a string search where ☞*wild cards* are also permitted. Unlike locate, find actually searches the directory specified, not just in its own database.

Commands to Access File Contents

cat [option(s)] file(s)

The cat command outputs the contents of a specified file without interruption.

Options:

-n Numbers the output on the left margin

less [option(s)] file(s)

Conveniently view the contents of specific files. Move half a page up or down with (PgDn) and (PgUp) and a whole page forward with (Space). Move to the beginning or end of a document with (Home) or (End). End the output mode with (Q).

grep [option(s)] searchword file(s)

grep is designed to find a certain search word in the given file[s]. If successful, it displays the line in which searchword was found and the name of the file.

Options:

-i Ignores case

-l Only displays the names of the respective files, but not the text lines

-n Additionally displays the numbers of the lines in which it found a hit

-1 Only lists the files in which *searchword* does **not** occur

diff [option(s)] file1file2

The diff command was created to compare the contents of any two selected files and display them in the form of a list of modified lines. This is frequently used by programmers who need only send their program alterations and not the entire source code.

Options:

-q Only reports *whether* the two given files differ

File Systems

`mount [option(s)] [<device>] mountpoint`

>Any data medium can be mounted in the file system using this command. Mounting means the integration of hard disks, CD-ROMs, and other drives in a directory of the Linux file system.

>**Options:**

>`-r` mount read-only

>`-t filesystem` Specifies the file system. The most common are `ext2` for Linux hard disks, `msdos` for MS-DOS media, `vfat` for the Windows file system, and `iso9660` for CDs.

>For hard disks not defined in the file `/etc/fstab`, the device type must also be specified. In this case, only `root` can mount. If the file system should also be mounted by other users, enter the option `user` in the appropriate line in the `/etc/fstab` file (separated by commas) and save this change. Further information is available in the man page for `mount` (`man mount`).

`umount [option(s)] mountpoint`

>This command removes a mounted drive from the file system. Before you remove a data medium from the drive, use this command. Otherwise, run the risk of data loss. Only `root` can `mount` and `umount`. Exception: When the option `user` is set for the drive in the `/etc/fstab` file.

System Commands

System Information

`df [option(s)] [directory]`

>The `df` (disk free) command, used without options, displays statistics about the entire disk space, disk space used, and disk space available on all the mounted drives. If a directory is specified instead, the drive on which it is located is shown in the statistics.

>**Options:**

>`-H` shows the number of occupied blocks in gigabytes, megabytes, or kilobytes — in "human readable" format

>`-t` Type of file system (ext2, nfs, etc.)

`du [option(s)] [path]`

When called without parameters, this command shows the total disk space used by all files contained in the current directory. If subdirectories exist, their total sizes are listed as well.

Options:

`-a` Displays the size of each individual file

`-h` Output in human-readable form

`-s` Displays only the calculated total size

`free [option(s)]`

`free` displays the sum of the total and the working memory being used and the swap space.

`date [option(s)]`

This small program displays the current system time when called. As `root`, also use this command to change the system time. Details can be found in the man page.

Processes

`top [options(s)]`

`top` displays a quick overview of the currently running ☞*processes*. By pressing Ⓗ, a page of the most important options with explanations is displayed, allowing the program to be adapted to the individual needs of the user.

`ps [option(s)] [process ID]`

When run without options, this command returns a table of all "your own" — user-started programs or processes. **No** prefixed hyphen should be used with the options to this command.

Options:

`aux` Displays a detailed list of all processes, independent of the owner.

`kill [option(s)] process ID`

Though the Linux system itself may be considered fairly stable, there are unfortunately programs (usually poorly programmed) that do not close down in the normal way. With the `kill` command, nearly all process "corpses", identified by their process IDs (see `top` and `ps`), can be "killed". It sends a "TERM" signal, which instructs the program to shut itself down. If this does not help, there is one more useful parameter.

Options:

-9 Sends a "KILL" signal instead of a "TERM" signal, whereby
    the process really is "annihilated" by the operating system.
    This brings the specific processes to an end in almost all cases.

`killall [option(s)] processname`
This command functions like `kill`, but, instead of a process ID,
the specification of a process name is sufficient to "kill" all processes with that name.

Network

`ping [option(s)] hostname or IP address`
ping is strictly a means of examining TCP/IP networks for their
basic functional efficiency. The tool sends a small data package
to another computer with the instruction to send it back immediately. If this works, ping displays an appropriate message that the
network is essentially up and running.

Options:

-c `number` Determines the total number of packages to send and
    ends after they have been dispatched. By default, there is no
    limitation set.
-f "flood ping": sends as many data packages as possible. A
    popular means, reserved to `root`, to test networks.
-i `value` Specifies the interval between two data packages in
    seconds. Default: one second

`nslookup`
The "Domain Name System" converts domain names to IP addresses. This tool allows queries to be made to the corresponding
information services (DNS servers).

`telnet [option(s)] hostname/IP address`
Telnet is actually an Internet protocol that enables you to work
with other computers across a network. Telnet, however, is also
the name of a Linux program that interprets exactly the same protocol and enables you to work with other computers without having to physically sit at the respective console.

Do not use telnet over a network on which third parties can
"eavesdrop." Particularly on the Internet, you should use en-

crypted transfer methods, such as `ssh`, to avoid the risk of malicious misuse of a password (see the man page for `ssh`).

Miscellaneous

`passwd [option(s)] [username]`
> Users can change their own passwords at any time with this command. Also the superuser `root` may use it to change the password of any user.

`su [option(s)] [username]`
> `su` allows you to change user login during a session. Used without further parameters, the command prompts you for the root password and, if you enter it correctly, grants supervisor rights. After entering a user name and the correct password of a user, you can use the environment of that user. As ☞*root*, you do not need to enter a password. With supervisor permissions, you can simply assume the identity of every user.

`halt [option(s)]`
> To avoid the risk of data loss, always shut down the computer with this program.

`reboot [option(s)]`
> Functions in the same way as the `halt` command, but the computer is immediately rebooted.

`clear`
> From time to time, the console may become cluttered with text lines. Use `clear` to "clean up" the console. This command does not have any options.

The vi Editor

Operating the `vi` editor takes some practice. For many, it is the preferred editor, partly because it is available on any UNIX-like operating system and is included in default Linux installations. Also, if nothing else works, `vi` will. The short instructions that follow should enable you to edit various configuration files and other types of files with `vi`.

vi recognizes three operating modes:

- *Command mode:* Keys are interpreted as command elements.

- *Insert mode:* Key are interpreted as text entries.

- *Last line mode:* Used for more complex commands, which are edited in the last line.

The most important commands in command mode are:

i   Changes to insert mode (characters will appear at the current cursor position).

a   Changes to insert mode (characters will appear *after* the current cursor position).

A   Changes to insert mode (characters will be added at the end of the line).

R   Changes to command mode (overwrites the old text).

r   Changes to insert mode and overwrites *each* character.

s   Changes to insert mode (the character where the cursor is positioned will be replaced by the next entry you make).

C   Changes to insert mode (the rest of the line is replaced by the new text).

o   Changes to insert mode (a new line is inserted *following* the current one).

O   Changes to insert mode (a new line is inserted *preceding* the current one).

x   Deletes the current character.

dd   Deletes the current line.

dw   Deletes up to the end of the current word.

cw   Changes to insert mode (the rest of the current word is overwritten by the next entries you make).

u   Undoes the last command.

J   Joins the following line with the current one.

.   Repeats the last command.

:   Changes to last line mode.

A number can be added to the front of each command that specifies the number of objects the command should affect. Delete three words at once by entering `3dw`. By entering `10x`, delete ten characters after the cursor position. With `20dd`, delete the last 20 lines.

The most important commands in last line mode are:

`:q!`	exits vi without saving any changes
`:w` ⟨*filename*⟩	saves as ⟨*filename*⟩
`:x`	saves the modified file and exits the editor
`:e` ⟨*filename*⟩	edits (loads) ⟨*filename*⟩
`:u`	undoes the last edit command

Table 22.3: *Complex Commands in the vi Editor*

Switch to command mode by pressing (Esc).

Part IV

Help

Help and Documentation

If you have questions about your SuSE Linux system, an answer may already be available. Find a wealth of documentation in the classical formats: man pages, info pages, HOWTOs, READMEs, FAQs, and more. SuSE Help combines all these formats within one system and makes them more systematic. Together with comprehensive search performance, this should provide the answers to your questions. This chapter introduces SuSE Help and provides an overview of the traditional documentation sources.

Installation Support

If you experience difficulties during the installation, we will gladly assist you with installation support. Some computers have special characteristics that complicate the installation. However, these problems can quickly be tackled with competent assistance. The free SuSE Installation Support is a special service for such cases. Detailed information about the installation support is available at `http://www.suse.com/us/support/inst_support/index.html`.

All support-related information, contact partners, and topical hints are published on the SuSE Support pages at `http://support.suse.de/en/`. If you cannot able find a solution here, contact us by e-mail at support@suse.de.

We have already found the answers and solutions to many questions and issues. This information is available around the clock in the form of several hundred articles in our online Support Database: `http://sdb.suse.de/en/`.

SuSE Help

SuSE Help can be started with the lifesaver icon (the one with the Geeko) in the control panel on the KDE desktop or via the 'SuSE Help' item in the K Menu or in the SuSE menu.

Users of other desktops can view SuSE Help in any browser. Start SuSE Help outside KDE by entering `help` in a console or with the URL `http://localhost/hilfe/index.html.en` in a browser.

> **Note**
>
> The `inf2htm` package is required to display SuSE Help as a documentation server in HTML format. Instructions for configuring your help system as a documentation server in an intranet can be found at `/usr/share/doc/packages/susehelp/README`.
>
> **Note**

Working with SuSE Help

Individual search settings are made in the left window panel. View the search results in the right panel in the form of a list of links to the documents found. This list is normally restricted to ten entries per documentation source and ordered according to priority. Refer to Section *The KDE Control Center* on page 121 for information about configuring SuSE Help.

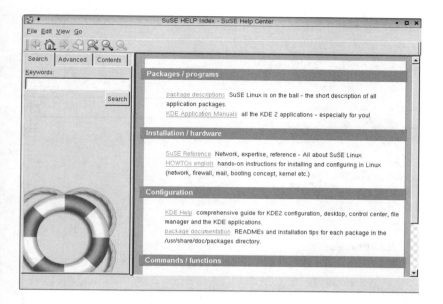

Figure 23.1: *The SuSE Help Home Page*

Home page After starting SuSE Help, see an overview in the right window panel of the subject categories. Open a listed documentation source by clicking it. Access the summary page at any time by clicking 'Home'.

Packages and Applications

- 'Package Descriptions' — Find short descriptions of each application package in SuSE Linux, regardless of whether it is installed. Obtain a summary of all the available packages and related information, such as the hard disk space required.

- 'SuSE Applications' — Obtain an introduction to applications designed for daily tasks on your PC (office, e-mail, graphics, and others).

- 'KDE Applications' — Provides information on all KDE applications.

- '/usr/share/doc/packages' — The classic Linux documentation directory containing documentation on application packages.

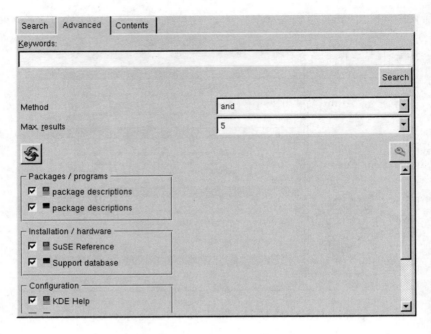

Figure 23.2: Advanced Search

Installation and Hardware

- 'SuSE Administration Guide' — Provides basic instructions on installation, network configuration, graphical user interfaces, and more — the SuSE manual in electronic form.
- 'SDB' — This link points to the locally installed support database and provides solutions to known problems (see Section *Support Database*).
- 'HOWTOs' — Offers hands-on installation and configuration instructions for Linux (see Section *HOWTOs* on page 331).

Configuration

- 'SuSE User Guide' — The configuration manual for KDE and SuSE Linux includes modem, sound, TV card, scanner configuration, and more.
- 'KDE Help' — Find everything you need to know about KDE. For example, find information about installation or configuring the graphical user interface.

Commands and Functions

- 'Man Pages' — UNIX system "manual pages" describe commands as well as options and parameters (see Section *Manual Pages* on page 329).
- 'Info Pages' — These help pages provide explanations and examples for using complex Linux commands and libraries. They describe the utilization of these items (see Section *Info Pages* on page 330).

Searching for documents In the left window panel, find the tabs 'Search', 'Advanced', and 'Contents' (see Figure 23.2 on the preceding page).

- 'Search' — For basic searches, enter the search word and click 'Search'. Normally, as long as they are installed and you have not specifically disabled the setup of the search database, the package descriptions, all SuSE manuals (Reference, Network, Configuration, Applications), KDE Help, and the Support Database (SDB) will all be searched.

  The label of the 'Search' button changes to 'Next' after you click it. When you click again, any remaining data sources will also be searched.

- 'Advanced' — This tab allows a refined search using several options. If you have entered at least two keywords, select via 'Method' if both ("and") or at least one of ("or") the keywords should appear in the document.

  'Max. results' limits the number of entries displayed per source or lets you view all the finds for each documentation source at once. For example, select "5" to only see the five most important entries for each documentation source. Reverse your selection using the button containing the two arrows.

  Additional documentation sources can be added to the displayed list by clicking the tool button. Now add the respective index database for the new source. Documentation sources can also be removed in this dialog. See page 121. The little flags symbolize the language of the documentation texts. Select the sources and languages to search with the corresponding check boxes.

  Once you have completed the settings, click 'Search'. The search results are displayed to the right, ordered according to subject categories.

- 'Contents' — The subject categories of the start page can be seen listed here (see Figure 23.3 on the following page). View the documentation sources belonging to each subject category by clicking

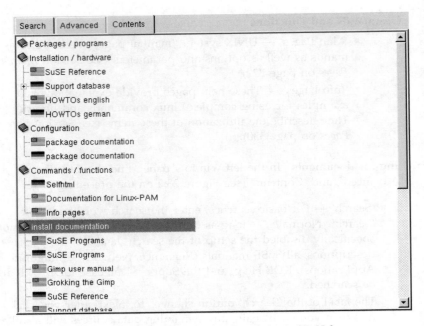

Figure 23.3: The Content Search in SuSE Help

the subject area with the mouse. Click again and the subject category will close. If you click the documentation source, the corresponding text appears in the right-hand window. This provides the only access to the KDE 'Tutors', which help you learn the KDE terminology and make it easier to use KDE Help.

To install additional documentation sources, click 'Uninstalled documentation' and select the corresponding documentation package from this list.

KDE Help

KDE Help contains information about KDE and its applications and about configuring the graphical desktop. It is completely integrated with SuSE Help. See Figure 23.3. If you prefer the original "KDE Help Center", start it with the lifesaver (without the Geeko) or under 'Help' in the 'K Menu'.

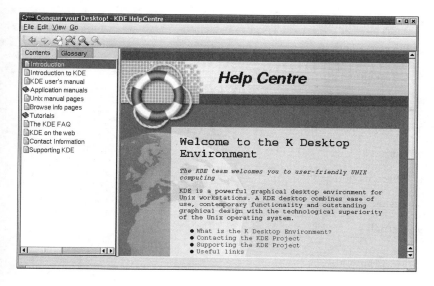

Figure 23.4: *The KDE Help Home Page*

Support Database

We have already found answers and solutions to many potential problems.
These are available online in the numerous articles located in our Support
Database: `http://sdb.suse.de/en/sdb/html/index.html`. You can
also find the contents of the Support Database in the `sdb_en` package that is
included on the SuSE Linux CDs. Read the articles using any browser.

─ **Tip** ──────────────────────────────────

Enter the command `sdb:` in the URL field in Konqueror followed by
the keyword to start the Support Database and search quickly.

───────────────────────────────────── **Tip** ┘

Manual Pages

Manual pages are the traditional way to access descriptions of application
usage and commands (such as C functions) in UNIX. All parameters and options for the command are included. Man pages are divided into the following categories, given when starting the manual pages:

1. User commands

2. System commands

3. C functions

4. File formats, device files

5. Configuration files

6. Games

7. Miscellaneous

8. System administration

9. Kernels

n   New commands

Access man pages in the following ways:

Console   Use the sequence `man <category> <command>` to access man pages in a console or terminal. Use the option "-k", such as `man -k <command>`, to display the command from all categories.

Konqueror   Enter `man:/<command>(<category>)` in the URL field.

SuSE Help   Browse the various man pages according to category or keywords. Find them in the subject category 'Commands / Functions' under 'Man Pages'.

Info Pages

Info pages have become standard for more complex commands. They not only describe options and parameters, but also offer a more in-depth explanation of how the commands are used and applied. These explanations are mostly accompanied by related examples. Normally, info pages are accessed with either the file viewer Emacs or the Infoviewer (`info`).

Console   You have three basic options:

- `info` shows a list of the available info pages

- `info -apropos <command>` shows info pages relating to `<command>`
- `info <command>` opens Emacs with a description of `<command>`

Konqueror Enter: `info:/<command>` in the URL field. Click the links in the browser as usual.

SuSE Help In SuSE Help (see Section *SuSE Help* on page 324), find the info pages in 'Commands / Functions'. The home page is a summary of all info pages, shown here in HTML format.

HOWTOs

HOWTOs are detailed, practice-oriented installation and configuration instructions for Linux located in the `/usr/share/doc/howto/` directory. For the HTML version, use the package `howtoenh`.

In the `docu/howto` directory of the first CD, find the current versions of the most important HOWTO files as of the CD release. These files are not compressed and can already be easily viewed, even prior to installation.

Console View the HOWTO text in a console with the `less` command, even if the text is compressed. To view the HOWTO text regarding Linux installation, for example, enter the following:

```
less /usr/share/doc/howto/en/Installation-HOWTO.txt.gz
```

SuSE Help Read the HOWTO texts in a more user-friendly environment via SuSE Help and perform searches.

Kernel Documentation

For problems with the kernel itself, the `/usr/src/linux/Documentation` directory is an extensive information source, which is only available if the kernel sources (packages `linux` and `kernel-source`) have been installed. You will also find several valuable tips in the individual subdirectories of the kernel sources and in the kernel sources themselves.

Free Books

The books package contains some books in PostScript format which can be viewed and printed with the gv. Before printing them, consider whether it may actually be more economical to purchase the book.

SuSE Linux FAQ

Here, we answer the most *Frequently Asked Questions*.

1. **I am the only person using my computer. Why do I always need to log in?**
   Linux is a multiuser system. Giving a user name and a password is necessary so Linux knows who is working with it. Only log in as `root` to make changes to your system (installing software or changing configuration). For everyday use, create a regular user. This prevents accidental damage to the installation.

2. **Where can I get more information about SuSE Linux?**
   As far as installation or SuSE Linux–specific matters are concerned, find information in the manuals. The PDF file is located in the package `suselinux-adminguide_en` (see `/usr/share/doc/packages/suselinux-adminguide_en`). Documentation on the programs can be found in `/usr/share/doc/packages` and instructions are provided in the "HOWTOs" in `/usr/share/doc/howto/en`. They can be read, for example, with the command:

   ```
   less /usr/share/doc/howto/en/DOS-to-Linux-HOWTO.txt.gz
   ```

3. **Where can I get special tips or help?**
   Enter the path `/usr/share/doc/sdb/en/html/index.html` in Konqueror. There, view our Support Database, which includes numerous tips and help entries. If the path does not yet exist, first install the packages `sdb` and `sdb_en`. On the Internet, our support database has the most recent updates at `http://sdb.suse.de/sdb/en/html/`.

4. **How can I enter commands in KDE?**
   Click 'K' → 'Tools' → 'Terminal'. Alternatively, press (Alt) + (F2) then enter `xterm`. This opens a terminal window in which to enter commands.

In KDE, start a konsole by clicking the icon with the screen and the seashell in the toolbar.

5. **I can't find many programs in KDE.**

   You can start all programs from a terminal window, such as xterm (see above), by entering the program name and pressing ⏎.

6. **What is a mirror? Why should I not get these things from ftp. suse.com?**

   Since there are many users who need to retrieve things from the server at the same time, it would be overburdened quickly if everyone used the same server. There are a number of other FTP servers that contain a duplicate of the SuSE server. A server such as this is called a "mirror". Access a mirror geographically near you — in the same country or a nearby area — so it is quicker to download. Find a list of mirrors at http://www.suse.de/en/support/download/index.html.

7. **I cannot find any .exe files. Where are all the applications?**

   In Linux, executable files normally do not have file extensions. Most programs are located in /usr/bin and /usr/X11R6/bin.

8. **How can I recognize executable files?**

   Using the command ls -l, see all the executable files in the directory in red. Also recognize them by the 'x' in the first column.

   ```
   -rwxr-xr-x    1 root    root    64412 Jul 23 15:23 /usr/bin/ft
   ```

9. **I want to remove Linux. How does this work?**

   With fdisk, the Linux partitions are deleted. You may need to run fdisk in Linux. Afterwards, boot from the MS-DOS disk and run fdisk /MBR in DOS or Windows.

10. **I need firewall, masquerading, mail, and a web server. Will your installation support help me with this?**

    No. The installation support will assist you in getting Linux up and running. For concerns extending beyond this, there are good books available at your local book store and excellent documentation in /usr/share/doc/packages, /usr/share/doc/ howto/en/NET-3-HOWTO.gz, and /usr/share/doc/howto/en/ NET3-4-HOWTO.gz.

    Furthermore, you can make use of our Advanced Support. For details, visit http://support.suse.de/en/.

11. **How can I access my CD?**
    You must first mount the CD with the `mount` command. Information about this command can be found in Section *File Commands* on page 313

12. **I cannot get my CD out of the drive. What should I do now?**
    First, unmount the CD. This is done with the `umount` command. More information about this can be found in Section *File Commands* on page 314. In KDE, you only need to right-click the CD-ROM icon and select 'Unmount Drive'. If YaST is running on your computer, exit it.

13. **How can I find out what space is available in Linux?**
    With the `df -hT` command. Also see Section *System Commands* on page 314.

14. **Can I copy and paste in Linux?**
    Yes. To copy and paste in the text mode, you must have gpm running. In the X Window System and in the text mode: *highlight* the text block by clicking and dragging with the left mouse button then *insert* with the middle mouse button. The right mouse button has a special function in most programs and applications.

15. **Do I need to be afraid of a virus in Linux?**
    No. In Linux, there have been no serious viruses found. Also, viruses cannot cause any serious damage if they are *not* activated by root. The only virus scanners available in Linux serve to search e-mails for Windows viruses (if Linux is being used as a router or server).

16. **Do I need to compile a kernel myself?**
    No, this is usually unnecessary. The kernel is currently so extensive that there are about eight hundred options to consider when configuring it. Since it is almost impossible to master all the possible configurations and their effects, we strongly discourage inexperienced users from recompiling the kernels. If you still proceed with this, you are doing so at your own risk. We do *not* provide any installation support in such cases.

17. **Where can I see system reports?**
    Enter the following command in a terminal window as `root`:

    ```
    tail -f /var/log/messages
    ```

    Additional interesting programs relating to this one are `top`, `procinfo`, and `xosview`. The boot messages can be displayed with `less /var/log/boot.msg`.

18. **I cannot log in to my computer with** `telnet`. **I always get the answer "Login incorrect".**
    You are probably trying to log in as `root`. For security reasons, this is not possible via `telnet` by default.

    With YaST2, set up a normal user account. Log in with this user name. Then change to the user `root` with `su`. It is much better and safer, however, to use the program `ssh` instead of `telnet`. The `ssh` program uses encoded, secure connections.

19. **How do I connect to the Internet in Linux?**
    Chapter *KInternet — Connecting to the Internet* on page 115 provides information on this.

20. **Where is OpenOffice.org?**
    Use YaST2 for the installation. Simply enter OpenOffice.org in the search dialog and start the search. The installation module will tell you which CD to insert.

21. **I found a bug in SuSE Linux. Where should I report it?**
    First, ascertain whether it is actually a bug in the program or just an error in operation or faulty configuration settings. Also read the documentation in `/usr/share/doc/packages` and `/usr/share/doc/howto`. The bug may have already been discovered. Check it at `http://sdb.suse.de/sdb/en/html/` in the support database. Enter a keyword or work your way forward or backward via the "History" link. If it really is a bug, send a description of it by e-mail to `feedback@suse.de`.

22. **How can I install applications?**
    Applications included in the SuSE Linux CDs are best installed with YaST2.

23. **I "only" have an application in source code. How can I install it?**
    Some know-how is required with some applications. Find more information in a good Linux book.

    Briefly, decompress the archive with `tar xvzf name.tar.gz`, read the `INSTALL` or `README` files, and follow the instructions. Usually, the following command sequence needs to be executed: `./configure; make; make install`.

    We cannot offer any installation support for the phases of compilation or for self-compiled programs.

24. **Is my hardware supported?**
It is best to refer to the component database at `http://hardwaredb.suse.de` or `http://cdb.suse.de`. Also, `less /usr/share/doc/howto/en/Hardware-HOWTO.gz` can provide some information.

25. **How can I defragment my hard disk?**
Linux has an intelligent file system. This file system makes defragmentation superfluous, because it prevents fragments from occuring. Your partitions should not be more than 90 % used (`df -h`).

26. **What is meant by partitioning?**

Partitioning means dividing the hard disk into individual sections. Windows and MacOS also are located in their own partitions. For the default configuration, SuSE Linux requires at least two partitions (one for Linux itself and one swap partition for the virtual main memory).

27. **How much space do I need for Linux?**
This depends on how many and which packages you install. A default installation with office requires about 1 GB. 2 GB is recommended if you want space for your own data as well. To install just about everything, you need 3 GB to 6 GB, depending on the version.

28. **I need more space for Linux. How can I add another hard disk?**
You can integrate free hard disks or free partitions of hard disks into a Linux system at any time to make more space available. If you need more space, for example, in `/opt`, mount an additional hard disk partition there. The exact procedure is:

(a) Install your hard disk and start Linux. Pay attention to the instructions specific to the hard disk.

(b) Log in as user `root`.

(c) Partition with `fdisk`, in this example, `/dev/hdb1`.

(d) Format the partition with `mke2fs /dev/hdb1`.

(e) Enter the following commands:

```
earth:~ #      cd /opt
earth:/opt #   mkdir /opt2
earth:/opt #   mount /dev/hdb1 /opt2
earth:/opt #   cp -axv .  /opt2
```

Check thoroughly to see whether all the data has been copied. Afterwards, you can move the old directory and add a new one — an empty ☞*mount point*:

```
earth:/opt #   mv /opt /opt.old
earth:/opt #   mkdir /opt
```

Add the new partition to the /etc/fstab file using an editor. This could appear as in File 2.

```
/dev/hdb1          /opt        ext2        defaults     1      2
```

File 2: *Sample Line in* /etc/fstab *for an Additional Partition*

Now, shut down the computer and reboot.

(f) Once you have rebooted the computer, be sure that /dev/hdb1 has actually been mounted in /opt using the command mount. If everything is working as desired, remove the old data in /opt. old:

```
earth:~ #   cd /
earth:/ #   rm -fr opt.old
```

29. **My computer crashed. Can I just press the reset button without risking anything?**

If your computer no longer reacts to your mouse or keyboard, this does not necessarily mean that your whole system has crashed. Possibly one program is blocking the mouse or the keyboard, but all other programs are still running. If your machine can be accessed remotely (serial terminal, network), log in elsewhere and abort the respective program with killall ⟨*programname*⟩. If this does not work, try killall -9 ⟨*programname*⟩.

If this is not possible, try to get into another console using Ctrl + Alt + F2 to kill the faulty process from there. However, if the computer does not respond to any of the keys, wait for at least ten seconds before pressing reset to make sure there is no hard disk activity.

30. **How can I switch from a virtual text console to the graphical user interface?**

By default, there are six virtual text consoles that can be accessed with Ctrl + Alt + F1 to F6. Press Alt + F7 to go to the graphical user interface.

Glossary

This glossary is limited to UNIX-specific and Linux-specific terms, because a complete introduction to electronic data processing is beyond the scope of this book. The reader of this glossary should already be familiar with terms such as *bits* and *bytes*.

access permissions
The account is defined by the user name or login name and the password. The access permissions are generally set by the ☞*system administrator*. The access permissions define to which user group the new user is assigned and the resulting permissions.

account
see ☞*access permissions*.

ADSL Asymmetric Digital Subscriber Line
Transmitting procedure that transmits data about one hundred times faster than ISDN in the telephone network.

AGP Accelerated Graphics Port
A high-speed slot for graphics cards based on PCI, but offering a larger ☞*bandwidth*. Furthermore, AGP graphics cards can revert directly back to the ☞*Random Access Memory* and ☞*main memory* in contrast to PCI models (without routing around the processor) to swap graphics data there.

ATAPI
ATAPI is a type of CD-ROM drive that is connected to an (E)IDE controller. Apart from ATAPI drives, there are SCSI CD-ROM drives, handled by a SCSI controller, and proprietary CD-ROM drives that use their own controller or are connected to a sound card.

backup
A backup is a duplicate of data used to restore data that has been damaged or lost. Backups should be done regularly, especially the important files.

bandwidth
Maximum load capacity of a data channel.

BIOS
Small component that takes on the initialization of important hardware processes. This essential procedure is complete when ☞*LILO* appears on the screen.

bookmark
A mostly personal collection of interesting web page or file references directly accessible in the browser.

booting
The sequence of computer operations from power-up until the system is ready for use.

browser
Program that searches and displays contents. Today it is mostly used for programs that graphically display contents of ☞*World Wide Web* pages.

cache
In relation to the ☞*main memory*, it is rather small, but still a fast memory buffer. For example, open files are saved to the cache to spare the hard disk next time the file is loaded.

client
Workstation in a computer network operated by a ☞*server*.

command line
Text-based mode of operating where commands are entered at a prompt. A command line can be accessed from within a graphical environment as well as from virtual consoles.

console
In former times, this was synonymous with *terminal*. In Linux, you have *virtual consoles*. This enables you to use one screen for many independent, but parallel sessions.

CPU Central Processing Unit
☞*Processor*.

cursor

The cursor is normally a block character that marks the place for input on a computer screen. This term also often refers to the symbol representing the location of the mouse in graphical interfaces.

DDC

Communication standard between the monitor and the graphics card, which transmits various parameters, such as monitor name or resolution, to the graphics card.

daemon

A daemon *Disk and execution monitor* is a program that monitors in the background and comes into action when required. Such daemons answer FTP or HTTP requests, for example, or control activity in the PCMCIA slots.

desktop environment

A desktop environment, often mistaken for a window manager, is not required for working in a graphical environment. Desktop environments, like GNOME and KDE, provide extra features to users and developers and unify appearance and configuration. A window manager is required to use a desktop environment.

directories

Directories are electronic folders in which files, programs, and even subdirectories can be stored. They build a ☞*file system* structure, which is standardized in Linux.

DNS

A system that converts name-based addresses to ☞*TCP/IP* addresses and vice versa.

driver

A program between the operating system and the hardware that "translates" the communication between these two layers.

EIDE

Improved ☞*IDE* standard that even allows hard disks with a size over 512 MB.

e-mail electronic mail

The means of transporting mail electronically between registered users via a network. As with "normal" mail (often referred to as "snail mail"), the address has to be entered. In e-mail, it is in the form "sender@sender's-domain" to "recipient@recipient's-domain". E-mail not only lets you send text, but also sound files or pictures. It has many advantages: it is inexpensive and mail usually reaches its destination within minutes.

environment

A ☞*shell* normally provides some kind of environment where you can temporarily set options, such as paths of programs, the user name, the current path, and the appearance of the prompt. This data is stored in an ☞*environment variable*. These variables can be assigned, for example, by the shell's configuration files.

environment variable

A storage location in the ☞*environment* of the ☞*shell*. Every variable consists of a name (usually written in capital letters) and a value (such as path name).

ethernet

Popular standard for less expansive computer networks.

EXT2 Second Extended File System

EXT2 is the native file system used by Linux.

file system

A file system is a system for structuring files. There are many file systems available, which differ (sometimes quite extremely) in performance and power.

firewall

Connects a local network to the Internet using various security measures.

free software

see ☞*GNU*.

FTP file transfer protocol

A ☞*protocol* based on ☞*TCP/IP* for transferring files.

GNU

GNU stands for *GNU is Not Unix* and is a project of the Free Software Foundation (FSF). The aim of the "GNU Project", with which the name of Richard Stallman (RMS) is closely linked, is to create a "free" operating system compatible with Unix. "Free" here means less *free of cost* than free in the sense of *freedom* — having the right to access, modify, and use software. To guarantee the freedom of the *source*, the program code, every modification must also be *free*: in particular, software may not be compromised in the sense of this freedom by modifying or adding to the program code. How this should be guaranteed is explained by the classical GNU Manifesto (`http://www.gnu.org/gnu/manifesto.html`). GNU software is legally covered by the GNU General Public License, in short, "GPL" (`http://www.gnu.org/copyleft/gpl.html`) and in the GNU Lesser General Public License[1], "LGPL" (`http://www.gnu.org/copyleft/lgpl.html`).

In connection with the GNU Project, all Unix help programs are being redeveloped and, in part, provided with more or enhanced functionalities. Even complex software systems, such as Emacs or glibc, are integral components of the "Project".

The ☞*Linux* kernel, subject to the GPL, profits from this "Project" (especially from the tools), but should not be seen as the same thing.

GPL
> see ☞*GNU.*

home directory
> Your own private directory in the Linux file system. This belongs to a specific user (usually in `/home/<username>`). Except the superuser ☞ *root*, only the user has full access rights in his home directory.

host name
> Name of a machine in Linux, usually the name by which it can be reached on the network.

HTML
> The most important language used in the ☞*World Wide Web* for designing the contents. The layout commands made available by HTML define how a document looks and how it is displayed in a ☞*browser.*

HTTP
> A protocol used between the ☞*browsers* and Internet servers to transmit ☞*HTML* pages over the ☞*World Wide Web.*

IDE Integrated Drive Electronics
> A widely-used hard disk standard in low-grade and middle-grade PCs.

---

[1]previously known as the "GNU Library General Public License".

Internet

World-wide computer network based on ☞*TCP/IP*, which is used by a very large population.

IP address

A numerical 32-bit Internet address, appearing in four decimal series separated by periods (for example, 192.168.10.1), which is uniquely assigned to a machine connected to ☞*TCP/IP* networks.

IRQ Interrupt Request

A request to the ☞*operating system* carried out by a hardware component or a program to assign it processor capacity.

ISDN Integrated Services Digital Network

A popular digital standard for high-speed data transferral over the telephone network.

KDE

A popular desktop environment for Linux. KDE with its corresponding window manager is the default graphical interface in SuSE Linux.

kernel

The kernel is the central core of the Linux operating system. It manages memory, contains the drivers that enable communication with the hardware, and handles processes and tasks. Applications run on top of the kernel.

LAN local area network

A LAN is a local ☞*network* and is usuallly rather small.

LILO

Small program installed in the boot sector of the hard disk that not only can be started by Linux, but by other operating systems as well.

link

A link is a pointer to a file, just as widely used in the Internet as in the Linux file system. In Linux, there is a distinction made between "hard" and "symbolic" links. While "hard" links refer to the exact position in the file system, the symbolic link only points to the respective name.

Linux

High performance UNIX-like operating system core distributed freely under the GPL (☞*GNU*). The name is an acronym ("Linus' uniX") and refers to its creator, Linus Torvalds. Although the name, in a strict sense, only refers to the kernel itself, the popular understanding of the term "Linux" usually entails the entire system.

login

Authentication of a user by user name and password to gain access to a computer system or network.

logout

The procedure of closing down an interactive Linux session and getting back to the ☞*login* prompt where you enter your user name and password.

main memory

Physical memory of limited capacity that can be accessed rather quickly. This is often referred to as RAM, Random Access Memory.

man pages

Traditional documentation for Unix systems, which can be read using the command `man`.

MBR

The first physical sector of the hard disk from which the content is loaded to the main memory and executed by the ☞*BIOS*. This code then loads either the operating system from a hard disk partition or a more sophisticated boot loader such as ☞*LILO* .

mounting

This describes the "insertion" of file systems into the directory tree of the system.

mount point

A mount point is the directory where a partition or other device is attached to the Linux file system.

MP3

Very efficient compression procedure for audio files that reduces the size by a factor of ten in contrast to an uncompressed audio file.

multitasking

Operating systems that can invoke more than one program simultaneously are called multitasking systems.

multiuser

Enables more than one user to work simultaneously on the same system.

network

The pooling together of several computers, accomplished normally using ☞*servers* and ☞*clients*.

NFS Network File System

A ☞*protocol* for accessing a ☞*file system* shared over a network.

NIS Network Information Service

A centralized data administration system in networks. User names and passwords can be simultaneously managed network-wide by the NIS.

operating system

The operating system is a process running permanently in the background, controlling the basic operation of the computer.

partition

Logically-independent section of a hard disk, each possibly containing different file systems. In Windows, also known as "drives".

path

Unique description of a file's position in a file system.

plug and play

Automatic hardware component configuration technology. Resources, such as IRQ and DMA, are configured and managed separately from the system.

PC *Personal Computer*

In contrast to mainframes, a "personal" computer is a small one. Since the early 1980s, this has usually meant a small computer from IBM, based on the Intel x86/88 processor — although the first machine of this kind was an Apple — the name is now making a comeback in the form of the PowerPC.

process

In Linux, started programs or executable files run as processes, often referred to as tasks. Processes can be controlled by commands like top entered in the ☞*shell*.

processor

The processor is the "brain" of every computer, working through and performing commands given by a user or a program in machine language. The processor has control over the entire system and is responsible for the actual performance of the computer.

prompt

See ☞*command line*.

protocol

Standard specifically defined for regulating communication for hardware, software, or networks. There is a multitude of these standards. The most common examples are ☞*HTTP* and ☞*FTP*.

proxy

Most commonly used cache implemented by Internet providers that stores frequently requested contents in a database to allow other machines requesting those pages to load them directly from it. This process not only reduces the time it takes to download this information, but also conserves the available bandwidth.

RAM *Random Access Memory*

See ☞*main memory*.

root

The user undertaking the configuration and maintenance of a complex computer system, such as a network. This system administrator is usually the only person who has access to all parts of the system (root permissions).

root directory

The directory at the top of the file tree, at the beginning of the ☞*file system*, which, unlike other directories, is not a subdirectory. The root directory is denoted in UNIX with a '/' symbol.

SCSI Small Computer Systems Interface

Hard disk standard implemented in servers and other high-level machines because of its high-speed performance. See ☞*server*.

server

A server is usually a rather powerful computer that offers services, such as HTTP, DNS, and FTP, or data to other machines connected via a network. There are also programs called servers, like the ☞*X server*.

shell

An especially flexible command line often equipped with its own specific programming language. Examples of shells are bash, sh, and tcsh.

SMTP Simple Mail Transfer Protocol

☞*Protocol* for transferring ☞*e-mails*.

SSL Secure Socket Layer

Encryption procedure for transferring ☞*HTTP* data.

superuser

see ☞*root*.

system administrator

see ☞*root*

task

See ☞*process*.

TCP/IP

Internet communication protocol finding increased use in local networks, known as "intranets".

telnet

Telnet is the ☞*protocol* and command for communicating with other hosts. Normally, the user only sees telnet as a means for logging into a remote system.

terminal

Previously, a keyboard and monitor combination connected to a central computer. This combination, when connected to a multiuser machine, does not have its own computing power. This term is also used to describe programs that emulate an actual terminal.

UNIX

UNIX is an operating system that is widely distributed, above all on workstations in networks. Since the beginning of the 1990s, there has been a freely available version for PCs: Linux.

URL Uniform Resource Locator

Unique Internet address that contains the type (e. g., `http://`) and the name of the host (e. g., `www.suse.de`).

user account

see ☞*account*.

VESA Video Electronics Standard Association

Industrial consortium that defines, among other things, important video standards.

wild cards

Placeholder for one (symbol: `'?'`) or more (symbol: `'*'`) unknown characters, most often used in commands (especially search commands).

window manager

A window manager is the layer that interacts between the ☞*X Window System* and the user. It is responsible, among other things, for your desktop display. There are a wide variety of window managers available, one of the more popular ones being kwm for ☞*KDE*.

WWW World Wide Web

Based on the ☞*HTTP* protocol, this is a hyperlinked collection of documents, files, and images that can be viewed with a web browser.

X11

see ☞*X Window System*

X Window System

The X Window System is the standard for graphical interfaces in Linux. In contrast to other operating systems, it is simply the middle layer between the hardware and the preferred ☞*window manager*, such as KDE or GNOME.

YP

see ☞*NIS*

Index